England
1175–1425

Edmund King

Department of History, University of Sheffield

Charles Scribner's Sons
New York

First published 1979
by Charles Scribner's Sons
597 Fifth Avenue
New York, N.Y. 10017
Copyright © Edmund King 1979
Copyright under the Berne Convention

Library of Congress Cataloging in Publication Data

King, Edmund.
  England, 1175–1425.

  Bibliography: p.
  Includes index.
  1. England—Civilization—Medieval period, 1066–1485
I. Title.
DA185.K56   942.03   78–21614

ISBN 0–684–161640–0

Printed in Great Britain

Series Editor's Preface

It is a truism that 'of the making of books there is no end' but, at least with regard to the study of history, there are two cogent reasons why this should be so. One is that each decade sees the examination of more and more source material as the increasing flood of research continues to rise. This, in itself, can necessitate the revision of older views and older certainties in the light of new knowledge. But even if no new material were available there would still be a need for new books because every generation asks its own questions and demands its own answers that make, or at least attempt to make, sense to contemporaries. The nineteenth-century student of history was concerned mainly with the world of politics, with the growth of constitutional monarchy and of religious and personal freedom. Then with the turn of the century men began to ask different questions, questions concerned with the industrial society in which they lived, and Archdeacon Cunningham produced his pioneering work *The Growth of English Industry and Commerce*. For the first decades of the twentieth century the emphasis was on economic rather than social developments, though to begin with there was no very clear distinction between them. As economic history became more technical there also emerged a growing interest on the part of the non-specialist public in the everyday life of their ancestors, and the success of G. M. Trevelyan's *Social History* demonstrated how widespread the appetite for this kind of information was. Meanwhile the growth of the welfare state incited more and more people to ask questions about the history of the society in which they lived. How, for instance, had the relationships between the various layers which comprised it altered over the centuries? How far was social structure determined by economic factors? To what extent did the distribution of wealth within a society determine its form of government, both national and local? To what extent were ways of thought and attitudes towards religion, social problems, changing as the structure of society changed? The questions are endless.

It would be presumptuous to suggest that this series on *The Development of English Society* can even begin to answer them. Its aim is the much more modest one of sketching out the major ways in which English society, seen as an entity, has developed from the England of the Normans to the England of Elizabeth II. Each volume is a separate study of a period of significant change, as seen by a specialist on that period. Because each period presents different problems there can be no uniform pattern of treatment. Each author must make his or her selection of where to place the emphasis on each period. Nevertheless it is hoped that, taken as a whole, the series will provide some answers to the question 'how did we get from there to here?' This series is not intended for specialists or to make specific contributions to research. It is designed primarily to meet the needs of students in the hope that other courses which they may be following, not necessarily in History, will be enriched by a deeper understanding of the main trends and developments in English society. It is intended to provide background reading not text books. It should therefore also appeal to that increasingly wide circle of readers who, while not wanting to be bombarded by too much detail and too many facts, are interested in tracing English society as we know it today back to earlier times.

The mid-twelfth century is a convenient point at which to begin this investigation. The foundations had already been laid. With the victory of William the Conqueror the diverse strains of Saxons, Danes and Normans, superimposed on the earlier strata of Roman-British culture, were slowly being fused together to form a society and way of life that can be described as English. During this period too, though not yet definitive, territorial boundaries within Britain were sufficiently defined to make it possible to speak of Scotland, Wales and England. A dominant theme therefore of Dr King's book is this growth of a national consciousness both at the cultural and political level. The centuries covered by this volume saw the origins of parliament, which brought the political life of the nation into a single focus. A unified political community was only possible in a society whose members shared a common culture, in which ideas of lordship and of the Christian religion played an important part. It was a period of substantial but fluctuating growth and adaption in the economic sphere. Recent research has emphasised the effect of changes in the size and distribution of population on both the social and economic life of the country and in this volume Dr King brings out the close links between these changes and contemporary developments in politics, administration and government. The teaching of English history has too long been kept in watertight compartments and nowhere has this been more the case than in the field of constitutional studies. Dr King's analysis of English medieval society should provide a useful corrective to this more specialist approach by making his readers aware of the soil in which the roots of our Constitution grew.

Contents

Plates

Figures

Acknowledgments

This book presents a view of English society over a period of two hundred and fifty years. It is intended less as a textbook than as a series of essays on a common theme, the unification of a single society. I have wished to stress at all times the interdependence of the different essays, and to argue that society cannot be fully understood if it is studied piecemeal. Inevitably I have been selective, and my main debt is to those historians whose specialist work makes possible a book of this kind. Some but by no means all of them are listed in the bibliography. Direct quotations have been acknowledged, but I cannot unscramble the ideas and the lecture notes of more than ten years' teaching, and if any academic colleague feels that some of my text should be directly attributed I can only ask indulgence for an error that is not intentional. I am grateful to those who have allowed me to use illustrations, and particularly to Mr John Hurst for supplying some information on Wharram Percy in advance of its publication elsewhere. I am also grateful to R. S. Thomas for permission to quote from his poem 'Tenancies'. I must thank Dr Dorothy Marshall for the invitation to write in this series, and for some valuable criticism of my draft text. I have been fortunate also in being able to call on expert criticism from two colleagues, Robin Jeffs and Bob Moore, and the book owes a great deal to their learning and good sense. The text was typed by Mrs Christine Gandy. My wife did not waver in her view that my writing should not be confined to the minutiae of twelfth-century feudal history. That there is a book at all is very largely due to her, and the book is for her.

Edmund King

Chapter 1

The Development of English Society

Men in the middle ages did not boast of historical development. Their standards of proper behaviour and of the right ordering of society lay in the past. Kings at their coronation had to swear to follow the customs of their ancestors. Members of the aristocracy looked back to the Norman Conquest of 1066, and traced their lines of descent from ancestors who had come with the Conqueror, whether or not they had indeed done so. The bulk of the unfree peasantry were 'customary' tenants—they held their lands by services that were fixed by custom. The law of England was a customary law, not written but based on precedent. In the king's courts as in the manorial courts, the relationships between individuals were governed by custom. Individuals and communities needed to cultivate a long memory. Magna Carta in 1215 took its inspiration from the charter which Henry I had granted to his barons in 1100, and it in turn dominated political discussion for a further century. Magna Carta established, at least in the eyes of the baronage, that the king was subject to the law just like anyone else within the kingdom.

Thus only by claiming continuity with the past could men hope to legitimise their actions in the present. The mental categories of medieval individuals were 'conservative', and so inevitably the sources that historians have to study are conservative also. It is a challenge to look for social development in such material. Yet change there was. During the period covered by this book, from the late twelfth to the early fifteenth century, English society developed in many ways that make it easier to recognise today.

The most important area of development and innovation was in government. Government in the twelfth century needed to develop or atrophy and there were forces in twelfth-century society which made some aspects of its development very rapid indeed. There was in the first place the area which the kings of England ruled, or meant to rule. These kings were Frenchmen, and the most important of their concerns lay across the channel. The period that has been taken for this book starts with one warrior king, Richard I, and finishes with another, Henry V. A concern to rule as much as possible of France, a legacy of the Norman Conquest of 1066 and of successive campaigns, informs the whole period and gives it a measure of unity. It culminated in the Hundred Years' War. Political history cannot be ignored in this period of the development of English society, and military history least of all, for warfare was a significant driving force in social change. Warfare needed large and increasingly sophisticated armies, and these men had to be paid. The financial needs of the monarchy in a time of war were the stimulus to the development of a system of taxation which involved the whole country. It involved individuals, and it involved communities, for the ability to withhold money gave a form of political strength to the representatives of the local communities of England. Parliament is the creation of the later middle ages: its development reflects social changes of major importance. Taxation and representation are the common change of modern English history. It was in the later middle ages that they came together, and put their hallmark upon English institutions.

The stories of kings and their battles are not normally central to social histories, and they will not be to this one, but they have their part to play in it. It was not only that warfare involved taxation, and that taxation both embodied and forwarded social change. There is the further point that kings and their military exploits provided the focus, the only possible focus, for national feeling and national consciousness. Kings stood at the head of their nations in the fifteenth century. There is nothing fanciful in the speech which Shakespeare has Henry V give to his troops before the battle of Agincourt, in which they were assured that men in England hung on news of their deeds, and would long remember them:

> Old men forget; yet all shall be forgot,
> But he'll remember, with advantages,
> What feats he did that day. Then shall our names,
> Familiar in his mouth as household words—
> Harry the King, Bedford and Exeter,
> Warwick and Talbot, Salisbury and Gloucester—
> Be in their flowing cups freshly remembered.

There was nothing fanciful either in the pageant which the Londoners gave to the king on his triumphant return, which will provide the final scene in this book. Such a degree of cohesion in the national community was a new thing. In part at least it was the creation, and the conscious creation, of the monarchy.

The links with Normandy, formed by the Conquest of 1066, were broken in the years around 1200. Few men in England were much concerned with the preservation of the Anglo-Norman state. The concerns of the monarchy outside England awakened little interest in the thirteenth century. Henry III's dream of capturing the Norman kingdom of Sicily for his son Edmund, foisted on him by the papacy, provoked scorn and led to financial and military disaster for him within England. It might have seemed to men in the mid-thirteenth century that any involvement with France was part of a history that had been discarded. It turned out otherwise. The monarchy came to appeal to a more remote past, to an age of chivalry and romance. The military energy of the aristocracy was harnessed to the assertion of monarchical rights over the extremities of the Plantagenet state. War involved taxation, and as taxation was raised the monarchy harnessed public opinion and provided popular support for military adventure. In this way it involved what I shall argue was a much wider political community than had existed in the twelfth century with one man's fight for an inheritance within France.

An example of political cohesion, and of the way that it focused on monarchy especially in time of war, may be found in a manifesto issued to explain the causes of the war with the French in 1337. It gave a detailed, and so far as can be seen, an accurate account of the diplomatic negotiations that had preceded the declaration of war. The king complained that his lands in Gascony were being withheld by the French king, who had said that he would only do him justice if the king of England came to France:[1]

> trusting in this promise, the King of England crossed secretly into France and came to him, humbly requesting the delivery of his lands, offering and doing to the king as much as he ought and more.

Edward III explained further his attempts to avoid conflict by a diplomatic marriage. He had made various suggestions, and 'when one was refused, he put forward another': the first of them had been 'the marriage of his eldest son, now Duke of Cornwall, with the daughter of the king of France, without taking anything for the marriage'. There had been further fruitless negotiations about a crusade. The French king's bad faith was transparent in all his doings;

and now he was engaged in succouring the Scots. This was a document intended to be read, and no doubt glossed, at meetings of the county courts, the traditional meeting places for all the freeholders of the county. The text is propaganda, but when it is compared with the propaganda involved in twentieth-century warfare there are some interesting contrasts. The people were to be treated not to slogans, but to the details of diplomatic manoeuvrings. They knew without being told, though now it is a world away, what was involved when the king of England promised to do 'as much as he ought' towards the king of France. They knew the considerations involved in the various marriages listed, and they were fully aware of the close links between Scottish and French affairs. The whole tone is that of *The Times* and not of the *Daily Mirror*. And the tone can be in modern terms so serious because the culture is unified. The technicalities of feudalism and of feudal marriage were the common concerns of everyone in the society. There were no cultural barriers between the different levels of society. The political involvement of the whole community was an important development of the later medieval period.

Such involvement would not have been possible had it not been for other twelfth-century developments, which made for the integration of a single culture. In the western monarchies the growth in the authority of the territorial state and the spread of literacy and of written instruments of government went together. In the mid-century the kings of England ceased to address writs to all their men 'both French and English'; the distinction was no longer real. So at the same time, the distinction made between all men 'both lay and literate', mainly in ecclesiastical records, referred to a world that was passing away, in which an educated laity had no proper function. From one point of view the history of the later middle ages presents us with a series of studies in the uses of literacy. The universities, a new creation of the twelfth century, performed the two functions of passing on the culture of the past, and of training men in the techniques required for the present. The men it trained were clerks, and the word clerk meant a religious as opposed to a layman: an early thirteenth-century charter from Lincoln records a sale of land by two brothers, Ivo the clerk and William the layman. It is not anachronistic to think of clerks in a modern sense, for a good number of those trained in the schools were to be largely engaged in clerical work.

The records of the late twelfth and early thirteenth centuries show very clearly the need for trained men, and the importance of written records. A series of letters survives, sent in the late 1220s by the steward of the estate to the bishop of Chichester, who was royal chancellor at the time.[2] The steward saw his lord only rarely, and his tone though polite is sufficiently direct to make it clear that he would have liked to see him more frequently. An age in which rights of lordship could only be exercised personally had been succeeded by one in which they were based on written documents and exercised by correspondence. The steward asked the bishop to send him 'a writ of the lord king' to enable him to pursue a fugitive villein, and 'letters of the lord king' about rights of common. The latter case was urgent, for the offending landowners were about to purchase a writ of novel disseisin, and 'you must get your letters in first'. The bishop was asked to speak with the lord king to get the guardianship of a Sussex estate, which had useful equipment and stock; he was told that his letters ordering iron had been misunderstood, and that if he wanted fish sent from Sussex to his London house he must send pack-horses down for their transport. The steward's administrative resources were clearly overstretched when the time for hearing the Michaelmas accounts came round, and he asked for help, 'for I don't believe that master Reginald of Winchester your official will have the time to be continuously engaged in this work.' Particular attention was given to getting a proper record of permanent transfers of land. Reginald Aiguillun had agreed to sell to the bishop his wood called Depemers. A draft of the charter was sent from Sussex to London, and the covering letter explained:

> I asked him most pressingly that he would deliver to me the charters of those from whom the right and claim descended; he replied that he had no charter which mentioned *Depemers* separately. Then I asked him to let you have the charter of the heir from whom the right descended. He replied 'no way', and so I left him.

The steward was unsuccessful. It was only comparatively recently that landowners had needed such records. The need for written documents to prove title to land was one of the most basic of the uses of literacy.

This was true both of church government and of secular government. The two were not opposed, if only because they were alternately staffed by the same people at different stages of their careers. It may seem strange to say this of a period that starts in the immediate aftermath of the Becket controversy, but Becket's was a bad appointment, if only because the apprenticeship which he served was so short. A better example of a clerk who made good is Walter Langton, who was attached to Edward I's household from his early years and had been a clerk of the Chancellor Richard Burnell. He served in the private office of Edward as king, becoming keeper of the wardrobe in 1290 and treasurer of the exchequer in 1295. He served in Wales and in Gascony, and in the late 1290s in missions to France and the Low Countries. He was Edward's chief minister in his later and more unpopular years. Between 1289 and 1295 he accumulated a whole series of rich livings, fourteen in all, which must have given him a baronial income even before his appointment as bishop of Lichfield in 1296. He was bishop there until his death in 1321. It was as well that he had the security of episcopal office, for while accompanying Edward I's body to London for burial he was arrested by Edward II's knights, his lands were confiscated and complaints against him invited. A series of trials lasted until 1312, and his career at the centre of power was at an end. It must have been in this semi-retirement that he built a new palace at Lichfield, in which a six-teenth-century antiquary recorded 'a goodly large hall, wherein hath been excellently well painted, but now much decayed, the corona-tion, marriage, wars and funeral of Edward I'. There he lived with his memories, surrounded by the glory in which he had shared. In all save the drama of arrest and trial, Langton's career was typical of that of the successful civil servant. The line of such men stretches from Hubert Walter in the late twelfth century to Henry Chichele in the early fifteenth. These were the men who ran England. Their careers make nonsense of any attempt to divide church and state. They served to unify the two.

Men like Langton rose to power on a sea of paper. The late twelfth century was a period of striking advance in the importance of the written word. From the 1150s there survives a continuous series of financial records of the central government, the pipe rolls of the exchequer. In the 1190s there came a more striking innovation, with the keeping of a permanent record of the letters sent out by the central government. Historians thereafter can study the day-to-day work of government. They can trace in quite new detail the network of political relationships within English society. What they know about individuals, they know only because it is to be found in the records of the royal administration. What they know, the king knew, or at least had access to. This detail of royal control over, and royal knowledge of, men's lives was undoubtedly responsible for a part of the unrest which led to Magna Carta. The barons were made to feel that Big Brother was watching them, in much the same way as some now fear that they may lose their liberties in a new, computerised society. At some point, clearly, a change in technique has become a change of substance. At the time of Stephen's reign, in the second quarter of the twelfth century, some of the most important documents can only be dated to within a period of ten years. In John's reign the political discussions which led to Magna Carta can be followed almost from day to day. The world had changed very rapidly.

The important development came not so much in the quantity of written records, though it increased, as in their technique. Those trained in the new universities were taught to make distinctions, to sort out the merits of conflicting authorities in theology and in canon law. It was a technique well suited to secular government. *Glanvill*, the English legal textbook of the 1180s, was rigorously organised by means of a long series of either/or distinctions. To take one example, on the procedure to be followed to establish who was the lord of a piece of land in dispute:[3]

> When both lords are present the tenant's lord will either acknowledge that the land in question is of his fee, or he will deny it. If he does acknowledge it, then he will have a choice of undertaking the denial himself or committing it to the tenant; whichever he does, his rights and those of his tenant will be preserved if they are successful in the plea; but if they are defeated, then the lord shall lose his service and the tenant the land without any right to reopen the issue.

This is dry certainly, in the legal manner, but at the same time clear. The reader of this book, or of *The Dialogue of the Exchequer* which deals in question and answer form with administrative procedure a decade before *Glanvill*, can easily get the feeling that he could go back in a time-machine and take up a clerical job at Henry II's court.

The later middle ages saw a rapid expansion of the civil service. There is a document recording the staff of the chancery in the latter years of Richard II. They were arranged in three grades, the clerks of the first bench, the clerks of the second bench, and those described simply as *cursitores*, the men who wrote the standard documents. The senior clerks had other clerks working for them. All told there were well over a hundred clerks in the central chancery. There were other clerks doing chancery work in the royal household. And the chancery was only one of the departments of state. By contrast, at the end of Stephen's reign in the mid-twelfth century, only two clerks have been identified by their handwriting as at work in the chancery. The English monarchy had been temporarily reduced to the staffing level, and to the authority, of an aristocratic household. The use of writing, the growth of the bureaucracy, were developments which changed the nature of government. Only one thing remained stable, and that was the scale of fees. The fees fixed for chancery work by a constitution of 1199 remained substantially the same for the rest of the middle ages.

'England was a much-governed country.' The idea is a popular one, and what has been said so far would seem to substantiate it. Yet it is important to realise how thinly spread the new bureaucracy was, and how far we are away from a society in which, in our terms, the power of the state was a daily feature of men's lives. England was a compact and well-integrated country, and it had a strong and well-established monarchy. That monarchy had grown out of and shared the general characteristics of medieval lordship. Its basic purpose was subsistence; its surplus could be used for display. As subsistence grew more strained because of foreign war in this period, and the amount of display demanded by a developing theory of monarchy increased, so the monarchy pressed more hardly on the community. The furnishing of troops and the seizure of supplies brought the demands of war home to individuals in a new way. The lay subsidies and the export taxes on wool were burdens borne by the whole community. From this point of view, warfare had its repercussions on the English countryside. But the nature of government was not changed, for the men collecting money and supplies for the crown were part of the local structure of lordship.

Lordship over individuals was exercised by a wide variety of men, and even over communities by a good number. At the top of the scale there were at the beginning of our period a number of earls who each might have an income of around £2,000 a year. There were twelve earls in 1189; and the same number in 1294. The earls had a distinctive title, but they were not a separate social group. Below them there stretched a large number of men who were tenants-in-chief, which is to say that they owed lordship to no man save the king. In 1166 Henry II sent a circular to each of these men via the sheriffs, asking them to list those who held of them by military service, and the services which they owed. The earls and greater barons sent in long lists, but in many ways the most interesting documents were those

which came from the more minor characters.[4] The charter of
Alexander de Alno of Compton in Somerset was as follows:

> To his lord the King of the English Alexander de Alno sends
> greetings and service. You have ordered me to declare to you the
> service of my fee; and I would ask your reverence to accept that all
> which is of my fee defends itself by the service of one knight; and
> thus my ancestors did service to your ancestors. Further your
> lordship should know that since the death of Henry I I have not
> enfeoffed any knight, but my father gave his brother Hugh de
> Alno a part of the land of his estate so that, if it were required, he
> should do the service of one knight to defend the whole of my
> father's land. This gift was made to him and his heirs in the time of
> King William.

William of Colechurch of Henstead in Norfolk, had an even smaller
holding, and was even more straightforward.

> I William of Colechurch owe my lord King Henry the service of
> half a knight in Norfolk, an established holding since the Conquest
> of England. I have no intention of hiding this service, for I shall do
> what I ought to do, which is to do homage to you, my lord, and to
> my lord Henry your son, and to do service to your sheriffs.

Each of these documents shows a certain prickly pride, which is a
pride in service, and in an established position in the land. The land
was defended by military service to the king. Each man stressed the
hereditary nature of his tenure, that the same services had been
performed by their ancestors to the king's ancestors. William claimed
that the land had been in his family since the Norman Conquest.

These men were the descendants of the Normans who had settled
England in the Conqueror's reign, some of whom had moved on to
other parts of the British Isles in successive generations thereafter.
They had come as foreigners, and many of them had come as
warriors. From the twelfth century onwards, it can be seen that their
descendants were neither foreign nor military. In some areas there
was a military ethos. In 1216 the earl of Chester issued his own
Magna Carta, which gives a very clear impression of a county still
organised for war. The English knights of the honour of Chester
were to do castle-guard, provided there was no sign of anyone to
fight; fighting was the work of the Cheshire knights. Elsewhere,
particularly in the marches, there were at least the echoes of war. Earl
Patrick's reply from Wiltshire in 1166 listed 40 knights, 'which I owe

you in the field', and Hugh de Lacy in Herefordshire stated that 'several of my knights reside with me, and I find their equipment; and several are in my houses in Wales, and I find their equipment also.' Even Alexander de Alno's uncle was prepared to jump on horseback when summoned, but we may be sure that the call never came, while the half knight offered by William of Colechurch was hardly an effective deterrent to an adversary. The image of a half knight on horseback is a vivid illustration of the decay of feudal tenure. Tenure of land was divorced from military obligation. The whole structure of feudalism, of wardship, marriage and its other paraphernalia, was maintained for fiscal profit and not social necessity.

By the late twelfth century no distinction between Norman and English can be drawn. Around 1200 only a very few laymen had large estates both in Normandy and in England, and with the loss of Normandy to the French after 1204 those families with interests in both countries were forced to resign one or the other. Some families had divided their Norman and English lands between different branches. In the course of the twelfth century, many landowning families were quietly dropping the names of their Norman homeland in favour of the name of the English village in which they had long been settled. A thirteenth-century family history tells us that around 1170 Walter de Grauntcourt (in Normandy) became known as Walter de Clopton, 'because of the difficulties the local people had in pronouncing his Norman name.' In much the same way, we are told that it was the coming of the railway in the nineteenth century that destroyed many distinctive rural pronunciations of names; the needs of the travelling public overrode local traditions.

In the twelfth century the divisions in society can be seen more clearly in the cloister than at the court. Around 1100 there was in many monasteries both a Saxon and a Norman party: the monks of Peterborough in 1098 paid a large sum to the king to be able to elect a Saxon abbot, who was forthwith deposed for simony, and the Anglo-Saxon chronicle was continued there up to the middle of the twelfth century. Around 1200 communities divided on different lines. In 1214 the abbey of Bury St Edmunds was split down the middle, with thirty-five monks on each side, between two candidates for the abbacy, one supported by the king, the other by the pope. The winning side, as it turned out, comprised monks from the immediate locality of the abbey, reared on a tradition of St Edmund's defence of his men against tyranny, and also men who had until recently been studying in the schools. There seems to have been a powerful division at Bury between the scholars and the plain blunt Englishmen. In the discussion of the previous vacancy, reported by Jocelin of Brakelond, one of the monks prayed: 'From all good clerks, O Lord deliver us; that it may please thee to preserve us from all Norfolk barrators, we beseech thee to hear Us.'[5] He was to be disappointed. God was on the side of the big battalions, and there was no fighting against the army of clerks.

The integration of the political nation went side by side with the integration of the economic nation. From the twelfth century onwards there was a national market in the main commodities, and a rapid growth of inter-regional and international trade. Population increase led to an increase in demand, and demand opened up new markets, so that by the end of the thirteenth century England had an active international trade with the Baltic, north-west Europe and the Mediterranean. In the fourteenth century, a contraction of population, and the increased nationalism which accompanied international warfare, decreased the total volume of trade and closed off some markets to English commerce. There was no similar decline in local trade. The mobility of the population increased. While in an economic sense the village may have been as self-sufficient at the end of the period as it was at the beginning, it was in no other sense as self-contained. Warfare took men from English villages to Scotland and to northern France. Pilgrimage took them to Canterbury and to shrines the length and breadth of the land. The local and regional communities of the nation appear very clearly during the Peasants Revolt of 1381. For the Dunstable annalist it was the communities of the land that had rebelled: first 'the community of Kent and Essex', then 'the community of the Londoners', and then closer to home 'the community of the lands of St Albans and the community of Barnet'. The men of St Albans boasted when at the height of their brief power that they had allies in thirty-two villages. These villages were the lands of the monastery, bound together by the ties of lordship.

There were considerable changes in the later middle ages in the way in which lordship was exercised over individuals. The one important legal division in medieval English society separated those who were free from those who were not. The distinction between freedom and servility was made much clearer in the later twelfth century, when the Angevin government offered the protection of the king's court to all those who held by free tenure. By the fifteenth century, the distinction was ceasing to be of much importance. In the intervening period it was to mould the lives of the majority of

Englishmen. Domesday Book in 1086 was a list of manors, the houses which were the centres of lordship and often of considerable estates. With the houses were listed the tenants, the men who provided the agricultural services within the estates. The two went together: dependent tenure underpinned the position of the lords. By the late twelfth century the freeholding classes had established rights of ownership over their lands. The peasantry had no such rights. The lands they held were not theirs to transfer. The disabilities of villein tenure were systematised by lawyers, and reduced to writing. The lawyers and their records were prime objects of attack in 1381. There were some good bonfires.

There were changes also in what we would now call 'the standard of living' of the peasantry. Evidence of this comes from a wide variety of sources, but many of the crucial proofs have been provided by recent archaeological work. The reconstruction of abandoned villages is going a large part of the way towards providing us with a range of material bearing on peasant life comparable with that available for the gentry and the aristocracy. It is one of the aims of this book to see whether at the village level what has been dug up from the ground fits easily into a historical landscape so far based largely on written records. From the thirteenth century onwards it became customary to build many peasant cottages in stone, rather than as previously in wood. Excavation of these cottages will often start to produce far more artifacts—pots, pans, pieces of ironwork and of agricultural equipment—from the fourteenth and fifteenth centuries than from any previous period. It may simply be that materials were more durable, rather than that the conditions of life had changed, but durability was a factor in stability. It is perhaps simplistic, in any age, to measure prosperity by the possession of consumer durables. But the extension of such possessions in the later middle ages was important, for it suggests that the peasantry were retaining more of their surplus, and using it in a way that provided a much more broadly based demand for the English craft and other industries. It is in fact within the village, and in the economic position of villagers, that some of the most striking developments of the later middle ages occurred. The horizons of most Englishmen, both political and social, were broader at the end of the period than they were at the beginning.

This chapter has presented in outline many themes that will be developed in the later chapters of the book. It has looked for change, and has concentrated on some of the more obvious areas of development. There is considerable cyclical change within the period, linked for the most part with the changes in population, its rapid growth and equally rapid decline. These changes are important. They mean that a comparison of English society at the beginning of the period with that at the end of it will not provide an adequate measure of the changes over time which altered men's attitudes and their institutions. The Black Death provides a bar to a straightforward understanding of the development of English society. It is a check to our imaginations, just as it was a check to the lives of so many Englishmen. We may not believe that all change is progress, let alone that all change is for the good, but we may well—at least unconsciously—take it for granted that history is concerned with measuring the pace and estimating the effect of changes which operated in a single direction. In the later middle ages that is not the case. To understand why not, it is necessary to look at the level of population, and to see how the population was settled on the land.

The level of population in England in 1175 and in 1425, at the beginning and at the end of the period covered by this book, was probably around two and a half millions. Behind this uniformity, however, there was both a major rise in population and a major decline. To appreciate these movements is of crucial importance for an understanding of medieval English society.

The population figures that are available present a mixture of precision and uncertainty, and uncertainty predominates. The mixture reflects the sources. In the late eleventh century there was the nationwide survey of Domesday Book, and in 1377 there was the first of the national poll-taxes. These are the twin piers from which we have to bridge the long period which intervenes. Otherwise the sources are strictly localised. From the thirteenth century, there is information for population levels for the area of Taunton in Devon and for a number of fenland villages in southern Lincolnshire. If the sources are difficult to interpret in detail, the main lines of development are none the less clear.

From around the year 1000 the rate of increase in population speeded up; it probably increased particularly rapidly from 1100; and it continued to increase throughout the thirteenth century. By around 1300, the peak of medieval population in England, the figure had almost doubled since 1175, reaching between four and five millions. In the first half of the fourteenth century the rate of growth evened out, and population may have declined slightly. There was a serious crisis in arable and pastoral farming in the period 1315 to 1322. From the middle of the fourteenth century the population of England fell dramatically. Dominating the demographic history of the later middle ages there was the plague. It crossed the Mediterranean in 1348, and attacked western Europe with devastating force. If contemporaries are to be believed, then up to half the population of England died from the plague between the years 1348 and 1350. This, however, is highly unlikely. The balanced reporting of contemporary disaster has always been difficult. In the middle ages it was impossible; both the strictly localised knowledge of individuals, and the assumptions they used, alike stood in its way. A figure of around 25 per cent, specifically for the plague mortalities of 1348 to 1350, would seem much more likely.

Between the 1340s and the 1440s the population of England fell by at least 50 per cent. The Black Death was the first of a series of plagues which, when combined with other epidemic diseases, kept the population down. There were major outbreaks of plague in 1360-1, in 1369, and in 1375; if the plague diminished in severity thereafter, it was still a frequent visitor. Mortality figures amongst the nobility had been calculated as follows: 7.75 per cent in 1349, 18.7 per cent in 1361, 5.75 per cent in 1369 and 5.3 per cent in 1375. For the nobility it was the 'second pestilence' that was the most serious. The nobility, in their stone-built dwellings, arguably enjoyed a relative immunity from the plague. The permanent decline of population, when all other factors should have led it to pick up again, is a remarkable phenomenon. For it is normally famine, rather than disease, that provides a permanent check on population increase.

There is more than one explanation possible for the decline in population in the century after the Black Death. It is possible that a decline in fertility both preceded the plague, and then served to prolong its impact. This would be one explanation of the negative replacement rates recorded for the aristocracy between 1341 and 1441; that is, that there seem to have been more deaths of men than there were sons surviving to replace them. It is also possible that the explanation is to be found in the continuance of high mortality working in a way that destroyed the normal balance of the population, and hence its capacity to recover from disease. The chronicler Knighton said that in 1360-1, 'those of greater and lesser rank died, but especially young men and children.' The chronicler of Meaux abbey described this as the 'children's plague'. Several of the later plague epidemics are reported to have had the same effect. Some allowance must be made for the borrowing of ideas, but the chronicle reports are not mere copyings. One chronicler, comparing 1360-1 with 1349-50, said that the later plague spared women, but that it proved 'more destructive of the nobility and prelacy', a verdict which later study has confirmed. Whether or not there was a decline in fertility, the century after the Black Death was undoubtedly a great age for disease.

Population studies give rise to a number of related questions. How long did people live in the middle ages? In what areas did they live? And what were the results of changes in population on the nature of medieval settlement? These questions concern fundamental developments in the nature of English society.

There survive from this period the first reliable figures for life expectancy. The figures again are for the landholding classes. They show that in the best years recorded, in the early thirteenth century, life expectancy for men at birth was 35 years. Infant mortality was high, but even for men who reached the age of 20, the life expectancy was no better than 49 years in all. These are the highest figures. For the whole of the fourteenth century, life expectancy was much lower than this. In the plague generations, from 1348–1375, it was down to 17 years at birth, so that at least half of the people born then would not have survived long enough to raise a family. Table 1 shows for every 1,000 children born the number who survived to reach the 15 to 19 age group.[1]

Table 1

up to 1276	1276–1300	1301–25	1326–48	1348–75	1376–1400	1401–25	1426–50
715	689	688	644	373	494	479	689

The ten kings of England from Henry II to Henry V lived out the following numbers of years: 56, 42, 48, 65, 68, 43, 64, 33, 46, 34, the average being 50 years. The expectation of life of those paying animal heriots in five Winchester manors was 24 years on entry to the tenement between 1245 and 1299, and 20 years from 1300 to 1348. It varied between 17 years in the decade 1310 to 1319, and 28 years in 1260 to 1269. A man had, on average, between 20 and 24 years to farm his own land.

The population of England was small by modern standards. At its peak in 1300 it was only a tenth that of present day England. The gap in scale seems enormous—certainly so wide as to make any imaginative reconstruction of medieval England extremely difficult. But the figures tell only a part of the story. With the history of settlement, the differences of scale are less apparent. The population of England was widely spread over the countryside. The great majority of the settlements which appear on the Ordnance Survey map today will be found in Domesday Book. A sample from a region in Oxfordshire showed over 71 per cent of the parish names to have occurred in Domesday Book; and there is other evidence for settlement in a large number of the parishes which remain. And if the settlement was almost as widespread as in our own day, in many villages it was also as dense. Shipton-on-Cherwell in Oxfordshire was as large in 1086 as it was to be in 1921. The wapentake of Elloe in Lincolnshire seems to have been as heavily settled in the late thirteenth century as it was in the census of 1841. If we want to explain the vast differences between medieval and modern population figures, then we must look not at the density of rural settlement but at the size of the towns.

We may start by looking at the towns around the year 1300 as they might have appeared through the eyes of a visitor to them. The first impression of the largest towns would be of their walls, the defences of the Roman or Saxon periods, which still served to contain most of the population. Overtopping the walls would be the spires of the churches; Lincoln had 46 parish churches, Winchester 57 and Stamford 15, in addition to chapels, hospitals and the houses of religious orders. As dominating would be the castle, the single focus of royal or other magnate lordship within the town. In some towns, such as Stamford, spared by modern development, the modern skyline is still much as it would have appeared in medieval times. As the visitor then went in through one of the town gates, he would walk straight into narrow streets in which craftsmen were working; nearer to the centre there would be fewer craftsmen and more retailers, of food, drink, or clothing. He would come across specialist markets, within broader and more central streets, for cattle, sheep, horses and pigs. And there would be open market places, in which cattle could be penned, and the stalls set out in rows, one for each of the main specialities. 'Those engaged in business of various kinds', said William fitz Stephen of London, 'sellers of goods, hirers of labour, are distributed every morning into their different districts according to their trade.' In all but the very smallest towns the pattern would have been the same.

Taking an impression from half a mile away, and a five-minute stroll through the streets, the visitor could see those features of the town which we must imaginatively reconstruct. The town's functions first of all. The castles, which the Conqueror and his successors and followers had built to subdue the Saxons, continued in more peaceable times to dominate their towns: they were the centres of lordship and administration. The towns were administrative centres not just for laymen but also for ecclesiastics. The Christian church had settled in the towns of the later Roman empire, and in so doing contributed to their survival. The bishops had always been based in the towns; the kings were increasingly to be so; but the lay magnates were not, although a variety of business brought them there. The universities and the major schools were urban. The new religious orders of the thirteenth century, the Dominicans and Franciscans chief among them, had an urban mission. The towns were the centres of various sorts of social and institutional control. Along with this there went their service function—they provided goods and exchanges for the surrounding countryside. The peasantry sold their agricultural surplus, and bought what clothing and household equipment they could afford. The weekly rhythm of the market represents the heartbeat of the medieval towns. A quite different rhythm, and a quite different type of trade, was transacted at the major fairs: the range of goods was catholic and the clientèle cosmopolitan. In the late thirteenth century a burgess of North-ampton was given a house for the service that during the fair he should provide a kitchen and the stabling for nine horses for a London merchant family. This man's experience may offer us a guide to the long-distance trade of the larger county towns; he knew all about it when it was going on, but yet it was a small part of his life and responsibilities.

In the light of these basic functions we may look at the size of a number of English towns, and the nature of the settlement. It is the market, with its exchanges and the specialisation which these make possible, which distinguishes the country from the town. At the height of its development in the late thirteenth century the average market town might have no more than 500 inhabitants, with that figure reduced to 300 a century later. There were many villages of this size, for the distinction between town and village was one of function, not of size. A town might well have over 1,000 inhabitants without there being any basic changes in its function. At Banbury in Oxfordshire, for instance, the provision trades still predominated in the market; but it was an important centre of lordship, that of the bishop of Lincoln, and it was a regional as well as a local market. The king's officers bought livestock here; and its cheese, cakes and ale were developing a national reputation. It is with towns five or six times the size of the average market—say 3,000 plus before 1300, and 2,000 plus in the late fourteenth century—that it becomes necessary

to look away from the market place, however favoured it had become, to understand the position which the town enjoyed. There
were only about thirty towns of this category in medieval England.
With but a few exceptions these were either regional centres of
importance, many of them county towns, or they were ports. From
Coventry, with 7,000 after the plague, down through Norwich,
Lincoln, Salisbury to Hereford and Worcester, with 2,000 after the
plague, there is a descent from first division to amateur football at the
time of writing, but in the middle ages these were all episcopal towns
and important regional centres. Then King's Lynn, Colchester
and Boston, the seventh, eighth and ninth ranking towns in 1377,
each with a population of between 4,000 and 5,000, and Newcastle,
Great Yarmouth, Plymouth, Exeter, Hull and Ipswich, were the
main ports. These were of similar size to the county towns, but they
had a quite different social structure. They were more recent settlements, all but insignificant administratively, with a predominance of
craft and distributive trades.

Above the regional centres, there were at various times the provincial centres of Winchester, York and Bristol. In the twelfth
century Winchester, the capital of Wessex in the Anglo-Saxon
period, was the second city of the kingdom, with 7,000 inhabitants:
Norwich and York had around 5,000 each at this time, and Bristol
3,000. But its administrative role was lost to London, and Winchester
atrophied—in 1377 it had around 2,000 inhabitants, and we are told
that in the fifty years previous to 1440, 11 streets, 17 parish churches
and 987 dwellings had been ruined through pestilence and the
withdrawal of trade. Bristol had by then replaced it as the second city
of the kingdom, in terms of population. York, though it had to suffer
the competition of its outport Hull and a general decline of northern
trade, was the second city administratively—it was a metropolitan
see, and at various times between 1298 and 1337 the whole royal
government moved there in the course of the Scottish wars. London,
with 25,000 inhabitants in the mid-twelfth century and 50,000 by the
end of our period, went from strength to strength. It kept its size
through the population checks of the fourteenth century, as did
others of the metropolitan centres of the later middle ages. The
development of society and government made by then reached the
point at which it could support towns on this scale. Yet although fitz
Stephen could proudly boast that London was 'pre-eminent among
the great and celebrated cities of the world', in fact it was not, and
earlier empires—before the fragmentation of power in the dark

ages—had supported urban settlements of much greater extent than those of medieval Europe. Around 1300, when London may have had 50,000 inhabitants, Cordova had 60,000, Paris and Milan 80,000, and Venice and Florence 100,000 each. The period we are considering is important for the rise of major ports, for the establishment of a considerable number of market towns, and for the final confirmation of London as the capital city of the land.

Thanks to the work of recent archaeology we can see the physical reconstruction of many of these settlements on the ground. The gains for the later medieval period have not been as considerable as those for the Anglo-Saxon period, for which written evidence is so much scantier. For an imaginative reconstruction of the medieval town the archaeological evidence is unrivalled. As a multi-storey car-park goes up in Finsbury, or additions to the president's lodging of an Oxford college, or a new Marks and Spencer's in what was once Jews Lane, Norwich, the new wealth of the 1960s and 1970s offers a brief glimpse of the life of the medieval town beneath. Sometimes we find little more than that Houndsditch in Aldgate, London, 'contained much 14th century rubbish and the remains of more than six dogs', which is satisfying but hardly sensational. But from the sustained digs in such places as Winchester, York, Southampton, and King's Lynn we can glimpse the men as well as their animals. The store of a late thirteenth-century merchant's house, that of Richard of South-wick, in Southampton has preserved a considerable range of imported pottery, ceramics from Spain and claret-jugs from Saintonge, woollen cloth and silk, some tally sticks for business, traces of a wide range of foodstuffs and fruit, the stave of a long-bow, two *ampullae* from Canterbury embossed with portraits of St Thomas, and the skeletons of cats and of a pet monkey. In fourteenth-century Southampton archery was more than just a gentlemanly sport: the town was burnt to the ground by the French in 1338.

Away from the centres of the towns there were the industrial areas. At Winchester one such area has been found in excavation. It shows a series of workshops in the fronts of the houses, used by fullers and dyers in cloth-finishing. Specially constructed water channels in the front of each house provided the water that these occupations required. The living quarters often contained only a single room, though some of these dwellings had a hall also. Behind these, the yards contained vats for boiling the cloth, and racks for stretching it and for drying it out. In the same area, at different periods on two different house sites, there are rows of cottages, 5m by 5.3m, which

WINCHESTER   Lower Brook Street 1967
              Early Fourteenth-Century Levels

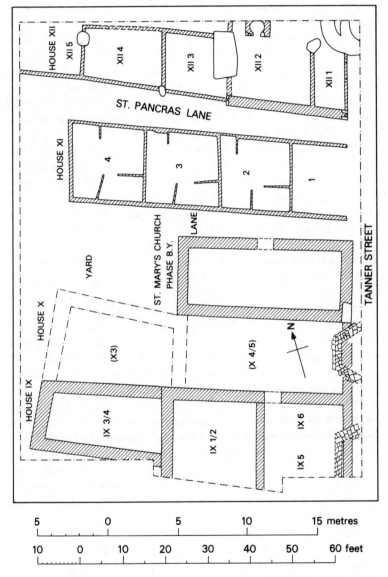

Figure 1 *Artisan housing from the Lower Brook Street site in Winchester, showing St Mary's church and a row of cottages. This was a cloth-making area, and the cobbled drainage channel in front of the houses was an important feature of the town landscape*

seem to have been built speculatively by landlords as cheap housing for artisans. Figure 1 shows one of these rows, and a small parish church in the midst of the grime and dirt, which served as an industrial mission.

This small industrial area at Winchester had a comparatively short lifespan. Before the late twelfth century the area was much less intensively occupied, and there is no sign of industrial activity. By the mid-fifteenth century it was out of use also, and had become an open space once more. What happened at Winchester had its parallel in many other major towns in the same period: the wave of town population flowed and, as suddenly, retreated.

The towns could only expand by receiving considerable immigration from the surrounding countryside. Stratford-upon-Avon was a new town founded by the bishop of Worcester in the 1190s: he obtained the grant of a market, and laid out his new borough in uniform building plots or 'burgages', held for 1s a year in lieu of all services to the lord. The town expanded, and a document of the 1250s shows where much of its population had came from. Of those men whose surnames indicated their place of origin, 90 per cent came from villages and hamlets within a 16 mile radius of the town. This represents the range of the medieval market; the men who settled there would have known the town well. Not only did immigrants often come from the town's market area, but they tended to settle near the town gate leading to their own locality. Such towns must be seen primarily as market centres, as providing the basic exchanges, the goods and the specialised services for the area of countryside immediately surrounding them.

The market is thus the central feature both of small and large towns in this period. That of the town of Northampton may serve for many. There was a single large open space around which were set up rows of stalls devoted to particular trades: there was the butchers' row, mercers' row, cobblers' row, cooks' row, and a malt row. These stalls are now represented by a row of shops which separate the market square from a street called Drapery. Off Drapery was Goldsmith's Street; elsewhere a Fullers' Street and a Weavers' Street. Speed's map of Northampton in 1610 is reproduced as Figure 2. In such towns the central market functions shaded off into a large number of specialist craft areas, as we have seen. It is the range of these crafts, not the size of the settlement, which marks off the countryside from the town. We have some figures from the west midlands. In Stow-on-the-Wold there were 28 separate crafts or trades; in Chipping Camden 35; in Cirencester 43. In towns of this size retailing was more important than manufacturing. There was a clear preponderance of retailers of food and drink and articles of clothing. Individual manufacturing crafts were less important, whether metal, leather, wood or textiles. In the larger towns the manufacturing crafts had a greater place: in York in Edward I's time 30 per cent of the new freemen were in the leather trades, and 17 per cent in metal crafts. This rather overshadowed the 29 per cent engaged in provisioning, and the 7 per cent concerned with textiles. And both services and manufacturing individually outweighed the 10 per cent who were engaged in commerce and shipping. It was the merchants who had the wealth, but it was the service and craft industries which occupied the majority of the population and dominated the settlement.

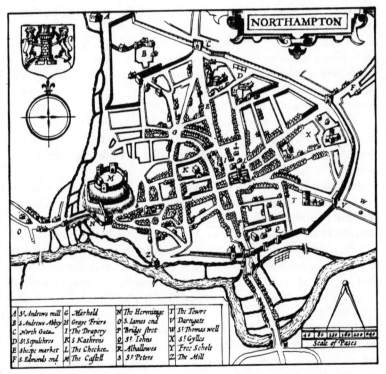

A	St Andrews mill	G	Marhold	N	The Hermitage	T	The Towre
B	S Andrews Abbey	H	Graye Friers	O	S. Iames end	V	Darngate
C	North Gate	I	The Drapery	P	Bridge ſtret	W	St Thomas well
D	St Sepulchres	K	S Kathrens	Q	St Iohns	X	St Gylles
E	ſheepe market	L	The Checker	R	Alhallowes	Y	Free Schole
F	S Edmonds end	M	The Caſtell	S	St Peters	Z	The Mill

Scale of Paces

Figure 2 The map of Northampton from John Speed's Northampton Shire, 1610. It offers at least the illusion of a three-dimensional town-plan, and the castle and the main churches appear prominently

There is for the countryside no counterpart to the kind of description of London provided by William fitz Stephen. There are very few medieval maps. But the story of the medieval countryside is written on the surface of the landscape itself. It has a strong plot, with the many twists and yet the basic simplicity of a good whodunnit. The simplicity comes from the stability of the main characters. The physical geography of England has determined land use over centuries, offering little scope for experiment. The boundaries of the main settlements, the parishes and villages of England are substantially the same today as they had been in the thirteenth century. Those boundaries, following the main features of the landscape, go back well beyond the age of written records. At Wharram Percy in the East Riding of Yorkshire, the excavators have suggested that 'the basic plan of the medieval village was determined by the layout of the Romano-British fields'.[2] This is one of the major deserted medieval village sites in England, and is now in the care of the Department of the Environment. In the two centuries before the Norman Conquest, the numerous distinct settlements which were grouped together to form the earliest manors in England, became the tenancies of individual lords, and went their own ways. Population grew: agricultural exploitation became necessarily more intensive. The growth of smaller units of production in part grew from, in part led to, the growth of exchanges. That could only strengthen the individuality of the main regions of England. The development of trade made possible the specialisation of function of large areas of highland, of forest, and of lowland England.

For the history of settlement, and much else besides, the distinction between highland and lowland England is a key division in English society. A line drawn between Teesmouth in the north-east and Weymouth in the south-west is conventionally taken as defining the two halves. It divides varieties of farming practice first of all. On the grass uplands the principal form of capital was stock—cattle, horses, and sheep. In the lowlands the farmers had a greater choice of land utilisation. In the great mixed farming areas of the midlands, they could choose between arable and pastoral husbandry with some element of freedom. It is clear that along with the expansion of settlement in the thirteenth century, there came a movement of the frontier between arable and pastoral husbandry in marked favour of arable. Thousands of acres of the most unpromising arable land were put under the plough in the thirteenth century. Much of this land went right out of cultivation after the Black Death, and has remained so to this day: land high up on Dartmoor, and the region of Long-wood Warren in Hampshire, described by Cobbett on one of his rural rides as 'amongst the most barren of the Downs of England'. It is a rare car or rail journey across the midlands that does not show sheep grazing on the ridge and furrow of old ploughed land.

The different topography and farming use of highland and low-land England in turn led to two different sorts of settlement. The distinction between the nucleated villages of the lowlands and the hamlets of highland England is a commonplace. As important, how-ever, was the division between enclosed and open-field England, a

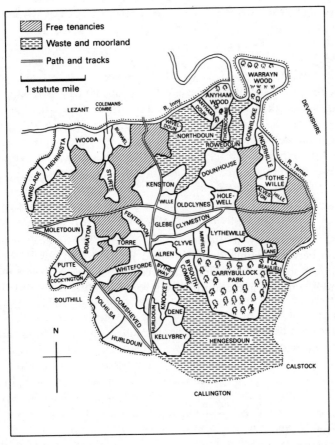

Figure 3 A manor from the highland zone of England: plan of the Duchy of Cornwall manor of Climsland

division that cut right across highland and lowland and the different settlement types. The first settlements that will be considered are villages, one of them from the highland and one from the lowland zones of England. The village of Climsland in Cornwall shows the structure of manorialism in the highland zone (see Figure 3). The manor was bounded on the north by the river Inny, and on the east by the river Tamar. Within the manor, almost one hundred conventionary and villein tenants held around 2,500 acres of land and 500 acres of waste. The free tenants held a further 500 acres, which like the waste and the woodland lay largely on the boundaries of the settlement. In the heart of the manor there was a deer-park, one of the most distinctive features of medieval lordship. Alongside the deer-park there were the holdings of the peasantry, each of whom had about 25 acres of land. The landscape was one of small closes, not of large fields, and within the closes the tenants had compact groups of land.

In lowland England it would be possible to take many well-documented examples of what would probably be regarded as the classic form of English medieval settlement, the open-field village. One of the most famous of them, Hitchin in Hertfordshire, was taken by Seebohm a hundred years ago as the starting point for his book, *The English Village Community*. Figure 4 shows the two main streets, with the church at the junction between them, and the way that the lands of the tenants in the eighteenth century lay scattered through the fields, just as they had done in Hitchin and hundreds of other villages throughout the middle ages. There is no doubt, from the results of excavations of dozens of deserted villages, from maps of the early modern period, and from the clear evidence of the landscape today, that this was a pattern to which many medieval villages conformed. As a typical if not the universal medieval English community, it can serve as a 'model' in the reconstruction of medieval society. The life of the fields and the life of the community went together: this was a form of land tenure which made communal agriculture unavoidable. In such a situation it might well seem that any idea of development would be foreign to the very soil itself. Such an idea merges easily with the modern romanticism of village life. It is important not to make the medieval village immutable. Settlements were formed and abandoned, grew and declined, as population shifts and other social and economic forces acted upon them.

There was no contemporary description of the medieval countryside, but several survive for the early modern period. What most struck foreigners in the sixteenth century, and what the English tended to take for granted, was the amount of woodland and pasture. If this was true of the sixteenth century it must have been all the more true of the twelfth. Beyond the areas of settlement there were large areas of woodland and waste. One belt of woodland stretched almost without interruption from the west country through to western Lincolnshire. Further north the Forest of Arden, in the south the Weald and the New Forest, presented major obstacles to the expansion of settlement. A considerably wider area, in the late twelfth century possibly up to a fifth of England, lay under forest jurisdiction, which while it did not necessarily indicate the presence of woodland none the less hindered the expansion of cultivation. In the twelfth and thirteenth centuries particularly, there was a continuation of a long process of land clearance—the larger areas of woodland

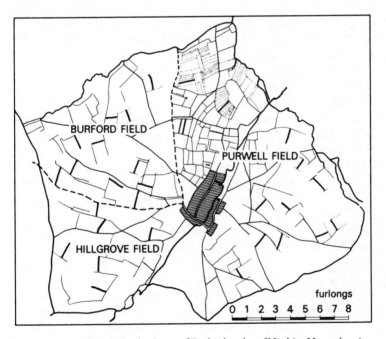

Figure 4 A manor from the lowland zone of England: a plan of Hitchin, Herts, showing the strips of a single tenant scattered among the three open fields of the village

were whittled down, and many smaller tracts disappeared alto-
gether. In considering both population and settlement two periods
can be distinguished, dividing around the year 1300. Up to this date,
it was the expansion of the cultivated area which was the main feature
of the history of settlement.

The great majority of medieval settlements, even if they were not
individually recorded in Domesday Book, were in existence by the
eleventh century. The number of new villages founded after this time
was small. It is the expansion of established settlements which we
must consider first of all. Figure 5 gives an interpretation of the
development of settlement in what are now three parishes in eastern
Hampshire. Chalton and Blendworth were villages founded in the
tenth century. The original common fields were extended in the later
middle ages, to provide resources for communities that were
growing in size. Idsworth was probably an eleventh-century foundation, and by the late twelfth century it was an established village. It
was to lose ground at the expense of Finchdean, which had earlier
been a hamlet. Now the twelfth-century church is all that remains of
Idsworth, standing in isolation in the midst of fields. On the frontiers
of the three settlements, each in different ways evolving and expanding their concerns, forest and waste ground were steadily
cleared. The later middle ages saw the establishment and expansion
of numerous small farmsteads. Their names, and their structure,
preserve the record of their foundation: Woodcroft and Wick in
Chalton parish, Woodhouse and Woodhouse Ash in Blendworth
parish. The pattern of small closes, the clearances of individual
families, stands in marked contrast to the open fields that surrounded
the villages.

It is the expansion of settlements such as these, and in particular the
small enclosures of individual freeholding families, that are the most
characteristic development of our period. The expansion of settlement broke down the barriers between villages, the most basic of
frontiers in a society whose concerns were localised and whose
communications were poor. Expansion was the chief but not the
only feature of the development of these villages. Other changes
were not in themselves tied to population growth. Settlements
grew, and declined. Not only was there the virtual desertion of
Idsworth in the century after the Black Death, but Blendworth, a
longer established village, slowly migrated to a new site a quarter of a
mile to the west of the initial one. Settlements moved, manor houses
moved, only the churches remained fixed points in the midst of

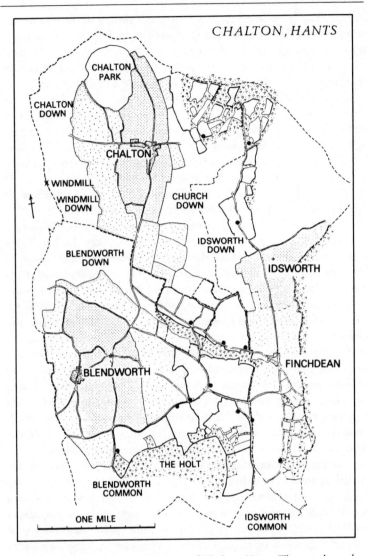

Figure 5 Medieval settlement in the region of Chalton, Hants. The map shows the distinction between the village fields, and the downland and the woodland that surrounded the villages. The original fields and their extension are stippled; the downland is unshaded; and the black dots represent the farmsteads from which the waste was colonised

change. The 'new' Blendworth only got a church in the nineteenth century, and the original parish church was demolished in 1960. What this example shows very clearly is that the history of individual villages will not of itself give us an adequate picture of the dynamics of settlement change. The idea of the village as a model of stability in a changing world is one which we must put out of our minds.

The colonisation of the medieval period was primarily the work of the free peasantry. This proves to be true even of areas which at first sight seem to be dominated by the major landlords, and whose colonisation seems to have taken place on a scale beyond the capacity of individuals to organise. The soke of Peterborough was an area of active colonisation both of forest and of fenland. The abbey of Peterborough owned nine-tenths of the property within it. It was the abbey that stood at the head of the community when it purchased the disafforestation of the area in 1214 for nearly £1,000. And yet if we look rather more closely at the records for this period we get a different picture. The records of assarts made before the disafforestation give long lists of tiny parcels of land, most of them of no more than one or two acres, recently cleared by freeholding families. An active market developed in these assart freeholds. In some areas the abbey slowly bought up much of the land thus cleared: in Paston, by the fourteenth century, it had made a new manor, which it farmed in demesne, from the consolidation of numerous small parcels of assarted land. The enclosures of which it was built up still preserved the names of the families responsible for clearing the land: 'Gernouniswong, formerly the land of Robert Gernoun', 'Nevilswong', 'an acre and a half which belonged to Thomas Underwood'. In the 1970s, in a further stage of colonisation, the 'new town' of Peterborough has spread into the areas cleared from the forest in the twelfth century.

The monasteries had their part to play, as entrepreneurs. If one new Peterborough manor was created through the consolidation of small freeholds, another at Biggin Grange to the north-west of Oundle proceeded from large-scale clearances which the monastery organised. At Biggin 1,000 acres were carved out of Rockingham Forest in the century after 1170, and this grange became the largest and most prosperous manor on the abbey estate. On the other side of the forest, at the same time, the Cistercian monks at Pipewell were engaged in assarting. The Cistercians are the best known colonising landlords of the day. They settled 'far from the madding crowd' as much from necessity as from conviction. To support a large community in the life of gentlemen, albeit gentlemen of ascetic tastes, needed several thousand acres of land, and in the twelfth century estates of this size could only be created on the frontiers of settlement. The aristocracy were happy to give woodland and waste, holdings which they lacked the manpower to exploit, to the new order. In the mid-twelfth century Roger Earl of Hereford gave to 'St Mary and the order of Citeaux':

> a certain place in the valley of Castiard called Flaxley to construct an abbey, and all the land which is called West Dean which belonged to Wulfric, and a forge at Erdlandam and all the land below the old castle of Dean to assart, and a fishery at Rodley called Newerra, and meadow in Pulmede and all their rights within the forest of Dean, and the whole demesne of Dymock and the land which belonged to Ernald the clerk, and the land of Ernald and the land of Wulfric.

The programme before the monks was thus marked out in the very charter of foundation. They were given land in the Forest of Dean, which they had to assart. Their predecessors in the area were a small number of free peasant settlers, the rights over whom were transferred to the new abbey. The meadowland, the pasture for the animals which would work the new estate, was the most vital of the resources transferred to them. It sounds hard work, and very likely it was; after the twelfth century the foundation could not sustain the basic community of thirteen (the abbot and twelve monks) laid down by the Cistercian rule. There were around seventy Cistercian foundations in England and Wales, and the majority of them grew to a greater substance than did Flaxley.

In forming a picture of the process of colonisation up to the end of the thirteenth century, the campaigns of land clearance by the greater landowners have to be put alongside the piecemeal reclamations of peasant freeholders. We are best informed on the colonisation of the period 1150 to 1250. There was no start to land clearance in 1150, of course, simply a proliferation of written records. It seems likely, however, that the check a hundred years later was a real one, that the reserves of colonisable land were exhausted over large parts of England. Some new colonisation there was, even in the early fourteenth century. In the north of England in particular there were some large scale clearances during this period: in 1333 the abbot of Chester was accused of assarting 400 acres in the Wirral peninsula. But in the south of England the movement had long since spent its force. Some of the force of forest reclamation was transferred to the no less difficult task of colonising the fens.

The great fenland monasteries of Crowland, Ely, Peterborough and Thorney were at the time of their foundation themselves on the frontiers of settlement, perched on a series of islands in the fens which had been placed there by God, so one of their chroniclers thought, that they might be the dwelling places of His servants. To the west of Ely, to the north of Peterborough, and to the east of the parishes now lying on the fifty foot contour, hundreds of acres lay undrained and untilled. Some of it was land of exceptional quality. With the creation of a series of sea banks in the twelfth and thirteenth centuries, reclamation from the fen and the sea proceeded apace. In the wapentake of Elloe alone, about fifty square miles were reclaimed from the fen between 1170 and 1240. A notable feature of this process of reclamation was the way that groups of villages worked together. These were communities that depended on communal action not just for their growth but for their very survival. A Crowland Abbey chronicle described a year's work in colonising the fen at Deeping, and then continued:[3]

> the following summer the men of Holland at Moulton, Weston and Spalding followed the example of the men of Deeping. They made an agreement between themselves, with the consent of all the people, and man by man divided out their fens above our waters of Asendyke. Some of them tilled their portions, some kept them for hay and some of them, as before, allowed theirs to lie as several pasture for their beasts; and they found the earth fat and fruitful.

Lordship was weak in this area, and what strong lordship there was was resented by the fenmen. In 1189 the men of south Holland, hearing rumour of the death of Henry II, combined to invade the fens belonging to Crowland Abbey.

The monasteries founded granges in the fens, as they did in the forest, and here too they built up manors by consolidating the clearances of the free peasantry. The pace of fenland reclamation seems to have continued through into the fourteenth century. Abbot William Clopton of Thorney (1305–1322) was remembered in his monastery as a great encloser of fenland. The other great area of reclamation was on the south coast, in Kent and in Sussex. The sea–edge manors of the priory of Christ Church, Canterbury fought valiantly but with no great success against the encroachment of the sea. At Lydden in East Kent 405 acres were described as lying 'in peril of the sea'. This land was of marginal quality and grew mainly oats, and a considerable amount of labour and capital was needed to keep it in cultivation at all. In some areas of forest and fen, as in this case, the growth of cultivation was a growth into marginal land.

Just as the expansion of settlement characterised the thirteenth century, so contraction and desertion characterises the period after the Black Death. The evidence of expansion comes from topography and written records. Evidence of desertion, in the nature of things, comes rather from excavations of deserted villages. Around two thousand deserted villages have already been identified, and at least a tenth of that number have been excavated. Though much work remains to be done, the chronology of desertion is fairly clear. The period immediately after the Black Death saw fewer desertions than had once been thought. From 1350 to 1450 up to 20 per cent of deserted villages were abandoned, the proportion ranging from 12 to 30 per cent in four midland counties surveyed. The high peak of desertion came everywhere after 1450, with the enclosure movement of the early modern period. In part though these precise dates of desertion are a fiction; many settlements which are recorded as being late fifteenth- or early sixteenth-century desertions had lost population in the later middle ages to such an extent that they ceased to be viable as independent units. One such village was Woollashill in Worcestershire, which lay on a small and cramped site on the slopes of Bredon Hill, three miles south of the monastery at Pershore and close also to Elmley Castle, the centre of the estates of the Beauchamp family. It was a late settlement, probably post Conquest, and always a small one. In 1275 there were less than fifteen families in the village, none of them wealthy. The records that survive for the period after the Black Death suggest a community that was in decay. The population slowly declined. More and more holdings were returned to the lord's hands, for the mixture of high rents and comparatively poor land meant that tenants could not be found for them. In 1429 six out of thirteen tenants were presented at the manor court as having ruinous buildings; these men must either have lived outside the village, or have had more than one holding. By the mid-sixteenth century the village was deserted, and its arable converted to pasture. This picture of the atrophying of a small community may serve for many of the late medieval and early modern desertions.

The work on deserted medieval villages has done a good deal more than simply elucidate the chronology of desertion, and the physical extent of villages at different points of time. It has shown also the way

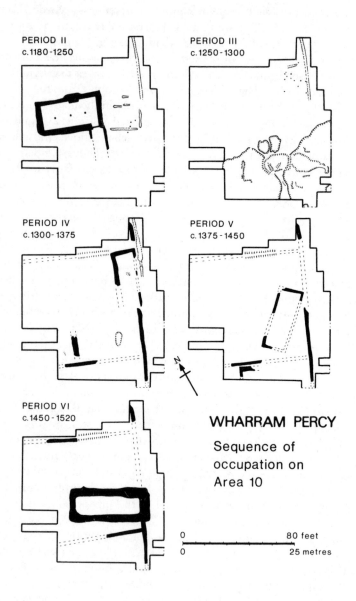

PERIOD II
c. 1180-1250

PERIOD III
c. 1250-1300

PERIOD IV
c. 1300-1375

PERIOD V
c. 1375-1450

PERIOD VI
c. 1450-1520

WHARRAM PERCY

Sequence of
occupation on
Area 10

0   80 feet
0   25 metres

Figure 6 A sequence of buildings on one croft in the deserted medieval village of Wharram Percy in Yorks, E.R. A manor-house of the late twelfth century was succeeded by a series of peasant farmsteads

that the physical appearance of the village changed. The houses themselves were rebuilt frequently, so frequently at times that it seems that every new tenant must have built afresh. On rebuilding, the houses might completely change their alignment. Building materials changed also. In the course of the thirteenth century, timber houses were replaced in many villages by houses made of stone. As an example of such changes, one of the first crofts to be examined at Wharram Percy produced evidence for not only a sequence of later medieval peasant buildings, but also the stone-built cellar of an earlier manor-house (see Figure 6). In the thirteenth century this manor-house was abandoned; thereafter there was only one manor-house, on the northern boundaries of the village. From the later thirteenth century till the time of the abandonment of the village at the beginning of the sixteenth century, as many as four houses were built on the area of the former manor-house. The earlier three of these were on an approximately north–south axis, whereas the last to occupy the site was orientated east–west. There might at the same time be major changes in the village plan. At Wawne, also in the East Riding of Yorkshire, between Beverley and Hull, there were in the early middle ages about twelve peasant houses set in an area in one corner of the village. In the fourteenth century these were destroyed, and a new and regular series of sixteen houses was laid out parallel to the street. This is a 'shrunken' not a 'deserted' settlement. Figure 7 shows the changes made. It would be difficult to find a clearer visual picture of the way that whole communities made a 'new start' after the Black Death. Within the village there was constant change. If we take as the measure of change the experience of an individual, we must recognise that a man aged 60 in 1400 would have seen in his own lifetime changes in his village far more radical than a man of similar age in most villages today. He would look out upon an attenuated area, whose structure would have changed out of all recognition. If he felt, as many old men feel, that all change is for the worst, then he would have seen a lot that he could only regret.

Excavations both in town and in countryside have offered for the first time reliable information on the living conditions of the medieval peasantry and the artisans. The normal village survey will state that each individual tenant occupied a toft and a croft, the toft being the site of the house and the croft the private enclosure. Within the croft there might be a whole complex of buildings—kilns, outhouses and barns; in terms of buildings the dwelling house was only a part of the peasant's wealth. The crofts themselves were fixed in size; they form the basic divisions of the maps that the archaeologists prepare, and their basic structure can be seen on the Ordnance Survey map and from aerial photographs today (see Plate 1). The visitor to a deserted village site will often be able to pace out several of these crofts, and in so doing start to form an impression of the peasant's environment. The solidity is given by the stone foundations, almost universal in the many areas that had building stone available. The stability is provided by the families themselves, for these units are family units, the crofts are the home farms of a race of peasant cultivators. Within the boundaries of the crofts, fixed over centuries, the changes were considerable. As the excavators work down through successive levels, they discover frequent rebuilding of the houses, constrained by the crofts but in no other way. The buildings at times seem almost as transitory as their occupants. Within this pattern of change and decay amongst the buildings, there were changes both in the types of dwelling and in the building materials used. The material comes to us piecemeal, as a series of blurred impressions of sites. It is important to examine the main feature of living conditions before examining change, and the implications of change.

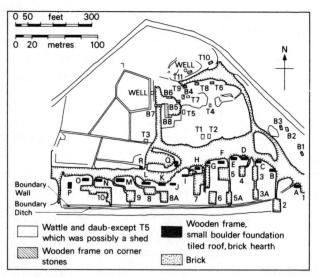

Figure 7 The buildings in an area to the south-east of the village of Wawne, Yorks E. R. The twelfth- to fourteenth-century timber buildings were succeeded by a new and regular layout of fourteenth- and fifteenth-century buildings on stone foundations. Behind some of the late medieval buildings there were cobbled yards

The main type of house found in the villages so far excavated has been the long-house; the larger part, of one or two rooms, was used for living accommodation, the smaller was used for animals, or occasionally for some trade or craft. At Wythemail in Northamptonshire excavation has revealed two stone long-houses, the first of them 11.3 m by 4.9 m, the second 17.4 m by 4 m, and built of limestone. The smaller house dates from the late thirteenth century, the larger from some time in the fourteenth. The larger house had two living rooms, each around 3.7 m square and heated, and two unheated rooms. The growth in size within a uniform structure of building, here that of the long-house, can fairly stand for the development of housing for most peasant families over the later middle ages. There are other house types, but they are found much less often, and we must presume them to have been less frequent. On the one hand there are the cottages, one roomed dwellings, found only rarely and presumed to be the houses of landless men or smallholders, men or women not supporting a family. More frequently we also find a complex of buildings constituting a small farm, in which the living accommodation was kept separate from the rest of the farm buildings. Some semi-deserted villages survived into the fifteenth century as a number of these small farms, which often spread over more than one croft. The change is one of scale rather than one of substance, for the long-houses themselves with their outbuildings formed self-contained farms.

At Faxton in Northamptonshire a croft 45.7 m by 30.5 m has been excavated, and shows a sequence of thirteenth- and fourteenth-century building. The site is interesting since it shows the development of building on a clayland site in the midlands, an area where stone for building is rare. The first building identified was 9.1 m by 4.3 m; it was built on a clay platform, with timber uprights placed in post-holes and supporting mud walls. The building dates from around 1200. In the course of the thirteenth century, a series of larger buildings, around 12.2 m by 5.2 m, were placed on the site, and the timber frames and mud walls were placed on a more permanent foundation of boulders and local ironstone. Part of the yard was cobbled, for better drainage; another part was a garden area, and contained rubbish deposits. At any one point of time, there were never less than two barns in use on this site, an oven, and a clay-lined water trough. The building sequence here has been confirmed from other clayland sites excavated, at Goltho in Lincolnshire and Barton Blount in Derbyshire. All of these are early modern desertions, in which the level of fifteenth-century occupancy seems to have been low.

The sites of deserted medieval villages will frequently show a sequence of buildings dating from the late twelfth to the early fifteenth century, precisely the period which is covered by this book. What do they tell us of the development of English society between these dates, of living conditions and of the wealth contained within the peasant croft? They show an expansion of size and an increase in the permanence of dwellings. They show the variety of building within the crofts, and a flexibility of use; thus a house in one generation might be preserved as a barn in the next. The greater use of stone for building made for greater permanence—a building material earlier confined to the landowning class was taken up by the peasantry at large. The evidence in short seems to show a steady improvement in the standard of housing. On and on, and up and up: the archaeologists would make Whig historians of us all. There are problems with this material. The dating of buildings, chiefly from pottery and coin finds, is relatively imprecise. But the sequence of buildings does not admit of serious doubt. And they do show a steady improvement in peasant living conditions, right the way through a period for which other evidence encourages us to believe that the standard of living of the peasantry was falling, with some of them perched precariously on the very margin of subsistence. An examination of peasant housing does not invalidate this view, but it makes it difficult to sustain in one respect. The villages revealed by excavation were composed of numerous small farms, each of them with a living house and a number of outbuildings. The hovels of the poor have defied the spade so consistently that it must be doubted whether they were ever there at all. This evidence is important. We can hardly form a proper impression of the medieval peasantry if we ignore what we can see with our own eyes, and touch with our own hands.

The change from timber to stone building came at a time when supplies of timber were being rapidly eroded in many regions. It is unlikely, however, that the change from timber to stone in building was made because timber was scarce. Stone stood for greater permanence. It was a sign of status. In many areas it was readily available: in Wharram Percy indeed the villagers quarried their building stone from their own crofts. There are signs of increasing durability in the contents of the houses also. From the late thirteenth century, the designs of expensive metalware were copied on mass-produced pottery. By the fifteenth century, in the south of England at least, all classes used metal vessels for cooking. At Wolverley in Worcestershire in 1405 a half-virgater bequeathed the following household goods: a two-gallon brass pot, a worn brass pan, a chest, a trough for pastry, a vat, a bed, a stand, a round trestle-table, and an iron-bound measure. He had a good range of farming equipment and gear, including a plough and a cart. The contents of his house were none the less sparse, even though the manorial documents record only the more permanent items. The range of metal goods surviving and recorded is impressive, right down to the hinges, locks and bolts from dozens of sites, interesting in that they prove that peasant houses had proper wooden doors rather than mat hangings. Glass is not found in peasant houses; the windows would have been shuttered. Roofs of houses were thatched or made of turf. It was probably the comparatively poor standard of timber and roofing and construction which led to the impermanence of medieval peasant houses. The period through from the thirteenth century seems to be one of an advance in technique, leading to buildings of greater permanence and sophistication.

We are left with the question whether at any point in our period English society had reached the stage of over-population, at which the pressure put by population on resources could not be sustained. The first point to be made is that so far as population is concerned it is unlikely that we are dealing with a single 'society'; there were too many regional differences to make generalisation in terms of the whole country helpful. Yet the expansion of settlement in the thirteenth century, and the contraction thereafter, were nationwide phenomena —from the cultivation of Dartmoor above the 500 foot level, to the desertions of clayland villages in the midlands or of villages like Wharram Percy in the Yorkshire Wolds. The tide of arable cultivation, sustained by the pressure of population, reached a peak around 1300, and then receded. The fall in population throughout the fourteenth century is not in doubt. What we see in population statistics we can see also on the ground, a society in the later middle ages in which there was more space, more elbow-room, for those that remained. There comes then the inevitable temptation to go beyond the archaeological evidence, and the description of the rise and fall of individual communities. There are from some areas detailed figures for landholding and for the size of population. It is from some very precise manorial records that the picture of a society confronted with a Malthusian crisis of subsistence has been drawn.

One of the regions studied in detail is Elloe in south Lincolnshire, which had seen rapid expansion in area and population since the time of Domesday. Here the absence of strong lordship, the easy availability of pasture and non-agrarian employment, and the richness of the land itself, offered ideal conditions for the expansion of population. The figures for the density of population in 1260 and then again in 1951, when the size of the modern towns in the area is discounted, come in each case to around 200 persons per square mile. To find that the density of settlement in the thirteenth century was similar to that of our own day is a striking discovery. But it gets us no nearer to the question of overpopulation. It is also possible to calculate the size of the holding available to each family, which after making allowances for fallow and for tithes comes out at rather under 1.5 acres per person, or—rather more helpfully perhaps—6 or 7 acres per family. It seems likely that this was the maximum density of population anywhere in England, for this was a fertile area at the height of its medieval level of settlement. If the amount of land available for each family seems small, it must be remembered that fish and fowl were readily available from the fens, that the herrings came ashore at the quay which still survives at Herring Lane in Spalding, and that livestock could be kept on the abundant pasture lands. The threat to the stability of this area came less from man than from the sea. The rising level of the North Sea in the thirteenth century threatened disaster, and did eventually make the salterns unusable. In the early modern period also, Elloe for the same reasons would take a more rapid increase in population than elsewhere in the region.[4]

The other area studied in detail is in the west country, on certain manors of the bishopric of Winchester and in particular the large and prosperous manor of Taunton. Figures for the payment of the hundredpenny at Taunton, which was due from all males of 12 years and over, show that population rose rapidly up to the 1260s. If these figures are to be taken at face value, then the population had doubled in fifty years. A selection of these taken at 20-year intervals runs as follows:

1212	588
1232	714
1252	891
1272	1,151
1292	1,154
1312	1,340
1332	1,228

But some of the jumps in this run of figures seem too rapid to be explained in terms of population increase alone; thus the increase from 998 in 1266 to 1,115 in 1268, and the more striking increase from 1,167 in 1309 to 1,344 in 1310. It is difficult to escape the feeling that while population was undoubtedly increasing, so also was the enthusiasm and competence of the manorial administration. If this is so, and undoubtedly attitudes to registering transactions on the land market changed rapidly in the late thirteenth century, then the Taunton figures for heriots become more difficult to use. And it is these figures that have been used to present the clearest argument for overpopulation in the late thirteenth and early fourteenth centuries.[5] 'A society in which every appreciable failure of harvests could result in large increases in deaths is a society balanced on the margin of subsistence.' Now the Taunton figures are most reliable for the more prosperous tenants; they show a fairly stable mortality rate of about 38 a year between the early thirteenth century and the Black Death, rising to over 40 in 1317, at the height of the great famine. It is only in this period of crisis, from 1315 to 1322, that the figures for death-rates show any significant correlation with the price of wheat. The figures for those who paid money heriots and are presumed to be smallholders show a greater correlation between death rates and wheat prices; but there are too many uncertainties in these Winchester figures to allow so weighty an argument to rest on their evidence alone.

Much of the evidence that has just been quoted is technical, and it is strictly local. But if the problems are glossed over, then the reader is deprived of evidence and of the opportunity to use his imagination upon it. And with this evidence a clear head is undoubtedly more important than a notebook stuffed with statistics. Malthus took it as axiomatic that 'population has this constant tendency to increase beyond the means of subsistence.' Englishmen may have been travelling along that road before 1300, but they stopped a long way before its end. Thirteenth-century England was no rural Utopia. The life expectancy of those entering Winchester tenancies was between 22 and 28 years in the thirteenth century, and lower in the early fourteenth. Infant mortality was high. The population was vulnerable to disease. Some of the land occupied was poor, and was later abandoned. But to go on to say that men lived in hovels would be wrong; we know that they did not, for their housing has survived. To say that they scratched a bare living from the soil is at best an over-simplification; the society, which we now turn to examine in more detail, was too sophisticated to be built upon a subsistence agriculture. Anyone turning from the works of George Ewart Evans, who has used interviews with farm labourers whose memories go back into the late nineteenth century, to the manorial court rolls and the agrarian treatises of the late thirteenth century, will find in the latter a world that he can readily recognise. The advice of the modern ancients, and that of Walter of Henley on agrarian practice, shows much similarity of technique; and we should not thereby be led to discount nineteenth-century British farming. The horizons of medieval countrymen were limited, their expertise less so. It shows the limitations of our imaginations, and not of their lives, if we make of our ancestors men whom we cannot understand.

While population changes provide a key to much of the development
of England during the later middle ages, lordship and the structure of
lordship provides a measure of continuity. Wealth continued to come
chiefly from the land, and the social structure was designed to pass
wealth into the hands of the lords. In dealing with medieval landlords
it is important, much more important than now, to accentuate the
second syllable. There was more to lordship than land occupancy, for
medieval lords were the lords not just of land but of men. Domesday
Book is the record of the wealth of the lords who had taken over
England at the Conquest. The currency of Domesday, the unit of
wealth and of lordship, was the manor. The manor was the house of a
lord. Thus at Folkingham in Lincolnshire in 1086, Gilbert of Ghent
had 12 carucates of land: 'Gilbert has five plough-teams in demesne,
and 24 villeins and 5 sokemen and 9 bordars.' The tenants were a part
of the stock of the manor, just as were the oxen. All represented the
jingle of cash in the pockets of the lords. It is important that the
distinction between land lordship and personal lordship be kept in
mind. There were changes in both in the later middle ages, but the
changes in the latter were the more important. In very general terms,
the service element in agricultural tenure, the link between the demesne and the villeinage which lay at the heart of the Domesday
extract just quoted, became less important. As it did so, the whole
idea of unfree tenure was called into question.

The greatest of the landlords was the king. In 1086 the king owned,
that is to say he had under the direct control of his agents, 20 per cent
of the area of England. This was around double the area that his
predecessors, the Anglo-Saxon kings, had owned. The increased
strength of Norman monarchy was due at least in part to the increased strength of its landed base. Below the king there were around
180 tenants-in-chief, men who held from the king the remainder of
the land in England. They were not owners, and they were not

occupiers; they were tenants. They were not owners, for under the theory of the new feudalism the king owned all the land in England. It was granted to them in return for a variety of military and other services, and on their death—always in theory and sometimes in practice—it returned to the king. The tenants were not occupiers either, for they took over large and scattered estates, and brought over large numbers of followers who sought their reward in land. The barons' own tenants were the knights; they were the lords of villages, though villages were often divided between several lords. These were the characteristic occupiers of medieval estates, the main farmers, the tenants of the manors which are the common currency of Domesday Book. Below them, and in some villages alongside them, were the peasantry, tied by bonds which varied a very great deal in their strength to the centres of feudal lordship. The villagers owed services in their turn; some of them a token amount of rent; others—an increasing number—owed a variety of agricultural services. Slaves there were also in 1086, but they need not concern us, for by the late twelfth century there were no slaves in England.

Below the king, in 1200, there was only one social line separating distinct classes, that which marked off the free man from the villein. The free men enjoyed the protection of the king's court; the villeins, in terms of civil jurisdiction, were still subject to their lords. In the ranks of the free no clear dividing line can be drawn, but clear categories can be established. At the top of the heap there were the barons, about 160 of them, who had an average income of around £200. The median income for a barony was £116, for some of these estates were very large. The baronage formed the political nation in 1215, their importance deriving from a strong economic base in a single or a group of counties and from a large following of men. Below them there were the lords of villages, the knightly class, although the title is a reminder of a military function that few of them performed. In the thirteenth century there were perhaps 3,000 men who had the wealth to support knighthood, but only 1,250 of them were knighted and no more than 500 of those could in fact be summoned for a military campaign. Just to hold by military tenure meant very little, for according to the lawyer Bracton anyone who paid even a halfpenny in scutage was a military tenant.

Below the lords there were the peasantry, the freeholders and the customary tenants. At the top of the category of freehold there were holdings of eight virgates, say 240 acres of land, which was the size of a small manor. At the other end of the scale nearly half of the tenancies recorded in the Hundred Rolls in southern England comprised five acres or less. To say that half the free peasantry had holdings of this size would not be warranted, however. Land transfers in eastern England show regular holdings of one or two bovates of land, or 20 to 40 acres. Alongside the freeholders in the village, their holdings much better recorded, there were the unfree tenants, the villeins. The range in size in villein holdings was less than that in freeholdings; 62 per cent of the villein holdings recorded in the Hundred Rolls were of a half-virgate, fifteen acres, or more, 29 per cent of the unfree had small holdings of five acres or less. With the peasantry, as with their lords, the terms of tenure do not provide a guide to wealth.

The paragraphs which follow will look less at the theory of land tenure than at the way lordship was established in the countryside, over the units of settlement considered in the previous chapter. In Domesday Book the units of lordship (the manors) and the units of settlement (the villages and hamlets) were intermixed; in terms of settlement there was little logic in their relationship. A century after Domesday, the units of lordship were coming to correspond a lot more closely to the units of settlement. To take one example, the knights in the eleventh century held small service tenancies carved out of existing estates, such as the land held by Alexander de Alno's uncle, which was referred to in the first chapter. Where the place-name Knighton is found, the knight's *tun* or settlement, it is usually on the fringe of an existing village. The knights of Domesday Book had on average only a hide and a half of land, little more than a large freehold. Some of the descendants of these men became the lords of villages, but many more did not. It required the rationalisation and consolidation of estates for them to do so. A stimulus to these changes, and possibly in part a reflection of them, was the protection given in the late twelfth century to seisin: to the occupiers of land rather than to those who had rights over land. The land which a family directly occupied became more clearly separated from lands over which it had a form of control, through rents or services.

The great magnates were the lords of regions. As an example of the position and influence of a magnate we may take the Beauchamps, earls of Warwick. They started with a secure landed base; they continued to produce male heirs; and they managed to avoid the ultimate penalties of the political career to which their wealth entitled them, and which their position forced upon them. Their wealth in these circumstances could not fail to increase, and in fact it did so dramatically. In the fifteenth century they were in the front rank of the English nobility.

In the twelfth century the Beauchamps had property in over fifty Worcestershire villages, but very little outside that county. Much of the land was in the hands of knightly sub-tenants, providing the Beauchamps with the foundation of their influence but with only a limited income. In 1210 the royal custodians in the vacancy could take over £500 from the Beauchamp estate, but over half this figure was tallage, and the annual income at the beginning of our period was probably nearer £300. The benefits of increasing trade were first felt in the revenues from the towns; it took far longer to tap agricultural revenues effectively. Sixty-six pounds was taken from the town of Worcester in the form of a tallage, an annual tax taken at the lord's will. At the same time the earls of Leicester took £172 a year from the town of Leicester in rent and £200 in tallage, which was half the total revenues of the estate in the vacancy of 1210. Feudal revenues came in spasmodically, and were difficult to collect. Agricultural revenues were fixed. The latter, however, represented the feudal aristocracy's real reserves, and their increased wealth in the thirteenth century came from the exploitation of their agricultural resources.

Careful management brought stability and a larger surplus. A good marriage could bring much greater rewards. And few thir-teenth-century marriages were more profitable than that of William Beauchamp to Isabel Mauduit, the sister and heir of the earl of Warwick, who died childless in 1268. The Mauduit and the Warwick inheritances were two separate baronial estates; when taken along with that of Beauchamp they must have increased the revenues of the Beauchamp family three-fold. They became national figures over-night, in the sense that in 1298 the Beauchamp lands were distributed over eight counties. Yet the base of their power remained, more strongly than ever, the west midlands. They had nine manors in Worcestershire, ten in Warwickshire and three in Gloucestershire. Their hereditary castle at Elmley, the royal castle at Worcester and now the castle at Warwick, each of them important fortifications, were—as they were intended to be—the clearest symbols as well as the instruments of their domination of the surrounding countryside. Lordship was power, and lordship was display. These castles dis-played the power of the Beauchamps over a wide area of the west midlands.

On the basis of this estate the Beauchamps could, indeed they were obliged to, enter national politics, and bid for the rewards and risk the dangers of this involvement. Though politics narrowly defined is not the concern of this chapter, the Beauchamps' further progress should be outlined. The increase of their income first of all, which seems to have been between £2,000 and £3,000 during the fourteenth century. The third earl was a minor in Edward II's last years, the fourth earl was condemned for treason in 1397, but the Lancastrian take-over released the earl from prison and saved the family's fortunes. At the very end of our period the fifth earl Richard managed by two marriages greatly to increase the size of his estate; the first wife brought him land worth almost £700, the second £1,250. At the end of his life the fifth Beauchamp earl of Warwick had a landed income of around £4,000 a year.

The long series of Beauchamp wills gives an idea of the scale of the family's surplus wealth, and the uses to which it was put. Earl Richard's was the greatest of these: as with all of them, 'there is the evidence of many legacies of gold and silver plate and household stuff, and a plentiful supply of gifts to pious uses.'[1] His executors were instructed to have made, 'four images of gold, each of them of the weight of twenty pounds of gold, to be made after my similitude with my arms holding an anchor between my hands.' These were to go to four of the most fashionable shrines in England. Both the extent and the form of this pious display, for the materials were worth £500 clear, are alike remarkable. The images do not survive, but his memorial chapel in the church of St Mary, Warwick does. The Beauchamps enjoyed wealth beyond the dreams of many of their peers. It set them apart in this world, as it was intended to do in the next.

The distinction in scale of wealth between noble and knight, for all that certain individuals may have blurred it, was very clear. In Magna Carta the baronial relief was fixed at £100, that for a single knight's fee at £5. The ratio between these two figures, of 20 to 1, was hardly an arbitrary one, when an average barony was worth around £200 a year and £10 would do well for a knight. In the taxation records of 1436 around fifty baronies and earldoms were worth on average £865, and the main range of baronial income was between £300 and £1,300 a year. Below them, around 180 greater knights had average incomes of £208, and 750 lesser knights averaged £60 a year. The latter figure might come from an estate of one or two manors, which was all that the majority of knightly tenants had. They should be thought of in terms of single villages, from which indeed many of them took their names.

The first example of a knightly estate is taken from Essex. The manor of Langenhoe was held in the second quarter of the fourteenth century by Lionel de Brabenham. It was his only manor. He took from it an average of £14 a year in rent, and £37 from sales of grain and wool, from a demesne of 250 acres. To the total of £51 a year should be added the grain consumed by his household, to the value of perhaps a further £10 a year. At the end of the century the same manor was worth nearer £35 a year, though this figure also must be supplemented by the value of the grain consumed by the household. This is a small manor, but in his own area it made Lionel de Brabenham a man of substance and influence, much of it malign, at least so far as the neighbouring burgesses of Colchester were concerned. In 1350 he and his cronies laid siege to Colchester with armed men, and took tribute from the merchants; and he similarly tyrannised the fishermen of the Colne estuary, on to which his manor abutted. He was a justice of labourers in 1355, and extorted money from his neighbours. The records may seem to be those of the abuse of authority, but the authority was clear. Such things a man could do from a manor worth £50 a year.

Further north, and further up the scale of the gentry, we can get a rather fuller picture of the family of Argentine. Sir John de Argentine, who died in 1318, had four manors: Melbourn in Cambridgeshire, Wymondley in Hertfordshire, Halesworth in Suffolk and Ketteringham in Norfolk. Some accounts for the first two manors survive, which are valuable in that accounts for small lay estates are rare. These will serve to establish our man, and a wide variety of other sources deal with the activities of the Argentines away from home. We have an account for Melbourn for the year just before John's death. He took £45 out of Melbourn in this year; a figure which again does not include the value of the produce consumed, and again is very close to our national figure of £50 for a single manor. There are also records of expenditure, and from them we can start to form an impression of the family's style of life. At Cambridge 12½ quarters of salt were bought, a good deal of linen, and 22 quarters of coal. Timber was transferred for building purposes from his manor at Wymondley. Slippers were bought, a small thing but very much a non-essential, and seven pairs of little socks for a nephew, presumably with a shrewd knowledge of their likely life expectancy. He spent £3 on geese for a feast that he gave to his men at the churching following the birth of an heir. This expenditure may be set in the balance against the £6 which he took from the same men as an aid at the marriage of his daughter. From the account there comes the impression of security and quiet comfort.

John de Argentine seems to have gone north in 1318, and may when he died have been on his way to fight against the Scots. If he did so, he may in part have wished to avenge the death of his younger brother Giles at the battle of Bannockburn four years previously. Giles de Argentine had been the leader of the king's personal bodyguard. He had earlier served abroad with Henry of Luxembourg, and had been imprisoned many times for illegal jousting. A contemporary text describes him as 'the best knight in Christendom'. The younger son as a knight errant seems almost an anachronism in the fourteenth century. It is interesting to compare his career with the quieter life enjoyed by his brother; and to speculate that at times at least he may have enjoyed the pleasures of a warm fire and clean sheets at Melbourn.

The grandfather of these two men, another Giles de Argentine, had a career that was a good deal less romantic, and which serves to complement the picture of the careers open to men of knightly rank. This Giles had been the most active of the political opposition to Henry III. In 1258 and 1259 he served on many of the different committees charged at various times with the work of reform. The committee of nine has been described as a council of lesser barons. Yet to describe Giles as even a lesser baron is misleading, for on his death in 1282 he held only Melbourn and Wymondley, and neither of them directly of the king. His career shows what could be done on a limited base by a man who must be presumed to have had energy, experience and a sense of involvement, rather than any great wealth.

The position in society enjoyed by both the magnate and the knightly class, suggested by these sketches of some of their activities, will perhaps become clearer if we move straight on to examine the comparative position of the peasantry. An income worth £50 at the most prosperous period before the Black Death may not seem very much for a knight, but at a time when £5 was possibly the average income of a priest, and half that sum would serve for a prosperous member of the peasantry, £50 in the context of the village community represents a very clear distinction in scale indeed. And while we must not become slaves to hypothetical figures, those for the knight and prosperous freeman differ in the ratio of 20 to 1, exactly the ratio suggested for the difference between magnate and knight. When we drop down to consider the peasantry, we again cross an enormous gap in terms of wealth as well as of status.

So far the ties of lordship, the exploitation of rights over individuals, have dominated our analysis. For we have been dealing with
the class of lords, men whose political ambitions were furthered and
whose comfort was guaranteed by the possession of large estates and
the labour of the peasantry. But we must beware of thinking that
lordship was all-pervasive at the village level. There are numerous,
quite clear indications that it was not. In the first place, and most
obviously, there was a large group of free peasantry, men such as the
nine sokemen of Folkingham with whom the chapter began. They
were tied to the manor, but their links with it were only tenuous. We
can form some impression of the balance between free and unfree
from the Hundred Rolls of 1279. What was intended was a record of
landholding to rival Domesday Book in its comprehensiveness, but
all that survives are the returns for Huntingdonshire, Cambridgeshire, Bedfordshire, Buckinghamshire, Oxfordshire and Warwickshire. Kosminsky sampled ten hundreds from these six counties.[2] He
found 5,814 villein households and 4,120 free households. The ratio
here is rather under 3 villein households to every 2 free peasant
households. In interpreting this ratio, we must remember that this
was the period of the greatest strength of lordship over the peasantry,
and that this was an area of greater than average strength of lordship.
Extending these figures over the west and the north of England, over
Lincolnshire and Kent, the percentage of free tenants would certainly
increase. To say that there were two villein households for every
three free peasant households, over the whole of England in the late
thirteenth century, is unlikely to be underestimating the number of
villeins.

The unfree are the best documented of the medieval peasantry;
while being careful not to make them a single 'type' we have to form
our picture of the peasantry by reference to the villeins. In turn, the
best documented of the villeins are those who lived in the villages
which surrounded the great Benedictine monasteries of the midlands
and the west country, which exercised a continuous lordship from
the tenth to the sixteenth centuries. They were exempt as corporations from the major uncertainties of lordship, the minorities which
could lead to dilapidation, the marriages which could transfer
control. The liturgical work of the church must have seemed as
immutable as the agricultural seasons themselves. The agricultural
surplus supported the *opus dei*. The monasteries were the most
tenacious of medieval lords.

The chief disability of peasant servitude was the obligation to perform agricultural services for the landlord free of charge, as a condition of tenure. The terms varied from estate to estate, but a common obligation attached to a tenancy of thirty acres of land would be three days' work a week. Smaller tenancies would usually owe less: at Melbourn the tenants of the Argentine manor owed two days' work a week. At harvest time the obligation was greater—it was then quite common for the larger holdings to owe a man's services on every working day. On top of this basic service between lord and man, there were drafted other and heavier obligations, which took their pattern from the 'incidents' of feudal tenure imposed on the higher ranks of society. An aid, or tallage, was sometimes taken: on some estates, this was a heavy, annual tax on the peasantry. Invariably there would be the equivalent of a 'relief', a fine upon entry to an unfree holding. These fines, adjusted to the size of holdings and to the new tenant's capacity to pay, could be very heavy indeed. On top of this, there were numerous petty, and irregular fines to be paid, for brewing ale, for fornication, for unsatisfactory ploughing, for permission to have your son educated.

The reader of medieval court rolls can have little doubt as to the careful regulation of the villagers' lives. It must be recognised, however, that such regulation was of itself a necessary feature of corporate agriculture. The chief disadvantages of villein tenure were first the performance of service to the lord, in recognition of dependent tenure, and second a series of regular payments to the lord, in recognition of dependent status. What is not clear in this relationship, and what is in fact much debated, is the relationship between lordship and peasant wealth. The lords took a certain amount of labour, and a certain amount of rent, from all their dependent tenants. In this way, they took a part of the surplus which the peasantry would otherwise have had available for their own consumption. The villeins were deprived not only of their freedom, but of a part of their working capital.

There were many villages in England in which the force of lordship played little part, and whose economic life was dominated by a class of peasant freeholders, whose only connection with lordship came from the payment of rent. One such 'freeholders' village' was Wigston Magna four miles south of Leicester. There was lordship here. At the beginning of our period two manors were formed; the larger was held by the earls of Oxford in the early fourteenth century, the smaller by the earls of Lancaster. These great men were of course absentee lords. The larger manor was directly farmed; the other was in the hands of members of the local gentry, for the most part absentees also. Each manor followed the normal pattern of having demesne and peasant holdings. In 1296 the Lancaster manor was described as consisting of 16 messuages, 16¼ virgates of land, a windmill, an oven, rents of 13s 3¼d, a pound of cummin and two capons. Little record survives of the relationship of the customary tenants of these manors to their lords, until the manors were dissolved in the late sixteenth century.

What is important at Wigston Magna is the absence of *resident* lordship. There were many manors of this kind in Leicestershire, and elsewhere in England. There were whole counties, such as Lincolnshire and Kent, where lordship was weak; and where indeed it remains weak to this day. By contrast, there are counties such as Northamptonshire, the county of 'spires and squires', which had large estates and a powerful landed interest. The strength and weakness of lordship in different areas is a point of fundamental importance. Studies, for instance, of the origins of dissent have shown how nonconformity took root in the freeholders' villages; it found it much more difficult to get a foothold in villages where there was a resident squire. The pattern that such modern studies have revealed is in essence a medieval one. The pattern of lordship was established by the late twelfth century, by which time landowners had sorted out much of the confusion of the Norman settlement.

The Wigston freeholders in the twelfth century were the successors, and in many cases the descendants, of the 31 sokeman households and the 6 'knights and Frenchmen' who held between them around 40 per cent of the land of a large village of around 3,000 acres. The charters which survive, in the archives of Wyggeston Hospital in Leicester, reveal about forty freeholding families in the thirteenth and fourteenth centuries. One of the families that can be traced from this material is that of Godwin, of which the first member who can be identified was a Robert son of Godwin who appears in the early thirteenth century. In 1330 the Godwin farm was transferred between brothers, and is described as comprising a messuage and a virgate of land with meadow and pasture and other appurtenances; there were seven selions of land attached to the messuage, and attached also was the reversion of 5½ roods of land held by Robert Godwin, who can safely be identified as a younger son, though of which generation we cannot tell. The existence of smallholdings, for the support of widows, of daughters and of younger sons, is shown in dozens of collections of medieval charters.

They helped to preserve the integrity of free peasant yardlands in manors such as Wigston, where in theory at least holdings could be minutely subdivided if the families so chose. The Godwins lasted only seven generations. The Herricks on the other hand can be traced from the mid-thirteenth century through to the twentieth in the same village. It is suggested that they may be descended from 'one Erik, one of the original Danish settlers';[3] like most neat and satisfying suggestions it is probably wrong, but let it stand.

What is not in doubt is that the freeholding families led their lives subject to no constraint of lordship, and in so doing in a sense they set the tone of the whole village. At least from the fifteenth century the customary tenants of the Domesday manors had held their lands by copyhold, or, to give it its full title, by the tenure of copy of the court roll. In the sixteenth century the copyholders claimed that they had rights of inheritance in their land, and entry by a fixed fine. In effect they claimed the rights of freeholders, owing only the most token acknowledgment to the lord. The landlords countered, as landlords had been countering for much of the middle ages, that the copyhold tenants had only an estate for life. Whatever the law, there is no reason to doubt that the copyholders had in practice the freedom which they claimed. Around 1600 the two manors broke up, and with them went the last remnants of a lordship that had at all stages been at best peripheral to the villagers' concerns.

All landholders in the twelfth century were farmers, in that they lived at one or more removes from the produce and the profits of agricultural exploitation. But the owners of great estates were most of them farmers in another and more technical sense; they were absentee landlords, and they leased out their properties, often to members of the local gentry, for a fixed sum of money known as a 'farm'. As *The Dialogue of the Exchequer*, a kind of catechism for the civil servants of the late twelfth century, put it:[4] 'the income from manors is rightly called *firma*, since it is firm and unchangeable.' Estates were leased out, in this sense 'farmed' out; thus the landlords escaped both the risks and the potential profits of direct management. From the 1180s this system of management of the great estates came to be replaced by one in which landlords used resident agents, and increasingly sophisticated forms of accounting, to administer their properties on their own behalf. The change took time, for contracts with the local farmer had to be honoured, and the properties of the great estates were widely scattered. But from the mid-1180s the trend to direct management is clear, and by the end of John's reign, though most estates still had some manors at farm, direct management predominated on the majority of them.

The reasons for the change are complex. The disadvantages of the farming system, its inflexibility in a time of rising prices, and increased expectations both of private consumption standards and public privilege, now went together with the means of replacing it, better communications, improved literacy—for the lay steward was as central to this administrative change as were men of similar standing to the concomitant development of Angevin administration. Here again, we are at the beginning of a movement that lasts well beyond the medieval period. The letters of Simon of Senliz, steward to the Bishop of Chichester in the 1220s, carry the refrain, 'all your concerns in Sussex are going well'; those of Daniel Eaton, steward of the earl of Cardigan at Deene in Northamptonshire in the 1720s carry an identical refrain, 'all things in and around Deen are well.' The estates directly farmed needed the work of the peasant farmsteads attached to the manor. The new administrators were following an established pattern in seeking to reduce to writing customs previously undefined.

The process of definition of services had as its chief purpose the maintenance of rights over individuals. Thus those surveying the estates of St Paul's Cathedral in the 1170s were asked: 'which of the peasants enjoy freedom, which are burdened with works, which are rentpayers and which are cottars.'[5] Fairly suddenly, in the 1180s and 1190s, the period of the origins of direct management, customary tenants found themselves losing the protection of the law. Along with the performance of services, there came the definition of other duties of customary tenure. There was merchet, the payment for marriage; the heriot, or death duty; the payment of a toll on the sale of stock; and tallage, an annual tax. The performance of any one of these, in the eyes of the lawyers, would be sufficient to establish unfree tenure. The changes of the period 1180 to 1200 can thus be seen to have been all of a piece. They bore severely upon the customary tenants.

In case this may seem a little theoretical, let us look at these changes as they affected a particular group of villagers.[6] In 1225 the men of Winkfield in Berkshire, who held of the abbey of Abingdon nearly thirty miles away, found themselves in court, and a jury of their neighbours was asked to declare the services they owed. The abbot claimed that they owed 3s a year rent, and a long list of services, including entry fines, tallage, and payments for marrying their children, all of these at the abbot's will. The men acknowledged only the rent, and some token customary services. The jurors, with two exceptions, agreed with the abbot, that the men owed the full range of services demanded of them. Of the two exceptions, one man said that he knew nothing of the matter, the other that he had never seen the men do the services, that he had indeed seen some of them as jurors before the justices itinerant, and thus he had presumed that they were free. It is tempting to see this as the classic English jury: ten good, solid citizens, one simpleton (or was he a rebel who understood only too well?), and one man who had something intelligent to say. There were many such cases in the late twelfth and early thirteenth centuries, and many similar verdicts.

Through an improvement in technique, then, the manor around 1200 appears in clearer focus. By 1400 the manorial system was in decay. Any book dealing with the development of English society during the same period has a structure clearly marked out for it by these changes. But what does it mean to say that the manor grew, and declined? And why exactly are these changes important? So far as definition goes, our interpretation will differ according to whether we put our emphasis on the direct exploitation of the demesne by the landlord, or whether we take a more strict definition, and stress the links between the demesne and the labour services of the customary tenants. That link was part of the *idea* of the manor. It was in consequence basic to the landlords' view of the proper ordering of society, in which they depended on the profits of agriculture for the maintenance of their position in the world. But in practice, in the period between 1200 and the Black Death, that link became less important; the exploitation of the demesne became less dependent on those labour services reclaimed with such effort around 1200. We are concerned with farms increasingly exploited in a modern sense, by agricultural labourers receiving a cash wage and a number of benefits in kind.

All estates needed a number of specialist agricultural workers, who worked on the farm full-time. There was a supervisory staff, the reeve, the chief man of the village, and possibly a hayward. There were men in charge of animals, shepherds, cowherds and swineherds; and other specialist staff, such as dairywomen and a miller. The largest group of specialists were the ploughmen, for while the tenants owed customary ploughing services, these were irregular and did only a part of the demesne ploughing. The work that was done by the labour dues of the customary tenants was more the seasonal jobs—haymaking, reaping—and irregular jobs such as fencing, and the carrying of produce from one manor to another. A heavier obligation of weekly service was usually due from customary tenants at harvest time. We can on some estates form some impression of the relative value of wage labour and customary services. At the Crowland Abbey manor of Cottenham in 1322 the bill for wages, including the value of food, came to £9 4s 6d, while the estimated value of the customary services was less than half that, under £4 10s. Almost invariably, the wages paid to the labourers (the *famuli*) were a good deal less than the value of the food supplied to them. At times of very high grain prices, that value could be considerable. The *famuli* were a class of smallholders isolated from the fluctuations of the market. The carrying services of the villeins performed two functions: to link the manors to the centres of consumption, monasteries, palaces and castles, and to link them also with markets and the centres of trade.

Thirteenth-century landlords, however, obtained only a part of their income from the profits of agriculture. In 1298–9 the income of the monks of Ely was made up as follows: 50 per cent came from rents, including the sale of labour services; 10 per cent came from seigneurial profits, including the revenues of courts and feudal dues; and 40 per cent came from the profits of agriculture. They had lordship over men, and lordship over land, and the profits of the two were at that date divided roughly equally. The maintenance of the landlords' position in the world depended on the maintenance of these two things. The demesnes of the great estates could either be farmed out directly, or leased out for rent. The choice between these two methods of exploitation depended upon many factors, among them the compactness of the estate, the quality of the land, and the lord's own inclinations. The great estates over this period show an increasing preference for rent. A century before the Black Death, even the great, compact monastic estates were retrenching in their level of demesne farming—neither Winchester nor Ely expanded its demesnes after 1250.

The retrenchment was selective. The accounts of Peterborough Abbey show that some of the more distant manors, in the claylands of Northamptonshire, saw a marked decline in the acreage sown. At Irthlingborough, on one of the poorest areas of the clays, the amount sown diminished from 179 acres in 1282 to 95 acres in 1310. Elsewhere on the estate, in the richer lands of Lincolnshire, the amount sown over the same period if anything increased; it was the weaker lands that were leased out. It is from the 1270s particularly that account rolls survive in most abundance, and that the various treatises on estate management were most widely copied. It was when demesne agriculture was declining that a huge weight of learning and effort was applied to its maintenance. Any increased profits in this period came from the development of rent. This point does not just apply to the century before the Black Death. It seems likely that the demesnes had been at best static since the Domesday commissioners rode around the English countryside in 1086. The expansion of settlement from that time onwards, the changes in methods of exploitation and in methods of management, should not disguise from us the fact that lordship over land was in decline.

The battle here was lost before our period opens. What it sees rather was the struggle to maintain the lordship over men. This was not solely a fourteenth-century concern; we can see it as clearly in the documents of the 1180s as in those of the 1380s. It is tempting to think that in the documents of the 1280s there is no such concern. The landlords seem to be on the attack; we see them charging higher fines for entry to villein tenements, and we see in the court rolls the detailed regulation of villagers' lives. The peasantry had not escaped in the thirteenth century from any of the disabilities of villein tenure. But it was the links with the demesne that were crucial to the lord's control, and those links were weakening. The virgaters and half-virgaters had their own 'servants in husbandry'. It was these men, or their own sons, who performed the required services on the demesne. There are frequent fines on the court rolls for sending youths who could not do a man's work, 'so that the work of the lord was less well done', or for bad ploughing. The more substantial amongst the peasantry could afford to be somewhat casual in their attitude towards their obligations. The estate administrations had to struggle also to keep some control over the acquisition of freehold land by customary tenants. On many estates, small parcels of land were purchased by villeins and added to their customary holdings. The lords tried to insist that such land was held at will, and that it was kept distinct from customary land. Thus they sought to ensure that none of their men enjoyed a freehold estate of inheritance, with all that might have implied for their status. But they could not stop, nor did they seek to stop, the purchases of freehold. At Forncett in Norfolk such freehold land was originally called 'rented land' (*terra solidata*), but the name that stuck was 'soiled land' (*terra soliata*), a description that possibly reflects the lord's feeling that such land was tainted by being held by villeins. The feelings were genuine, but it was a loser's jibe.

It has been shown that rising profits favoured the landlords in the thirteenth century, but that demesne acreages did not increase. It is usually assumed that these same conditions must have been unfavourable to the peasantry. The records of estate management show the regulation of the peasants' lives, and the disabilities of villein tenure. And yet some of these records can just as well be seen as showing not severe exploitation but the lord's need to keep control. The burden of feudal rent may not have been as great as appears when viewed from that great centre of bureaucracy, the episcopal city of Winchester. Here, considered from another angle, is the problem of the standard of living of the peasantry in the thirteenth century, when medieval population was at its peak.

Much of the argument which follows has been implicit in the way the evidence has been presented so far. Even in the thirteenth century, only a minority of the peasantry were customary tenants and subject to the burdens of villeinage. Within this minority group, the burden of rent would depend on the size of the peasant's holding, on whether or not there was resident lordship on the estate, and on the strength of any seigneurial impositions, which might compound the uncertainties of nature and heredity. The pressures of lordship on the peasantry were selective, and it is important not to construct a 'model' which presumes that they were monolithic. The heaviest burdens on the ecclesiastical estates fell on the full virgaters, men who held thirty or so acres of land. Here the force of lordship was working in more than one way. It was taking a large sum in feudal and money rents, but at the same time it was protecting the villein in the tenure of a holding which was much larger than that enjoyed by most freeholders, and which normally would have produced a surplus for sale.

Most of the seigneurial impositions were customary. It was in these terms that they were presented in the case quoted from Berkshire in 1225, and were maintained. The Taunton hundredpenny, whose figures were used at the end of the previous chapter, was a fixed payment. The random impositions, random in the sense that they could be varied according to circumstances and not that they were arbitrary, were court fines, sometimes the annual tallage, and in particular the fines taken for entry to peasant holdings. Entry fines were undoubtedly increased on many estates in the late thirteenth century. On many of them the normal range increased to between £1 and £5; at Winchester, for reasons so far unexplained, the normal range went up to £10, and there were occasional figures a good deal higher than this. The close supervision of the manorial administration, the bureaucratisation of the manor after the 1270s, made possible the extraction of these high sums. They were possible, however, through a more exact assessment of capacity to pay, and not through arbitrary severity. These were entry fines, after all, and not agreed mortgages. The great landlords may well have been taking a higher percentage of the peasantry's surplus at this time. The high sums that could be taken from that surplus in the years around 1300 in consequence tell more than one story.

The evidence for the burden of rent relates very largely to the peasantry on a few great estates. Absentee lordship was not always as tenacious as this, nor indeed was resident. The resident knightly lord was unlikely to take tallage, or heavy fines. The labour services on the demesne were what was important to him; these would have been carefully watched, and not always unsympathetically. The Melbourn account of 1318 recorded 82 days' work 'in breaking the soil in seed time for barley and drage', but added that each man who worked for a full day had two days' work credited to him. The eyes of such a man as Giles de Argentine were focused on the demesne and its yield, and far less than the aristocracy upon the paraphernalia of feudal lordship. There were many men with smallholdings. They owed less by way of agricultural service, and less also in rent. Some of them worked as labourers, receiving a money wage and also grain payments in kind. Others were craftsmen. Yet others, though mainly employed in agriculture, had some wealth other than in the land itself—some livestock, access to the forest and fenland, and the opportunity of non-agricultural occupation. Little has been said of the cottagers here, but they have an important place in the chapter which follows.

What then of the men in between, the landlords like Giles de Argentine, those whose lordship was restricted in scale: how did their economic position alter in the period from the late twelfth century to the Black Death? These men were the resident lords, the men who occupied the manor houses, found or identified in nearly all medieval excavations, the quality of whose buildings is a clear sign of the wealth and status which set them apart from the rest of the villagers. That wealth depended, far less than with the larger landlords, upon lordship over the villagers themselves. In general terms first of all. A survey of the hundred of Chilford in Cambridgeshire in the late thirteenth century saw over a third of the hundred occupied by 'small' manors. On half of those manors there were no villein tenants at all, and on the rest there was very little villein land. On lay estates in Leicestershire, the surveys of the demesnes of tenants-in-chief between 1272 and 1335 showed eight out of twenty-nine properties on which the villeins owed no services at all, and more significantly showed that on none of them was regular week-work demanded. The knightly manors were small farms worked chiefly by wage labour. There is no reason to think that such units were in any way vulnerable in thirteenth-century conditions. We have already examined the position of a couple of families whose accounts survive. It fits with all that we know of the position of the knightly class in the thirteenth century, a picture of stability and self-confidence gained from a wide range of records.

It has, however, been suggested that there was a thirteenth century 'decline of the gentry', of a kind similar to that found by some historians in the seventeenth century. There is no *prima facie* case for this; and this is true whether we look at their buildings, at the rare records for gentry families, or at the political history of the age. The evidence that has been adduced for it consists of the undoubted decline of a number of knightly families, whose land was bought up piecemeal by neighbouring great estates. The monasteries, corporations which never died, were particularly active in this land market. There were purchases not just of manors, of the bailiffs as it were going in to the chief messuage, the manor house, but of their freeholds. There is nothing in such records to make us suspect the decline of a class. There was considerable rise and fall of individual landed families within each of the social groupings with which this chapter is concerned. Any land which the monasteries gained in the late thirteenth and early fourteenth centuries was only a tiny fraction of what earlier they had granted out.

Individual examples of the decline of families, interesting in themselves, should not distract attention from the important fact that the general movement of property, from at least the time of the Conquest onwards, was down the social scale and not up. Feudal contracts were contracts of service, and servants required land. There was a constant haemorrhage of property down the social scale. The landlords' reaction could only be a defensive one: they sought to protect the integrity of any service tenancies, and to collect all the rent and feudal perquisites due to them. We have just seen that such income was increasingly important to the landlords from the mid-thirteenth century onwards. It was a desire to stop the haemorrhage that lay behind much of the land legislation of Edward I. It was most vexatious that the landlords should lose out in this way, as the preamble to the statute *Quia Emptores* calmly put it. We can see in this legislation, which is examined in more detail elsewhere, the general concern of the landowning class with the preservation of the units of property and in particular for the preservation of the services, which supported their estate. It is likely that the attitudes of the knightly class to this legislation would have been a supportive one; they were not the social group primarily involved.

The Black Death led to no immediate changes in estate management. Its effect indeed was to postpone change, for the instinct of landlords confronted by crisis was to continue farming at the old level, and in the old way. At Cuxham in Oxfordshire there were four separate bailiffs and three separate accounts rendered to the lord, 'the warden and the scholars of the hall of Merton in Oxford', for the period Michaelmas 1348 to Michaelmas 1349. The first of them to go was Robert Oldman, who had been reeve since 1311; his reward for long service no more than the laconic entry of the clerk, 'he died before he could say anything about the fodder given to the oxen.'[7] The work went on as usual. The *famuli* were given 12d in the summer, 'so that they might do the lord's work better'. The work of the demesne continued, but the rent collected fell off: it took five years to find tenants for all the vacant holdings. But the college did find them, and so did many landowners. What the plague once and for all destroyed was the reserve of landless men with holdings so small that they had to work for others. For a generation at least landlords came to require services in person from tenants accustomed to commutation, men whose fathers had been accustomed to send a 'servant in husbandry' to do the lord's work. This was the manorial reaction which followed the plague, a defensive conservatism.

It failed because general economic trends moved against it, not immediately but over a period of years. In the 1350s and 1360s both wages and prices kept at a high level. In 1370 prices rose to a peak, higher than they had ever been save in 1316 and 1317. In the early 1370s, prices fell slowly. In the late 1370s they fell fast. They never recovered. Over the same period, from the Black Death, wage rates moved steadily but not dramatically upwards; and they continued to climb even after prices fell.[8] An indication of the main trends in these statistics will be found in the Appendix. In its figures will be found one reason why the manorial reaction failed. The manorial reaction failed also because the peasantry reacted in their turn, dramatically in some areas in the Peasants' Revolt, but everywhere quite as effectively by refusing to take up tenures on the old terms. All tenancies became more difficult to lease, but the most difficult of all were villein tenancies held for villein services. To lease villein land on any other terms, as increasingly happened, meant a loss of control by the lord. And it made yet more expensive and more difficult the direct exploitation of the demesnes of the great estates.

It was the loss of cheap labour that finally undermined the manors directly farmed. The auditors of the Duchy of Lancaster reported in 1388 that the Northamptonshire manors of Higham Ferrers and Raunds were operating at a loss, and recommended that they 'should be leased at farm as elsewhere'. At Higham Ferrers this was done in the following year; at Raunds shortly thereafter. All over the country, auditors were asking the same questions, and getting the same answers. In East Anglia the process of leasing can be seen in the manors organised from Clare in Suffolk, the property of the earls of March. Bircham in Norfolk and Woodhall and Claret in Suffolk were leased by the mid-1360s. Walsingham in Norfolk and Standon in Hertfordshire followed around 1370; and the three other manors in the group had all been leased out by 1400. This was as true of ecclesiastical as of lay estates. At least eighteen of the demesnes of the archbishopric of Canterbury were leased in the 1380s and 1390s; the few that remained had all been leased by 1450. With the demesnes went the manorial stock, the buildings, and the customary services of the tenants. Thus Cuxham was leased to the rector of the church, for a period of seven years from 1361. He was granted the manor with all the lands attached to it, all rents and customs, the services both of free tenants and of villeins, and all the profits of the manor court, 'saving to the warden and scholars and their successors the wardship and marriage and heriots from the tenants as they fall due during the said term'. It will be noted that the college reserved those customs which gave it the basic rights of lordship over individuals.

There is no reason to suppose that the wealth of the landlord class was much affected by the new return to an ancient system of estate management. On the March and Lancaster estates income in the 1370s was no more than 10 per cent lower than it had been in the 1340s. At Canterbury there was a fairly close similarity between the valuation of the estates and the sums for which they were farmed; although these sums would certainly not have approached the actual profits of individual manors in the best years before the Black Death. To take our last example from Cuxham once more, the recorded profits before the Black Death were on average just over £40. The rent on the lease just quoted was £20. If the income of the manors declined, this was in large part because the manor itself declined. The manor was not a static thing, but a complex of lands, rents and services, all of them subject to decay.

The chief change in the century after the Black Death, as it affects the fairly static picture which we built up in the early part of the chapter, came not in the wealth of the landlords but in the status of the peasantry. The customary tenures which had supported the demesnes were over this period converted to copyhold, 'tenure by copy of the court roll according to the custom of the manor.' There was a general abandonment of the miscellaneous services attached to customary tenure. The 'incidents' of feudal tenure atrophied. It should be noted that this was true at all levels of society, and not just at the village level. The king in response to parliamentary pressure, as we shall see, progressively abandoned the minor incidents of feudal tenure. He also kept a firm hold of wardship and marriage, his rights over individuals, just as the village lords did. The concern with status was most acute at the village level. There were fewer tenants, and they were more mobile. They had larger holdings. To take some examples of this last point, from Leicestershire. At Stoughton, a manor of Leicester Abbey, there were in 1341 twenty-six holding land in villeinage, twenty-three of whom each held a virgate of 24 acres. In 1477 there were seventeen tenants, seven of whom held between 2 and 3 virgates, three held between 1 and 2 virgates, three half a virgate, and the remaining four had smallholdings. At Thurmaston in 1341 there were twenty-four tenants holding in villeinage; nine of them held virgates, and eleven of them half-virgates. In 1477 there were thirteen tenants of whom ten held between 1½ and 3 virgates.

To keep a hold over a more mobile and more prosperous tenantry the lords were forced to appeal, around 1400 just as they had done around 1200, to the idea that servility was in the blood. In 1391 the council of the earl of March instructed a reeve that he should not 'allow any male or female child or any other that is a villein by blood of my lord, to pass out of his lordship . . . so that my lord shall not be disinherited of their blood by their withdrawal from the lordship.'9 But just that was happening, whether the lords liked it or not. The situation at Forncett in Norfolk in the fifteenth century was that many of the customary tenancies were in the hands of women. The men appear in the records only as paying chevage or head money.

They lived outside the manor. They made a token payment in recognition of their origins, the maintenance of a link with the manor which was partly in the peasant's interest, in that it might establish title to land; as with copyhold itself, this might be a piece of record keeping for which the villagers were grateful. Peasants as well as lords could see the uses of literacy.

The discussion so far in this book has concentrated upon arable farming, and the remarks upon the relationship between lord and peasant should be referred chiefly to southern and open-field England. It may be helpful to conclude this chapter with some information on the wealth of the different regions, and the way that the sources of wealth changed during the later middle ages. Unfortunately there are no figures which will measure the changes in wealth over the period covered by this book. For this we rely on national taxation, and the earliest comprehensive records are those of the lay subsidies of the 1330s, the decade which saw the outbreak of the Hundred Years' War. The next set of figures, which are both reliable and independent of the lay subsidies, come from the early sixteenth century. The two maps which are printed in Figure 8 show for the different counties of England the distribution of lay wealth, first in 1334, and then in 1515. Figures taken county by county will give only a rough guide to the actual sources of wealth, but they show distribution, and they indicate the main features of development in the later middle ages.

The difference in the wealth of the various counties in 1334 was striking. At the top was the region of Holland in south Lincolnshire, assessed at £46 8s per thousand acres. In the south of this area lay the wapentake of Elloe, whose colonisation and population figures have been examined. Oxfordshire was assessed at £42 4s, and Norfolk at £38 18s. At the other end of the scale, Lancashire and the north and west ridings of Yorkshire were assessed at between £4 12s and £7 per thousand acres. The average figure was £21 10s per thousand acres. Two centuries later the range of wealth, already wide, had become a good deal wider. The average had risen nearly three-fold, to £66 per thousand acres. Lancashire had gone down to £3 16s, while Middlesex was now rated at £238 2s per thousand acres. Two distinct areas increased their wealth more than four-fold, the south-west peninsula and what we would now call, writing a southern bias even into the language, the home counties.

The earlier map, which shows the richest counties in a belt stretching across the midlands, suggests a correlation between high

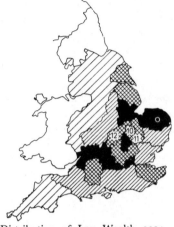

Distribution of Lay Wealth, 1334

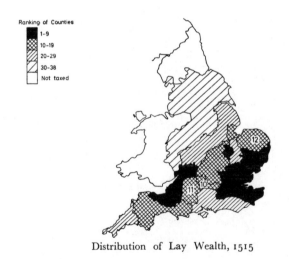

Distribution of Lay Wealth, 1515

Figure 8 Maps to show the distribution of lay wealth in England as assessed in taxation records, the subsidy of 1334 and the Tudor subsidy of 1515.

R. S. Schofield, 'The Geographical Distribution of Wealth in England, 1334–1649'.
Economic History Review, *2nd ser., xviii (1965), p. 506.*

assessments and the production of wheat. Two centuries later, it seems likely that the greatest wealth was no longer in agriculture, but in wool and in cloth. In order to complete a survey of the social structure of England, a place must be found for industry, a place which grew more important. The changes, when compared with those of the modern period, are not dramatic. But England in the later middle ages, in common with the other less developed areas of Europe, moved slightly from an agricultural to an industrial base, and became primarily a manufacturing nation. The various extractive industries brought wealth, inadequately represented on these maps, to the highland areas of England. The chapter which follows will look at industrial wealth, and show the social structure of England further from the constraints of lordship and of the open-fields.

Chapter 4 — Trade and Industry

The discussion so far has been much concerned with country matters. It has concentrated on the village, and inevitably may have suggested that the village was largely self-sufficient, and that the most important relationships in the medieval countryside were those between the peasants and their lords. The network of feudal relationships was not a mesh that was spread tight over the whole of the English countryside. Medieval England had an important agricultural and trading base. It had groups of wage earners whose only links with their masters were economic, and a much larger number of individuals whose contact with the market gave them a form of independence and offered a wider range of economic and political relationships than were involved in agrarian tenures. It is with these contacts that the following chapter is concerned. It will pay particular attention to the relationship between trade and industry and the structure of medieval lordship.

The twelfth century saw the beginnings of what can fairly be termed a national economy. The cells of that economy were the local markets. The peasant's surplus went to the market, where he could purchase a wider range of food, clothing and agricultural equipment than his own village could provide. Not only the economic structure but also the political structure was composed of hundreds of small, interlocking market areas. The majority of those frequenting the markets had to walk there and back in a day. A man's feet limited his horizons, and his imagination also. If there was not parish-pump, then there was market-cross politics—the difference was not very great. Superimposed on this there was a regional structure. The country towns and other regional centres were to be found not a day's walking but a day's riding apart. To these the king's justices would come, bringing the king's law and the king's commands. In these towns the greater magnates had their castles. In some of the larger towns there were sessions of parliament: Winchester, Northampton, Bury St Edmunds, Marlborough, Lincoln, Salisbury,

York, Carlisle, Stamford, Oxford, Gloucester. In these centres the range of goods and of political gossip was a good deal wider than in the market towns. The strength of the regional centres is an important feature of medieval and early modern history. Yet these centres were a world away from most Englishmen and their concerns. And the national centre of London, the 'capital' centre of the kingdom, where kings who had the itinerant concerns of medieval lords came none the less to spend an increasing proportion of their time, was one of the more distant of them. When the peasants marched on London in 1381 as many may have gone out of a sense of curiosity as out of political concern.

When we speak of the growth of a national economy, we are thinking of the disintegration of some of the barriers which separated the village and the local market from the financiers of London and the great men of the court. One of the forces here was warfare. As we look at the pipe rolls, the annual record of the central exchequer's dealings with the local sheriffs, we can see the economy come to life before our eyes. For the Normandy campaign in 1201 Essex sent cheese and bacon, Cambridgeshire beans and Gloucestershire horseshoes from the ironworks of the Forest of Dean. In 1205, 140 deer and 200 loads of beans were puchased for £40 6s 8d in Lincolnshire and this balanced diet conveyed to the king at Rouen. In 1203 John of Kempsey was given 43s 10d 'for chests and carts to take the king's books overseas'. There are dozens of such payments, which show the victualling of the king's forces as they strove to defend and then recapture Normandy. They show us a whole series of local economies harnessed to the needs of empire. The royal will moved cartloads of goods for other reasons also. Large numbers of herrings were sent to nunneries the length and breadth of the country if the king got indigestion after eating meat during Lent: 100,000 herrings purchased for this purpose cost £18 10s in 1204. The needs of diplomacy might move men as well as goods in due season: King John sent 300 loads of corn and 51 Welsh mercenaries as a gift to the king of Norway in 1201, and in 1193–4 diplomatic need of a rather more pressing kind had harnessed the whole economy to contribute to the ransom of King Richard, who had been captured in Germany on his way back from the crusade. Everyone contributed a quarter of his income for the year; the churches had to sell a part of their gold and silver plate; the Cistercian order contributed the year's wool clip. £2,000 came from the King of the Scots and was carefully carted down the Great North Road. And there they are on the pipe roll:

'£5 for the carriage of the pennies sent by the King of the Scots.'

The pipe rolls of the late twelfth and early thirteenth century show the involvement of the central government with the currency, and with weights and measures. The English currency had long been the envy of the rest of Europe. When Richard's ransom of £100,000 was paid to the German emperor, the 24 million silver pennies it comprised caused some havoc in the empire, where each lord issued his own coin and weights fluctuated considerably. The Emperor Henry VI made his currency an exact replica of the English. If his own name appeared on his coins it was only because he shared a name with Henry II of England. Neither Richard I nor John dared issue coins in his own name, for fear that the merchants of Europe would not accept them. The pound and the mark (13s 4d) were units of account, but the highest denomination of silver currency remained the penny until 1351, when a groat was issued valued at 4d. Experiments with a gold currency took place from 1257, and culminated in 1344 with the issue of the noble, worth 80 pence. The establishment of a strong coinage represents the earliest involvement of the English government with trade.

With weights and measures the government had more difficulty in trying to introduce an element of standardisation into local custom. To take one example, the dimensions of the sheaves of corn issued to labourers after the harvest were measured in a variety of ways. On some estates the binding was to be a length the circumference of the reeve's head, elsewhere the distance from the sole of his foot to the knee. Such local customs remained, but some standardisation was necessary in the weights and measures used for the main goods and in the main trades. The first detailed exercise of this kind was the Assize of Measures of 1196. It provided for uniform measures of grain and beans (equivalent to a 'good horse-load'), uniform measures of the different kinds of drink and uniform weights for different kinds of goods, and a uniform width for all cloth. Standards for all these measures were to be sent out, and kept under lock and key. The pipe roll of 1197 shows that £11 16s 6d was spent in London to make 'measures and gallons and iron rods and scales and weights to be despatched to all the counties of England'. It was an ambitious exercise but a successful one. The pattern of weights and measures established in 1196 was very similar to that of today. The iron rods were yards. According to popular belief, the yard had been established as the length of Henry I's arm. The hand of the monarchy lay, fixed and immutable, on the farthest parts of the land.

Medieval monarchs were not just kings but also the greatest of the lords, and they shared with the lords the desire for a life-style that would adequately reflect their estate. They were the most conspicuous of the conspicuous spenders. Records of this are also to be found in the pipe rolls, for no distinction was made between the king's public and private expenditure. In 1176 the king's daughter was bought a robe which cost £114. In 1212 King John spent £226 on precious stones and on gold for lances. He also bought a lion and a keeper and, possibly as an afterthought, a door also, for a total cost of £7. The profits of the king's manors, of judicial and other fines, went into expenditure such as this quite properly in a society which obliged its *noblesse* to display their wealth and to distribute it lavishly. Matthew Paris thought it worthy of remark that Henry III at the Christmas feast in 1251, 'did not distribute any festive dresses to his knights and his household, although all his ancestors had made a practice from times of old of giving away royal garments and costly jewels.'[1] The aristocracy did likewise. The great monasteries spent as much of the surplus as was left to them, after their subsistence at a fairly generous level was assured, in purchasing new vestments and costly jewels as in building up their capital in animal stock, in buildings and in other investment. The lay lords bought robes for their retainers, the quality carefully specified according to rank, and had their breviaries inlaid with precious stones. A mixture of subsistence and lavish spending was of the essence of the noble life in a feudal society whose wealth lay in land and whose surplus wealth was channelled into the pockets of the lords.

The science of estate management was organised to support the consumption needs of the aristocracy. The detailed calculation of yields and the avoidance of waste was necessary, 'so that in the end your stock will pay for your wine, your robes, your wax and all your wardrobe.' Thus Bishop Robert Grosseteste, in his eyes stating the obvious, in the *Rules* he drew up for the widowed countess of Lincoln in the 1240s. The countess's estate, like his own, lay in a number of different regions.[2]

> I advise that you make your great purchases on two occasions in the year. The wine, wax and clothing that you will consume in Lindsey, Norfolk and the Vale of Belvoir you should buy at the fair of Boston. When in the country of Caversham and of Southampton buy at Winchester; and when in Somerset buy at Bristol. Your robes you should purchase at St Ives.

The demand of the aristocracy for goods that their estates could not supply was the chief stimulus to the growth of trade from the tenth century onwards. There were two basic luxuries, the first of them cloth, the second wine. Not all could afford tame lions and precious stones, but anyone who had pretensions to stand apart from the common herd needed fine cloth and wine. It was in these commodities that there developed the most important international trade of the middle ages.

International trade represents only a small part of the network of exchanges. Regional trade was more important. Local trade, the trade of the markets, was more important still. It is none the less valuable to get an impression of England's place in the western European economy of the time. We have a brief list from a merchant's book made in Bruges in the 1250s: 'from England come wool, hides, lead, tin, coal and cheese'. The perspective is a valuable one. As seen from Flanders, England was a pastoral country which was rich in minerals.

Wool would have headed the list anywhere, but it was of particular importance for Flanders, an industrial area based on the production of cloth, and dependent on England for its raw materials. Francesco Pegolotti's *The Practice of Commerce*, written in Florence in the early fourteenth century, commented on the quality of the wool of each of the main regions of England. The best wool of all was on the backs of the sheep that browsed the hillsides of Herefordshire and Shropshire in the Welsh marches. Slightly behind came that from the Cotswolds and the Lindsey division of Lincolnshire. The midlands, that were sodden and unkind, produced the middle grade wool. The wool from the chalk downlands of the south and south-east was inferior to this, and the wool of Devon and Cornwall so coarse that it was not exported at all. From business accounts and correspondence, and from buildings which still survive, it is possible to form an impression of this trade in its heyday. At Northleach, the centre of the trade in the Cotswolds, the merchants came in May. Men such as Chaucer saw:

There was a merchant with a forked beard, who sat
On a tall horse; he wore mixed-coloured cloth,
And on his head a Flemish beaver hat.

(In Chaucer's day, the beaver still flourished in Europe.) There they made their bargains, often contracting and paying for the following year's wool from a major supplier such as a monastic house at the same time as they collected the current year's clip. The wool had to be packed under supervision, and sealed, in the county that it came from. From there pack-horses took it, along roads which had been used for centuries, over the Wiltshire and Hampshire downs, and thence by the pilgrim's way to the ports of the Medway. The same trade from other regions raised up ports that at the time of the Conquest had been tiny villages. The wool from the marches went overland to Nottingham, and thence up the Trent and out through Hull. The Lindsey wool, and much of that of the midlands, went out through Boston, which around 1300 handled more wool than any other port in England. The tower of its parish church, the famous Boston 'stump' is a reminder of its former glory. King's Lynn handled the trade of the Wash, and much of that of East Anglia.

The trade is well documented because so much organisation was necessary. The organisation was necessary because it had almost as many individual bases as there were peasant proprietors in England. In 1225 the monks of Glastonbury had on their manor of Damerham in Wiltshire 570 sheep, while their 200 tenants on the same manor had a further 3,760 sheep. The Cistercian monks may be the best-known sheep-farmers of the middle ages, but they are hardly the most typical. The real foundation of the industry was the peasant farmstead. In the Cotswolds, again in 1225, the average tax-payer had fifteen sheep, a horse and three cows. And there were many too poor to be taxed. The middle-man was a necessity here, but much of the business was found and secured by the merchants who handled the sales. Their capital, for wool was the cash crop *par excellence*, and the wool merchants were the great capitalists of their day, allowed them to dominate the countryside. Around 1300, the price of a sack of wool in the Cotswolds was about £6 10s. Its transportation and the export duty added £2 10s and it was sold at Calais for about £11, leaving a profit to the merchants of £2. By modern standards the cost of production was a high percentage of the final sale price, and the merchant's profit was small. Yet £2 was still a sizable sum. It was the yearly income of a peasant. The more prosperous merchants exported hundreds of sacks. Thus Lawrence of Ludlow had royal licence to export 300 sacks in 1275, and this was only one of his trading activities. His position in the countryside can be seen to this day, for Stokesay Castle, which he bought in 1281 and then rebuilt, set him apart in a magnificent residence which still survives. The royal castle in his home town of Ludlow lies in ruins. He died in 1294 and the chronicle of Dunstable priory recorded his death with some satisfaction: 'He it was who induced the merchants of England to grant the king 40s for each sack of wool . . . and because he had sinned against the wool mongers he was drowned in a ship laden with wool.'[3]

The chronicler was rather harsh. If Lawrence did carry a burden of sin in this matter, it was that of the necessity of politics. He inhabited what Tawney called 'the seductive border region where politics grease the wheels of business and polite society smiles hopefully on both.'[4] In the thirteenth century feudal taxation no longer served even for the basic needs of the crown, let alone for foreign warfare. A few figures will give an idea of the scale of the problem. In the late thirteenth century the ordinary revenue of the crown was normally rather under £30,000 a year. In 1294–5 Exchequer receipts were £124,790 and expenses £138,256. In 1296 it was estimated that the army being sent to Scotland would cost £5,000 a week. The monarchy could only meet such commitments by taxation, both direct and indirect, and by the raising of loans. It was through the taxation of trade, from the late thirteenth century onwards, that the English crown got the most substantial regular addition to its revenues. In 1275 a duty of 7s 6d a sack was imposed on wool. Taxes came and went, but this remained: it was known thereafter as 'the great and ancient custom'. The duty was raised to 40s a sack in 1297; this was the 'maltote' or 'bad tax' which brought such opprobrium upon poor Lawrence of Ludlow. It was then that it was said that the wool of England was half the value of the whole land, and that 'the whole community feels itself burdened by the tax on wools.' With the beginning of the Hundred Years' War in the 1330s the tax was increased again, and came to settle at the rate of 33s 4d a sack for native merchants and 66s 8d a sack for foreign merchants. In the 1340s there were added to this an export duty on cloth, a tunnage on wine imports, and a poundage on the import and export of general merchandise. The wool subsidy became a regular peacetime tax, and provided an important part of the government's income. It was the needs of government finance which led to the channelling of all wool exports through one or more fixed points, or 'staples'. From the late fourteenth century there was a single staple at Calais, which lasted until the port was lost to the French in 1558. The merchants engaged in the wool trade were formed into a single company, 'the Fellowship of the Merchants of the Staple of Calais', which had a monopoly of the trade in English wool north of the Alps. By the mid-fifteenth century the Staplers controlled 27 per cent of England's export trade.

By then, however, the trade in raw wool stood at less then 30 per cent of its level of around 1300. Its place as England's main export had been taken by cloth.

The pipe rolls show that the cloth industry was strongly established in the major towns in the late twelfth and early thirteenth centuries. There were fullers' gilds at Winchester and Leicester, weavers' gilds at London, Lincoln, Oxford, Winchester, Huntingdon, York and Nottingham, and other signs of major concentrations of industry at Newcastle, Beverley, Northampton and Stamford. The cloth industry provided an industrial base which diversified and hence added to the strength of the great provincial towns of England. It was not confined to them: there might be small groupings of cloth workers in market towns, men such as William the weaver, Gilbert the woolman and Hervey the fuller who occur in a list of tenants at Oundle in Northamptonshire shortly after 1215. There were similar groups of men in numerous villages in the countryside. The trend was none the less, throughout western Europe, to attract the industry to the towns, taking successive stages of production in from the countryside. The towns were the merchants' centres; their capital allowed them to dominate and closely regulate the lives of the small groups of craftsmen who lived huddled together in the back streets. The same concentration made possible specialisation of function. In the Flemish towns during the thirteenth century, there were more than thirty different processes in the production of cloth. Thus there were not only specialist dyers, but individual dyers specialising in particular colours. If English industry was to compete in producing high-quality cloth for the international market, it needed large concentrations of workers, and these in the twelfth century were to be found only in the larger towns.

Most of the English towns had a merchant gild, a corporation licensed by the crown, which controlled the town's trade and undertook much of its government. In some towns such as Leicester the records of the gilds have survived, and testify to a tradition of local control of urban government unbroken from the twelfth century to the present day. It was the gild that regulated the work of the craftsmen: thus at Leicester in 1260:[5]

> these customs were agreed to in the Gild of merchants with the consent of the merchants and the weavers and the fullers. The weavers swore that they will conceal no infidelity in their work and that they will have three shuttles in their work, and will not

weave at night. The fullers swore that they will not full unfaithful cloth without showing their defects to the mayor and bailiffs . . . and that they will not hold any morning speech except in the presence of two members of the Gild of merchants who shall have been chosen for this purpose from the community of the Gild.

The gild was a community. It was in the common interest that the quality of the town's cloth should be maintained. It was not in the common interest, or at least in the merchants' interest, that working people should meet privately to discuss conditions of work or the conduct of their trade. Prices and conditions of work were subject to detailed supervision. They were justified in terms of the need to maintain the reputation of the town's cloth. In 1264 one of the 1260 regulations was altered: 'it was agreed and published that the merchants who wish to weave in Leicester may weave both by night and by day, but so that no defect may be in their work.' There is no reason to doubt that a community of interest underlay such regulations.

If we remember the Winchester picture of these communities living close together, many of them plying their trades on the street front just as we can see in many areas of the continent to this day, we can see how easily the smallest breach of the regulations could lead to a fine of 6d or the pledging of a cask of ale at the morning speech, the 'parliament' of the gild. Not all accepted the authority without protest. Swearing went down in the book, and sometimes we are even told what was said. Sixpence was exacted from Nicholas the coverlet-maker in 1264, 'because he wove fullable cloth against the liberty of the gild'. When asked for the money he said to the Mayor:

> 'do you want to drive me from Leicester, you need my 6d so much?' And with other words he greatly abused and annoyed the Mayor and the community of the Gild. And so the Mayor said to the Nicholas, 'Thou mayest have the excommunication of God'. And he answering said to the Mayor, 'Put your excommunication where you put your other goods'.

If one impression of the Leicester roll is of the close regulation of individuals, another must be of their reluctance to be constrained, that individual enterprise was quite as strong a force as gild conservatism.

The late medieval towns have been likened to Mesozoic reptiles, constrained by the weight of their defences against change of any kind. This is a striking image, yet we are told that it was a change of climate that most likely was responsible for the demise of the dinosaur. Were there changes in the economic climate that operated against the urban cloth industry? One such has been suggested in the rapid spread of the fulling mill in the late twelfth and the thirteenth centuries, a piece of capital equipment which made fulling possible wherever there was water power. It seems unlikely that fulling in itself tilted any balance between town and countryside. What happened in the thirteenth century was that the high cost and high quality urban industry suffered from competition from Flanders, and lost not only exports but much of the home market on which it relied. The extra glamour of foreign goods is now a familiar problem, and in the thirteenth century no protection could be looked for. The great towns declined: in the 1270s cloth-making was said to have largely gone from Winchester to the bishop's suburban liberty and beyond. The number of weavers in Oxford fell from 60 to 15, and by the 1320s there were none at all.

The protection came in the fourteenth century, as a by-product of the heavy taxation of wool and the pressure put on Flanders by English warfare with France. The Flemish economy, that of an industrialised society based on a single high-cost manufacture the bulk of which went for export, was particularly vulnerable. In 1297, when the great powers were no more than sparring with each other, the people of Flanders protested to the count that their livelihood was threatened: 'without the coming of the English into Flanders and the passage of the Flemish into England we cannot possibly trade.' The imports of foreign cloth into England from Flanders fell dramatically in the 1330s and never recovered. The Flemings retaliated by prohibiting the import of English cloth in all but a few years from 1340 to the late fifteenth century. But this could do nothing to prevent the cost advantages which the English industry gained by the taxation of the raw material of the Flemish industry. And English cloth when exported was taxed only at the low rate of 2s the cloth. As with wool, a tendency towards monopoly proceeded from the needs of royal taxation and the basic contraction of trade. Towards the end of Edward IV's reign the Merchant Adventurers controlled 38 per cent of the exports from and nearly 70 per cent of imports into England. The Merchant Adventurers were the cloth dealers of each of the major ports, the counterparts to the Merchants of the Staple in the wool trade. In origin they were adventurers, seeking markets in distant lands, but by the fifteenth century the Merchant Adventurers of

London, dealing with the Low Countries, had a virtual monopoly of the cloth trade.

The cloth industry grew from the mid-fourteenth century onwards both in the town and in the countryside. A major rural industry developed, particularly in the fifteenth century. There were three main growth areas, the west country, East Anglia and Yorkshire. The west country was the most important of these. Such places as Stroudwater and Castle Combe came to specialise in the production of broadcloth. Since broadcloth required heavy fulling, the water-driven fulling mills were of particular importance, and here if anywhere we can speak of an 'industrial revolution' in the later middle ages. What had originally been small hamlets at the riverside came to overshadow the original settlements upon the hills. Thus Castle Combe was described by William of Worcester in 1454 as follows:[6]

> In the said manor are two vills. One is called Overcombe, in which reside the yeomen who are occupied in the cultivation and working of the land which lies upon the hill. The other is Nethercombe, in which dwell the men who make cloth, like weavers, fullers, dyers, and other artificers.

When he wrote, fifty new houses had been built in Nethercombe in the previous half-century. The account of cloth produced in Wiltshire early in Henry V's reign has a separate entry for Castle Combe, of 71 cloths. But this is still a small percentage of the total of 1,871 cloths produced within the county. The bulk of production, 1,309 cloths, was registered under the city of Salisbury. There was some new growth in the countryside, but the urban industry was not eclipsed.

In the thirteenth century, the weavers 'and other artificers' engaged in producing cloth were dependent folk, as the quotations from the Leicester gild rolls have made clear. It was the merchant freemen who regulated the trade, and marketed the cloth they produced. By the fifteenth century the craftsmen had a greater independence. They often owned their houses and workshops, and they had their own craft gilds. But the merchant class had not lost their hold on the government of the town or the production of cloth. The majority of clothiers or 'clothmen' in Salisbury came from the merchant crafts, men such as the draper William Doudyng, mayor in 1412, who bequeathed to his son in 1419 his share in the good ship *Katherine of Salisbury*. Their power came from capital. And capital was no less important in the countryside than in the town, though the actual organisation of the trade was different. The clothiers bought the wool, but the main stages of production were 'put out' to workers to be done in their own homes, sometimes on equipment that the clothiers had paid for. The process of putting out is clearly recorded in a case of 1459 when a Cirencester clothier was accused of folding and tacking cloth before he had paid duty on it. There had been no intent to defraud, he claimed. He had sent the cloths to Stroud, to six fullers, who had washed, fulled, dyed and shorn it. When, three weeks later, their work was finished the cloths had been wrapped and secured simply to ensure their safety on the eight-mile journey by pack-horse back to his house. In the west it was the Stour and its tributaries which saw the main growth of rural industry, and in the West Riding the upper reaches of the Aire and Calder valleys. In Yorkshire the units of production tended to be smaller, and the typical entrepreneur employed only a few workers within his own home. In Yorkshire as elsewhere many of those engaged in the trade were smallholders, and were thus engaged both in agriculture and in craft work within their homes.

If there is a sense in which the cloth industry moved to the country-side in the later middle ages, the other main industries were country-based from the beginning. Lead, tin and coal were in the Bruges short-list of English exports, while in scale iron-working was the most important of all. Taken together the mining industries show a number of common features. They produced wealth for some of the poorest and most sparsely populated regions of England, from the lead mines of Cumberland and the High Peak division of Derbyshire to the tin-mines of Devon and Cornwall to the forges in the wood-land fastnesses of the Forest of Dean. They are very far away in organisation and structure, though they may only be a few miles in distance, from the main centres of manorial England. They are not totally divorced from lordship, for the mines are there even in the skeleton outlines of Domesday Book, and Domesday Book is the record of the wealth of lords. But this lordship was not lordship over men but over land. Personal freedom was a basic requirement of all the mining communities of England. They added to it more specialist and particular liberties necessary for their work; many of them held their own assemblies and made their own laws. The miner shown in the brass in Newland church in the Forest of Dean, reproduced in Figure 9, is a sturdy individual.

There were three main areas of lead mining in England. In the north there were the 'mines of Carlisle', at Alston Moor on the boundaries between Cumberland, Yorkshire and Northumberland; in the north midlands the mines of Derbyshire; and in the south-west mines in the Mendip hills. Derbyshire is the best documented and was probably the most important of the three areas. It is the best documented because some of the best established mining areas were on manors of the royal demesne, such as Wirksworth, Bakewell, Ashford-in-the-Water and Hope. The lead from such remote centres played an important part in the economy of northern Europe. In the 1180s there were 100 carretates of lead sent from Derbyshire to the Cistercian house at Clairvaux in Burgundy: £33 6s 8d was allowed to the sheriff for the lead, a further £9 13s 11d was needed to get it to the Humber estuary, and another £6 13s 4d for its transport in two ships to Rouen. The important market centres were at Derby, Chesterfield and Wirksworth; and the bulk of the export trade was conducted via London.

A miner had the right to prospect for lead anywhere save in churchyards, gardens, orchards and highways. When he established a mine, he had to mark out three units of uniform size, one of which was reserved to the king. On the other two units, 'of the mine won in work of this kind in the king's fee, the lord king shall have in

Figure 9 Brass from Newland church, Glos, showing a miner in the Forest of Dean

recognition of his lordship the thirteenth dish which is called the lot';[7] in other words he took rather less than a tithe of the produce. The king has the first right to the produce of the mine, on paying the market price for the lead. The miners could dispose of their mines at will. Their court, the barmoot, had a fixed scale of payments; 2d for a small trespass, but 5s 4d for the shedding of blood for any crime committed in the mine itself. All this was established in the *quo warranto* proceedings of Edward I's reign. An enquiry which was intended to define the king's rights in fact produced a charter of liberties for the miners. And there was more to the same effect. Those who had died suddenly in the mines could be buried without the view of the coroner. The miners claimed the right to take timber from the king's forests for use in the mines. The king guaranteed them access to his highway; if the landowner could not agree a route with the miners, then the steward took two miners, and the three of them arm in arm took the most direct route to the road, which then became a right of way even had they trampled through growing corn. The image was perhaps more striking than the reality, for the High Peak has never been one of the great granaries of Europe, but the picture of the miners trampling down the corn will serve well for a community whose rights preceded and overrode some of the most basic principles of feudal lordship.

Despite the privileges which the miners obtained, it was the lords of Derbyshire, the king prominent amongst them, who took most of the profit and none of the risk. After the execution of Thomas of Lancaster the lead mines of the wapentake of Wirksworth and of the manor of Hartington were administered directly by the king's officers, and an account survives. The king in this manor was an industrial entrepreneur; he collected the lead from those who had an interest in the mines; he arranged for its smelting, and then for its sale and distribution. The bulk of the ore—621 loads from Wirksworth and 155 loads from Hartington—came from the miners themselves; 69 loads came from the various rectors as tithes. In addition to this ore, for which the king had to pay the market rate, he had his own lot free of charge. The ore was collected from the various mines to be washed at Bromyegg, and thence was taken to the wind-hearths at Ladyclif, where it was smelted. The produce amounted finally to 160 barge-loads—the importance of water transport in the trade is shown very clearly by the fact that the barge-load was the final unit of account. The king's share of the final product was either sold to pay for working expenses, or delivered to the sheriff of Derbyshire, or sold to Richard and William de la Pole. Only the king controlled whole wapentakes, but what he did the lay lords strove to emulate. The combination of mining freedom and the rights of lordship is an interesting one. The unit of production was the individual prospector and his mine, but the ore seems to have been manufactured and sold chiefly through the units of lordship, the largest of them representing manufacture on a very large scale.

Tin mining was an extractive industry very similar to lead-mining both in the processes involved and in the degree of independence from seignorial authority which the working tinners enjoyed. The tinners of Devon and Cornwall could also dig as and where they chose. In the first stannary charter that survives, which dates from 1201, they were given the right of[8]

> digging tin and turves for smelting it at all times, freely and peaceably and without hindrance from any man, everywhere in moors and in the fees of bishops, abbots and earls . . . and of diverting streams for their works . . . just as by ancient usage they had been accustomed to do.

They also were personally free, and had their own courts, presided over by the wardens of the stannaries. Yet they were very far from operating free either from royal control or from a dependence on capital which in fact constrained their independence severely. The royal control came from a tax on tin production called the coinage duty, which was fixed at the rate of 40s per thousandweight of tin in Cornwall. The dependence of the tinners came from the risks they bore, the capital they needed, and from the additional constraints which the coinage system put upon them. Coinages were held in Cornwall only twice a year, at Midsummer and then at Michaelmas; only then could it be exported from the county, and the tinner expect to be paid.

The distinct stages of production were in the hands of different groups of men. The labouring tinners sold the ore to the merchant tinners, who were responsible for smelting it and presenting it for coinage. The merchant tinners then sold to tin dealers, who sold the tin throughout Britain and abroad. The tin dealers provided credit for the local merchant tinners; they in turn provided credit for the individuals who worked the mines. The mines themselves might be bought up by the local merchant tinners, perhaps foreclosing upon a debt, in which case the mines would be worked by hired labourers who were paid a wage. The top group of such men were employers of labour on a large scale. Abraham the tinner in 1357 owned seven tin works in Fowey Moor and the upper Fowey Valley, and claimed to employ 300 men in all. The strengthening of capitalism within the mines was an inexorable development. The miners themselves paid a heavy price for a precarious independence. If they had their own courts, these provided rough justice for rough men, and they had their own prison, described with feeling by a former inmate as 'one of the most unsavoury, contagious and detestable places within this realm'. The tinners were poor men; they worked in appalling conditions, and earned wages which were both low and highly uncertain. It has been calculated that the number of tinners in Devon in the late thirteenth century varied between 300 and 450 souls, who produced tin worth no more than 20s a year. The greater number of these men had other employment, and many of them had their own smallholdings. At times when land was easily available, as it was after the Black Death, the number of tinners and hence the amount of tin produced tended to fall.

On this uncertain foundation and very tight royal control was based a trade which was central to the western European economy of the day. It was one of the basic commodities of northern Europe, bulky and thus largely dependent upon water transport, which provided a balance with the higher cost, more luxury products of southern Europe. It was this that made Lostwithiel and Falmouth cosmopolitan centres of European trade. The great centres of Lübeck and Hamburg had an agent in Falmouth around 1265; and it was from the great Hanseatic ports that tin was distributed in north, central and eastern Europe, down the great rivers which led south and east from the Baltic sea. It was, however, with France that England did her most important dealings in tin, with the channel ports and those of the south-west of England. Tin was one of the most important cargoes of the ships which sailed regularly to Bayonne, La Rochelle and Bordeaux. From Bordeaux the bulk of the tin imported was then sent along the river Garonne to Toulouse, thence being loaded onto pack-horses and shipped from Arles, Marseilles and Narbonne throughout the Mediterranean world. There is a detailed description of this trade, one of many, in the works of a thirteenth-century Arab geographer, Ibn Sa'id. In Genoese and Venetian galleys, tin went through their entrepôts on Asia Minor and the Black Sea. It was through the links with the national and international world, very largely provided by their mining industries, that some of the most distant parts of England were integrated into a national community.

I The 'shrunken' village of Blatherwycke, Northants. To the north of the present buildings there was a church. The line of the tofts, the enclosures which contained the peasant farm houses, appears very clearly

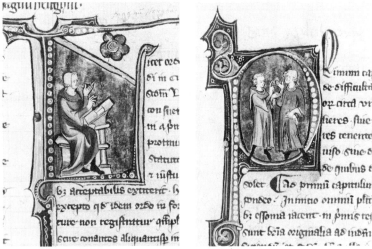

2 *Faces of the poor and of the professional classes: (a) pilgrims to St James of Compostella, from a wall painting at Wisborough Green church, Sussex. (b) lawyers from a legal manuscript; a judge wearing his coif, and two pleaders deep in argument*

3 The martyrdom of Thomas Becket, from a wall painting at South Newington church, Oxon. The blow of the first knight is warded off by the monk Grim, who stands behind the altar. The second knight cleaves Becket's skull, and his mitre falls to the ground

4 *Drawings by Matthew Paris: (a) four kings with monasteries they patronised—Henry II with Waltham Abbey in Essex, Richard I with the church of St Thomas at Acre in the Holy Land, John with Beaulieu Abbey in Hampshire, and Henry III with Westminster Abbey*

4 *Drawings by Matthew Paris: (b) in the margin of the chronicle, Richard, the earl Marshal (died 1234), shown on horseback with his coat of arms*

5 *The Wheel of the Five Senses from the wall paintings at Longthorpe Tower near Peterborough. The moral is that in each of his senses man is excelled by many creatures; by the boar in hearing, the cock in sight, the monkey in taste, the vulture in smell and the spider in touch. The king stands for Reason, the director of the senses, which are good only if they are controlled*

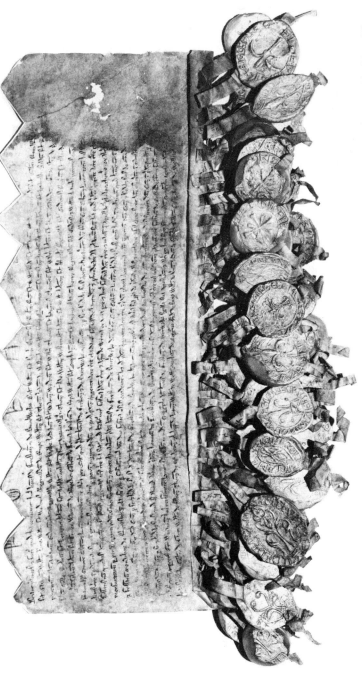

6 Charter of between 1217 and 1232 recording an agreement between earl Ranulf of Chester and the men of Frieston and Butterwick, Lincs. There are fifty seals on parchment tags, each inscribed with the individual's name

7 *Medieval housing, now demolished, from Great Butcher Row in Coventry*

In this way mining provided a part in the development of the nation which was not simply confined to the creation of wealth.

The extractive industries whose product could most conveniently be worked on the spot were sited where they had access to fuel. Of the main fuels of the modern industrial world only coal was produced in the middle ages, and its production was insignificant. Only in one region was coal important, that of Newcastle. Newcastle's coal trade grew rapidly in the fifteenth century; but it remained growth from a small base, and prior to 1500 exports from the Tyne, mainly to London, seldom exceeded 15,000 tons. Coal was dug on most of the present-day coalfields, but on a small scale. In the early fourteenth century manorial documents from Cannock Chase show that five pits were being worked, each of them by one or two miners, and each for only part of the year. The articles of the forest eyre in 1244 asked for enquiry to be made concerning 'sea coal found within the forest, and whether anyone has taken money from the digging thereof'. Some coal travelled long distances: receipts from the Forest of Dean in the thirteenth century included the customs on sea coal transported down the Severn, and coal found at an excavation at Goltho in Lincolnshire has been tentatively identified from its particular structure as having come from Barnsley in Yorkshire. Coal remained scarce, and something of a luxury. It was wood that provided the main fuel.

The most important extracting industry was undoubtedly that of iron, which was particularly tied to forest regions. Evidence is particularly abundant for those aspects of the industry that were concerned with war. In the twelfth century the Forest of Dean was the main centre of the iron industry. From the thirteenth century, however, there are increasing references to the purchase of iron goods from the Weald of Sussex and Kent. In 1254 30,000 horseshoes and 60,000 nails were purchased in the Weald; in 1327 a forge at Roffey near Horsham sent 1,000 horseshoes via the port of Shoreham for the Scottish wars; the horseshoes costing £4 3s 4d with 5s extra for carriage. It is clearly the second of these transactions, rather than the first, that indicates the organisation of the industry. At Bedburn forge in 1408 there were only four full-time employees—a bloomer (the smelting forges were called bloomeries), a smith, a foreman and a charcoal burner. At Tudeley also there were four men, there referred to as the master blower and three other blowers. They were paid on piece-work, earning a certain amount for every bloom of iron that they produced.

Dozens of such sites have been identified in the Weald, at places where ore was available close to water supply and timber for fuel. One of them recently excavated, at Minepit Wood near Rotherfield in Sussex, showed a medieval iron-working site of the fourteenth and fifteenth centuries on the site of an iron-works that had been in use in the iron age and then in the Romano-British period. The medieval site showed a roasting furnace, in which the ore was broken up and the water removed from it, a smelting furnace which probably had a timber hood to protect it from the elements, the mines from which the ore was produced, slag-heaps both with ore and refuse, the whole enclosed in a small paddock with wattle and daub fencing. It is interesting that so many medieval sites, both rural and urban, show evidences of earlier industrial workings. The continuity is the more striking with an industry such as iron, since there is practically no continuity of medieval sites with those of the modern industrial age.

Clay suitable for potting was also widely dispersed. Knowledge of the medieval pottery industry has increased enormously in the last decade, as hundreds of archaeological reports have drawn with loving detail and at vast expense practically every scrap of pottery brought forth from the ground. This material, when combined with documentary evidence, shows the methods of production, the scale of manufacture and the range of distribution of the finished goods. The pottery industry increased rapidly in scale during the middle ages, following an increase in demand both for clay and various types of metal goods. Along with iron artefacts, which show a similar distribution and increase in quantity, it was important not just in extending the range of manufactured goods, but in satisfying a consumer demand both for luxury goods for the aristocracy and for basic equipment for every hearth in the country. In this industry, as in most medieval industries, many of the workers had small agricultural holdings. At Poteria (later Crockerton) in Longbridge Deverill in Wiltshire there were twenty-five smallholders with four acres of land or less. Two of these were millers; the others were entitled to make pots if they so wished; they paid 7d for their fuel if they worked for a full year, 3½d if for only half the year. They also had to pay for their clay: 4d if they took it from the lord's land, 2d if they took it from their own, i.e. from their smallholdings. They ownd boon-works, but no other agricultural works. This is a rare example of a semi-industrialised community working within the framework of the manorial system, and recorded in some detail in manorial records.

The structure of the pottery industry presents a complete contrast to that of tin: it was very far from being capital intensive, and it met what was largely a local demand. On the fringes of the deserted medieval village of Lyveden in Northamptonshire, within the Rockingham Forest, there was a site used for iron-working in the twelfth century which came to be used for pottery-making during the thirteenth century. Excavation has revealed a potter's workshop, various yards and pits, kilns, a pot-bank and a store-shed. This small industrial site is not dissimilar to the iron-working site from Sussex which has already been described, save that it formed part of a small village within the forest bounds, a village which seems slowly to have decayed around it. The distribution of Lyveden ware, and of numerous other types of pottery identified, shows clearly that they chiefly met a local need. At Wythemail in Northamptonshire there were pottery sherds from Lyveden and Olney Hyde in Buckingham-shire (each 12 miles away), Potterspury (19 miles), Great Brickhill (26 miles). Humber Ware went to south Yorkshire and north Lincolnshire, within the range of the rivers which followed into the Humber estuary. The recent excavation of a tile factory at Danbury in Essex has shown another industrial site, on scrubland of poor quality, which also served a local area and the distribution of whose wares seems chiefly confined to the Chelmer valley. It is clear that the local market town would be the normal place of distribution of such wares, and that the potters' stalls on market day would be the meeting place of many styles.

The impact of this wide range of industrial activity on the structure and development of medieval society can only be appreciated when the different trades are considered as a whole. Geology and the need for fuel set the extractive industries well apart from the manorialism of lowland England. The individual nature of the work, as well as its geographical situation, set those engaged in it apart from the routine of the villages of open-field England. Many of these men, the miners of north Yorkshire or the tinners of Cornwall, would have a small agricultural holding, which might provide a basic continuity and a home for their families. Yet their homes for much of the year would be in a forest clearing, smelting iron, or within open-cast mines. Few areas of England were without a basis for employment outside agriculture. In constructing any picture of medieval society, it is important to leave the industrial smallholder an important place. It requires imagination to do so, for industry now is more concentrated and more specialised. A town like Corby now stands apart from the villages around in Northamptonshire, specialised and producing iron in bulk. In the medieval period there were by contrast numerous small settlements such as Lyveden, and villages and small towns with an industrial fringe to them.

Those engaged in trade became during the course of our period a professional class, living outside feudalism and with an ethos quite different from that of the lay aristocracy. A distinct mercantile culture developed in England. It took its tone and many of its techniques from the more developed parts of the western economy, particularly from Italy. It was not a secular culture, but it was a lay culture. 'In the name of God and of profit' was the standard beginning to the ledgers of the merchants of medieval Florence. It is the concern with profit that was distinctive, and from it all else followed, both in way of life and in the techniques of business. The merchant in a foreign land should stick with his own compatriots, and keep his own counsel, give little sign of wealth, and indeed make it appear that 'necessity was driving him to the grave'. All should be subservient to his vocation, which was to make money. He should spread his risks, and at all costs avoid the ultimate sin, which was to have his capital lying idle. Even if he made no profit, he could preserve the network of contacts upon which he depended against better times. Little separates the merchants' manuals in which such advice appears from the paperbacks about how to succeed in business today. By contrast, the difference between the merchant manuals and those of medieval estate management is complete. The latter were equally full of conventional wisdom and good advice, but they were designed to protect the lords against fraud not to maximise income. Indeed the calculation of profit was no part of their proper concern. The bishop of Lincoln's *Rules* were a world away from the invention of double-entry book-keeping, the complicated network of credit which sustained not only the merchant community but also the whole political structure of the day.

With the formation during the twelfth century of a single unified western European economy, this ethos could not fail to spread from Lombardy and Flanders to the less developed regions of Europe. In mid-twelfth-century London, it is difficult to identify a distinctive group of merchants, let alone a distinct culture. Two centuries later London, unhindered by the Black Death, was going from strength to strength, taking an increasing proportion of the nation's population and wealth. The merchants were a minority in the larger towns, but they all but monopolised their wealth. The survival from the 1390s of the ledger book of Gilbert Maghfeld, an iron-dealer, a rare English survival of a class of records that occur in their hundreds in Italian archives, can show the detail of the world of these men in the late fourteenth century. The staple of Gilbert Maghfeld's export trade was cloth, and its chief direction was to south-west France. In return he shipped not wine—or at least not in large quantities—but iron from the Bayonne area and from Bilbao in northern Spain, along with large amounts of woad and alum from Lombardy, the dye-stuffs used for making cloth. As a merchant in London he could find a market for most things, and it is a sign that his capital and space were not allowed to lie idle that he is found importing also wax, linen, copper, millstones and on two occasions even asses from Spain. His trade provides a useful corrective to the view that the trade of England with the south was chiefly confined to the transport of low bulk, high cost luxury goods.

It is difficult to get a single impression of the development of English commerce. There were changes in supply and demand, for a variety of reasons. Population change was important. There was a 50 per cent decline in population in the century after the Black Death. The first plague put a sharp check on every trade. But the rate of recovery of the different trades varied enormously. Political considerations, and in particular warfare, were also important. The Hundred Years' War with France had an immediate and continuing impact. In some trades the 1330s show checks and readjustments more striking than those caused by the Black Death. Warfare, either by restraining supply or by restricting commerce, could lead to abrupt short-term fluctuations in particular trades. The horizons of trade narrowed; in particular, the nature of English trade with northern Europe changed with the development and increased aggression of the Hanseatic League.

Of all the major trades, the pattern of development is most clear in the case of the English wine trade with France. Diplomacy, warfare, and population changes all precipitated its decline. The following figures show exports of wine from the Bordeaux region of France, taken at roughly twenty-year intervals:[9]

1308–9	102,724 tuns
1328–9	69,175 tuns
1349–50	13,427 tuns
1366–7	37,103 tuns
1380–1	9,041 tuns

1402–3	10,067 tuns
1429–30	13,222 tuns
1452–3	9,919 tuns

The figures are for exports from France, not for imports into England. The decline in imports is not as marked, for English consumers took a higher and higher proportion of the total. In the early fourteenth century, it may have been as little as 25 per cent, representing on average at least 20,000 tuns a year. By the 1390s, England took up to 80 per cent of the trade, which seldom amounted to more than 10,000 tuns a year. At the beginning of the fourteenth century, England was but one of many outlets for a flourishing export trade; at the end of it, it was almost the sole outlet for a much attenuated one. A narrowing of the horizons of trade was a general feature of commercial development in the later middle ages. It sprang in part from an increasing emphasis on imports by native merchants, which in turn were fostered by a differential tariff between native and alien merchants.

Warfare provided the biggest check to the wine trade. In the year 1336–7, at the beginning of the war, the figure shrank to under a quarter of that of the previous year. Henceforward, wine fleets had to be defended, to carry extra crew, and to sail in convoy. Merchants claimed that they thereby lost the rewards of enterprise; but they kept their capital and their contacts, and hoped for better times. But better times never came. During the 1360s trade picked up, but to a level less than a half that of fifty years before. All but irreparable damage was done to the trade of the *Haut Pays*, to the vintages of such areas as Le Réole, St-Emilion and Entre deux Mers, which lay in the disputed borderland between the kingdom of France and the duchy of Gascony. The borderland was frequently devastated, but the Duchy lacked the resources to defend it. In the first half of the fifteenth century, the wine trade remained fairly stable, but at an average of 12,000 to 14,000 tuns yearly it was at an even lower level than before. The figures for the *Haut Pays* slowly diminished, as the English hold on the area lessened. On 20 June 1451 Charles VII of France captured Bordeaux. The trade of the whole region, organised along the rivers—the Dordogne, the Garonne and the Tarn—which led out through Bordeaux, was destroyed by this combination of politics and geography. The history of the wine trade shows not only that trade was affected by warfare, but that a foreign import trade focused on a single outlet was particularly vulnerable.

The cloth industry was affected in its development from the 1290s onwards less by warfare than by the needs of government finance. Heavy taxation of wool provided the crown with a regular income from a staple trade, and it provided the necessary security for borrowing in advance of the customs collection. As had happened in the wine trade, differential taxation led to the concentration of trade in the hands of English merchants. In the wool trade, the need for borrowing had led to the emergence of the wool staple at Calais. In the cloth export trade, the dominance of the Merchant Adventurers of London slowly asserted itself. There was the tendency to monopoly even in a trade that was secure and expanding. Table 2 shows exports of wool and cloth, and converts the figures for cloth into their wool equivalent.[10]

Table 2

	Wool (in sacks)	Cloth (in wool equivalent)	Cloth (in cloths of assise)
1281–90	26,856		
1301–10	34,493		
1311–20	30,686		
1321–30	25,268		
1331–40	29,569		
1341–50	22,013		
1351–60	32,655	1,267	5,491
1361–70	28,302	3,024	13,102
1371–80	23,241	3,432	14,873
1381–90	17,988	5,521	23,926
1391–1400	17,697	8,967	38,856
1401–10	13,922	7,651	33,158
1411–20	13,487	6,364	27,580
1421–30	13,696	9,309	40,340
1431–40	7,377	10,051	43,559
1441–50	9,398	11,803	51,150

The wool trade declined, and the cloth trade grew. If the figures are to be used to show anything more than a general trend, however, some important qualifications are necessary. The first is that the sudden appearance of the cloth trade in the customs records is an illusion. Only in April 1347 did exports of cloth by English merchants start to be taxed, and so only from that date is it possible to estimate the total volume of exports. The second qualification is that these figures deal only with exports. If any estimate is to be made of the production and of the market for cloth in England, then it is necessary to consider both home-produced cloth and imports from abroad.

The first stage in the expansion of the cloth industry in the fourteenth century was its capture of the home market for good-quality woollens. In 1347–8 around 12,000 cloths were being exported, while the home market took between 5,000 and 6,000 home-produced cloths and between 9,000 and 10,000 imported cloths. By the last decade of the century more than 40,000 cloths a year were being exported, and around 10,000 a year retained for the home market. Imports of cloth had become insignificant. In the second half of the fourteenth century there were two periods of particularly rapid growth. The first was between 1353 and 1368, when the trade grew at the rate of 18 per cent a year. In 1368 the plague returned; in 1369 there was renewed warfare with France; and in 1370 famine in England. The loss of the Gascon market led to a short-term decline in the cloth trade, and, in the long-term, to a diversification of markets. The political difficulties of the English government in the 1370s were in some measure caused by this process of adjustment. Between 1380 and 1395 there was another period of expansion. In terms of volume, exports of wool were higher, as Table 2 shows, than exports of cloth. In terms of value, there was little difference between wool and cloth. Two cloths of assise were roughly equivalent in value to one sack of wool. In the fifteenth century England became an exporter of cloth rather than of wool.

The progress of England as a manufacturing nation during the later medieval period is important. But it is important also that it is put in perspective. Towards the end of the twelfth century, Lombardy and Flanders were industrial and mercantile societies, whose wealth and expertise set them quite apart from the regions which lay around them. Those regions provided them with raw materials, and a cosmopolitan culture and an expanding economy provided them with a European market for their goods. The political and economic developments of the later middle ages destroyed these advantages. Societies became more self-sufficient, as population levels fell, and warfare and conscious or unconscious economic protectionism put increasing barriers in the way of international trade. By the fifteenth century there was less discrepancy of wealth between the different regions of Europe, just as there was less discrepancy of wealth as between the different social classes. The development of manufacture in cloth is a part of a general process of levelling up in the western economy generally, not an isolated development, still less a sign of particular strength.

England was still an agricultural country. It would be misleading to over-emphasise the progress made by manufacturing industry, but the variety and geographical spread of English industry, and the number of market towns and of regional centres, means that a social history that concentrates on the country's agricultural base can equally mislead. The towns grew in size. London alone had nearly 10 per cent of the wealth of England in the early sixteenth century. Behind this figure lay the centralisation of government as well as the increase of trade. Much manufacturing took place in the towns; in cloth manufacture, for instance, the towns were more important than the countryside. But every region had its industry widely distributed. The bases were small. Many industrial workers were cottagers, who had smallholdings, an agricultural base of three or four acres of land. They should not be presumed all to have been on the verges of poverty, rather they lived on the verges of manorial England. William Cobbett, on his *Rural Rides*, extolled the virtues of the cottage economy which he sought to disseminate. The economy of later medieval England was also, in important respects, a cottage economy, one in which opportunities for employment were diversified. Industry was an important element in this diversification.

The force behind the shire town was the force of government, of lay
and ecclesiastical magnates and increasingly of the crown itself. One
of its functions was to act as a centre for what would now be called
government propaganda. The sheriffs were instructed to explain the
issues of the day, and the financial needs of the crown. At times of
great political debate, as during the civil wars of Henry III's reign or
the early years of Edward II, or during the late 1330s at the beginning
of the Hundred Years' War, the sheriff's post-bag was particularly
heavy. A lot can be learnt from what was said on these occasions,
when politicians, at least vicariously, went on the stump.

One such missive, which has already been referred to, was sent out
in 1337, at the very beginning of the Hundred Years' War.[1] 'These
are the offers', it began, 'which were made to the King of France by
the King of England to try to avoid war.' The king had sent
numerous diplomatic missions, asking for the return of lands in
France 'which are being withheld from him in the Duchy of
Guienne'. He had gone secretly to France, and had tried to settle the
dispute by marriage. First his eldest son had been offered to the
daughter of the French king, 'without taking anything for the
marriage'. Then he had offered other matches. Then he had offered
money. The French king had accepted none of these offers, but rather
had 'busied himself in aid and maintenance of the Scots, the enemies
of the king of England'. Edward had even offered truces to the Scots,
in the hope of starting peace negotiations with the French; but the
Scots had simply broken the truce, and 'captured several great men of
the King of England's allegiance'. The king, in short, could not have
done more to avoid war.

The rhetoric of these missives was supplied by the various magnates
and royal officials commissioned to do the job. The detail was
carefully edited; but how none the less could such a document manage
to hold a popular audience? There are too many documents of the same
kind for this one to be dismissed as the work of a scholarly and

over-enthusiastic clerk. The answer in brief must be that while there was a lot of detail, there were only a few ideas, and those ideas were shared by all ranks in society. The ideas were those of feudal lordship. The king sought rights over lands in France. Rights over land were governed by custom, and the English king had been scrupulous in performing his customary obligations to the French king. Disputes between equals in this society could most properly be settled by marriage, and great efforts had been made to settle the matter in this way. Kings and peasants followed the same rules in giving their children in marriage, so that the emphasis put on the marriage negotiations would have found a ready audience. Rights in land, and an awareness of the services attached to land in a feudal society, were shared also by all ranks in medieval English society. The document also presumes a political awareness, of the idea of the Crusade, and of the interrelationship of affairs in France, Scotland and England. Two things only were presumed of the listener: an involvement with feudal lordship, and a knowledge of the context of western European diplomacy.

The preceding chapters have shown how men were separated in rank and status, wealth and power. In spite of those divisions they shared—so at least the government believed—knowledge and assumptions which made political discussion possible amongst them. They inhabited the same mental world, which had its particular landscape, quite distinct from that of the present day. There was a community of ideas, and the chapter which follows will examine some of the more important of those ideas. The unity of the political nation was built upon, and served to strengthen, a single culture.

There were distinct orders in society. There were those who worked, those who fought, and those who prayed. Yet these divisions proceed from a kind of social contract; specialisation of social function was not something that destroyed a culture, any more than did economic specialisation. The ties of family and neighbourhood united the three orders, and these ties should not be ignored just because they are obvious. The ties of feudal tenure also united them. A freeholder might own land in several adjacent villages in one area, and in each of them experience a different type of lordship. One piece of land might be held of the local squire, an adjacent one from a Benedictine monastery twenty miles away, and yet another from a tenant in villeinage. The relationship between these four individuals would be expressed in terms of feudal service, but these services had largely lost their social content and been reduced to cash payments.

None the less the holding of land provided links between men of widely different wealth, experience, and aspirations. A close relative might be a monk in a local Augustinian monastery. A brother-in-law of whom he disapproved might have redeemed himself in part by war service in France. The common culture was built up from a wide variety of shared assumptions and shared experiences.

Opportunities to see the world beyond the nearest town were rarer for men of peasant status, but none the less available. Warfare against the French or against the Scots would take the ordinary soldier to the frontiers of the kingdom and beyond. This was a new development in the later middle ages. English kings in the twelfth century largely used mercenary armies. For his Scottish campaigns Edward I mustered men from the north of England, and for the Welsh wars chiefly from Chester and the Marches. Derbyshire and Nottinghamshire sent men to each theatre of war, and points south of the Trent were little affected. It was in the fourteenth century that the south of England was drawn into warfare. In Edward III's reign the northern counties still served against the Scots, and the rest of England sent troops to France. Thus in 1346 archers were sent from seventeen counties, in groups of between twelve and eighty men, to the channel ports. These were national armies. There can be no doubt that regular campaigning from the 1290s onwards gave ordinary people an insight into the politics of the country and the personalities of its leaders. Another microcosm of society is presented in the group of pilgrims who went on horseback to Canterbury, 'the holy blissful martyr for to seek'. Pilgrimage was another facet of a cosmopolitan society, taking men not only to local shrines a few days' distance from their homes, but also from far afield to the great shrines of Walsingham and Canterbury, and some of them to Compostella (see plate 2a), Rome and Jerusalem. Not only the doctrines but the physical geography of the Christian religion were imprinted on their minds.

Warfare then, and the needs of government with whose proclamation we began, was a powerful force for the unity of culture. The structure of government inherited from the Anglo-Saxon period made the shire the connexion between the freeholder and the central government. Not only diplomatic negotiations and requests for money came to it. The political debate between successive kings and their baronage was similarly accompanied by missives from London explaining the terms by which their differences had been resolved. From the paper wars of Henry III's reign, several important documents survive in all three languages—Latin, French and English—a clear sign that they were intended to reach the widest possible audience.

Much attention was given to publicising the Ordinances of 1311. First they were published in St Paul's Churchyard before a largely aristocratic audience. Then a few days later the earl of Gloucester and other magnates proclaimed the text to the people. Later still they were sealed with the Great Seal and sent to the counties to be published there. The earl of Lancaster erected a tablet in St Paul's for their better memory. The text of the Ordinances dominated the political discussion of a decade; with its successive revocations by the king and republications by the baronage it must not only have become extremely familiar, but have acquired a genuine moral force. That the Ordinances were intended to redress popular grievances was not open to doubt. They must have had the same publicity as the text of the scriptures and the lives of the saints, and like them (as we shall see) have been allegorised and assimilated into a popular culture which included a powerful political tradition. Small wonder that miracles were recorded as worked both at Lancaster's tomb and at the tablet in St Paul's, and that the commons in 1322 asked for Lancaster's canonisation. At South Newington in Oxfordshire a scheme of wall painting of the 1330s shows Lancaster's execution, though it is the executioner and not Thomas who has lost his head with the passage of the years.

The same church has one of the best surviving paintings of the execution of St Thomas of Canterbury (see plate 3, also from South Newington), the moral of whose death was a familiar one. It was part of clerical and popular not of royal historiography: the only record of Becket's death found in an English castle comes appropriately from Chester. Royal taste was rather different. A lot is known of the scenes that Henry III was fond of. The famous 'painted chamber' in the palace at Westminster contained 'all the warlike pictures of the whole Bible.' The story of Alexander was popular, and so was 'the story of Antioch and the duel of King Richard' with Saladin (see Figure 10). There were St Edward and St Edmund, the saints among his ancestors, the signs of divine approval of the traditions of the English monarchy. The ideas both of paintings and of texts were by their painting or writing fixed. Simon de Montfort's loyalty to the Provisions of Oxford and Thomas of Lancaster's loyalty to the Ordinances of 1311 may look like stubbornness, and possibly they were stubborn men, but to publish an idea was to preserve it. Any conscious appeal to popular opinion inevitably involved literal-mindedness and conservatism. Political debate was conducted in a series of images from past history.

It was the king's duty to follow the customs of his ancestors, and to protect the lands and liberties of his subjects. A real moral force lay behind the preservation of estates in land, and the king's rights over his subjects' property were circumscribed. Magna Carta said that no man might be disseised, 'save by the lawful judgement of his peers or by the law of the land'. This was good feudal law, but in practice any forfeiture was in danger of being reckoned as disinheritance. To disinherit men was tyranny. Early in May 1266, in the aftermath of several years of civil war, Henry III wrote to the sheriff of York, saying that it was being falsely reported that the king had arbitrarily

Figure 10 The duel between King Richard and Saladin, after a tile from Clarendon Palace, Wilts

ejected men from their possessions without trial. The sheriff was to take immediate steps to dispel this impression, and to announce in the county court, in towns and in market places, that if anyone had been unlawfully dispossessed he should come to the king's court. And sure enough, when the Dictum of Kenilworth was published that October, the lay and ecclesiastical lords charged with establishing peace declared: 'we wish to walk in accordance with God's will and on the path of equity, and so we have thought it right that the course to be followed is not disinheritance but redemption.' Men could buy back their lands, and the king's peace, for between one and seven times the estate's annual valuation, according to the gravity of their offence. Traitors were still liable to disinheritance. Thomas of Lancaster was executed in March 1322, but his brother was restored the bulk of his lands in 1327; and when Henry Bolingbroke was refused the same inheritance in 1399, the action led to the king's deposition. Up to the mid-twelfth century, rebels were treated

with compassion, but their estates severely; subsequent developments bore more hardly on individuals and more leniently on their
lands.

How then was the inheritance of land to be determined? What
considerations governed its transfer between individuals, and
between the generations? In the ideal world, it was service which
determined the tenure of land. The peasant ploughed. The knight
fought. They each had land holdings appropriate to their rank, to
sustain their service. And so service, again in theory, determined the
relationship between individuals. But feudal society changed. Land
lost its original social function of supporting service. Money made
the adjustment easy. Service could be rendered in cash. From the
twelfth century onwards, there are references to knights fighting *cum
denariis*, with their pennies, and to peasants ploughing with their
pennies also. The idea is logically absurd, but functionally quite
sensible. This means that the concept of service will often show an
ideal world, and not the forces behind custom. Those forces lie rather
in the land itself, and in the needs of the families occupying it.

At the manorial level, the links between service and tenure were in
large part maintained. The manor of Domesday Book and of the
manorial surveys was a unit of production whose manpower needs
were met from a series of tenancies, yardlands, half-yardlands and
smallholdings, which were of fixed extent and which provided
known services. The continuity of agricultural production was
secured by continuity in the occupancy of these fixed holdings. By
the custom of the central parts of England, that continuity was in turn
secured by a system of impartible inheritance. One person succeeded
to an undivided tenement. The most common of these systems at the
village level, which determined also the succession to the crown and
to most free tenures, was that of primogeniture. The eldest son
succeeded to the entire holding that his father had inherited. If there
were no sons, then it passed to the eldest daughter. If there were no
children, then to the dead man's eldest brother; and so on, according
to well-known rules. A man's heirs were his blood relations. Rights
in land were family rights, and they carried family obligations. In
some areas, the custom known as Borough English prevailed, in
which land went rather to the youngest son of the household; and, in
its simplest form, then to a younger daughter, to a younger uncle,
and so on. Either way, either by primogeniture or by ultimogeni-
ture, the service element was preserved intact. Each system had its
logic. The eldest son would be the most likely to be an adult when his

father died, and hence able to inherit his obligations. The youngest son, on the other hand, was the most vulnerable, the least able to make his own way. Lords, their tenancies intact, could be happy with either, though primogeniture was more familiar, and therefore seemed tidier. In regions where the manor was less dominant, and with it the force of feudal lordship, different forms of inheritance tended to divide holdings on a tenant's death.

Primogeniture and other forms of inheritance were a means of imposing order on the descent of land holdings. The land had not only to provide service but also support a family unit. A body of custom and law grew up by which the transfer of land between members of the family was controlled. Some transfer was necessary; men had by law to provide for their wives, and they would wish to provide for all their children in some way, either by marriage or by the grant of land.

What makes an old lady into a dowager is simply the possession of land, and in medieval society all widows were dowagers. In many villages a widow could hold her husband's tenancy for her lifetime, provided that the service due was properly performed. Up to a quarter of the main tenancies in the Winchester manor of Taunton between 1270 and 1315 were obtained through marriages with widows. And so we must not think that primogeniture necessarily meant a regular descent from father to son. Consider in diagrammatic form the descent of the tenancy of William de Chilkepathe in the years following his death in 1268:[2]

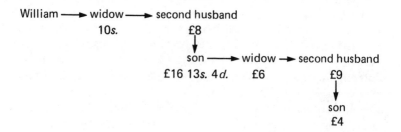

The last of these transfers took place in 1350; you have six transfers of property in the space of 82 years. Behind such diagrams we must imagine the frustration of youth and the power of the old:[3]

This is pain's landscape.
A savage agriculture is practised
Here; every farm has its
Grandfather or grandmother, gnarled hands
On the cheque-book, a long, slow
Pull on the placenta about the neck.
Old lips monopolise the talk
When a friend calls. The children listen
From the kitchen; the children march
With angry patience against the dawn.

That is from 'Tenancies' by R. S. Thomas, a poem written in North Wales in the 1960s. It is useful to keep his images in mind. The cheque-book: a farmer unable to work the land could negotiate a generous settlement as the price of his son's succession in his own lifetime. Thus an inheritance registered on the manor of Cranfield in Bedfordshire in 1294:[4]

> Elias de Bretendon surrendered in open court a messuage and half-virgate of land at money rent . . . to be held by his son John in return for the services due . . . John will provide suitable food and drink for Elias and his wife Christine while they are alive, and they will live with John on the capital messuage. And if it should happen, though it may not, that trouble and discord should in the future arise between the parties so that they are unable to live together, then John shall provide for Elias and Christine, or whichever of them should outlive the other, a house and curtilage where they can decently reside. And then he would give each year to the same Elias and Christine . . . six quarters of hard corn at Michaelmas.

The son paid £2 to have the agreement made and registered; but the terms of the agreement are those of the parties and not the lord. The parents were pensioned off in some detail and in some comfort.

Other members of the family could not dictate terms of this kind, but they were entitled by custom to a basic subsistence if they stayed upon their parents' holding. This might involve their board and their keep, or a more regular arrangement. Thus at Sevenhampton in Wiltshire in 1287:[5]

> Six pounds from Reginald Damemalde as the fine for one virgate formerly belonging to Maud, his mother, of the holding of John de Seinte Elene. And the same Reginald grants to Walter his brother a

house and every year at Michaelmas one quarter of wheat, so long
as he remains without a wife and on this land.

A life tenancy could support a son who could not, or did not wish to,
move from the land. It could not support another household. The
prohibition of alienation applied to the father's holding, the
patrimony. It was accepted that movable goods could be divided,
though here again there were customary rules, and also that land
acquired could be used to support daughters and younger sons. A
fringe of free tenures surrounded many villages, and free tenancies
might be acquired by those of villein status to provide extra holdings,
and a measure of flexibility in family arrangements. Thus with the
descent of the holding of Robert Alred, a tenant on the Peterborough
Abbey manor of Boroughbury. His elder son paid 66s 8d for the
capital messuage and a virgate of land. His younger brother Roger
paid 20s for a cottage and three acres of land in *le Stibbing*, land cleared
from the forest. The widow paid 6s 8d for a further cottage and 2½
acres of land. Each of these two small holdings of free land had been
acquired by Robert Alred in his lifetime. And he had provided from
capital for a third son also, who had been 'put to letters' in the abbey
in 1300. The abbey had confiscated a series of charters by which the
free land had been acquired.

These were men of property, with their own family archives.
Everything was subsumed to the family interest. There was a feeling
akin to that found in modern Ireland, that the family's name should
be 'on the land'. This can be seen on the Winchester estate, when a
man marrying a widow and therefore gaining his landed base from
her, would normally change his name. Thus in 1255 John of Half-
nakede married Edith, the widow of Adam of Shordich, and appears
thereafter as John of Shordich. The man takes his identity from his
holding. It is the family's link with the land which makes sense of the
tenurial structure of the village and of the village land market.

It is not a fanciful idea to say that the family and its possession of
land can be taken as a key to medieval culture, and it is a major part of
the argument for a common culture that the ideas we find in village
records relating to the tenure of land are common to the whole of
society. As Homans put it:

> in their main lines, the rules of family law were the same for the earl
> and the husbandman . . . in particular they all held to what we
> have seen as the central principle of the organisation of medieval

families: the permanent association of a given blood line with an established tenement unit.

With the gentry and aristocracy we have a much fuller range of records, and can see how family consciousness and the records of land tenure are the foundations of perspective, the means by which an individual related to the world around him.

The estate book of Henry de Bray, a Northamptonshire land-owner who was the lord of the village of Harlestone in the latter part of the thirteenth century, will provide an introduction to these ideas. Most of the book is taken up with the ordinary records of land transactions, with accounts and court records, and with lists of rents and services. But it was not where Henry de Bray started. He started with the date and regnal year, with a description of the world and lists of the English counties, and of bishops and kings. He then had the records of his own estate, starting with the Domesday description of it; and then there were details of the landlords from whom he held, and of their own estates. All this was done to provide information (literally 'to supply evidence') for his heirs. We should look beyond the basic compilation of record material to its arrangement, and to the philosophy that lay behind it. It was designed to place Henry de Bray in his position in the world, both geographical and social.

The only thing that marks this off from other lay records of the same period is the comparatively restrained treatment of family history. Both the Hotots of Clopton, the lords of a single village, and the Bassets of Weldon, a family of baronial rank with half a dozen demesne manors, start their thirteenth-century records with a family chronicle, which takes them back to the Conquest. The following extract from the Basset records comes from a feodary, a list of knights' fees, made in the 1240s:[6]

> From Robert de Bussy descended the inheritance to Geva his
> daughter, who married Geoffrey Ridel. And from the said G.
> Ridel and Geva his wife there descended one daughter called
> Matilda, who married Richard Basset the son of Ralph Basset.
> This Richard came at the Conquest, and was justiciar of England at
> the time of King Henry the son of the Conqueror, and he was the
> first man to ascend the Exchequer in England, and he gave laws
> such as frankpledge and other good laws.

The tenure was traced from the time of the Conquest of England, and the first Richard Basset, who had been an important royal servant at the time of Henry I, was taken back fifty years. He was the famous ancestor, the first justiciar, although it was clearly something of a struggle by 1242 to conjure up the details of his legislative work. A window once in Tamworth church showed the Conqueror granting the castle to Robert Marmion (see Figure 11).

Figure 11 Window (now lost) from Tamworth church, Staffs, showing William the Conqueror granting the castle to Robert Marmion. The Conqueror died in 1087; the Marmion family acquired Tamworth after this date, and the first Robert Marmion who occurs in England lived in the early twelfth century.

> They hail'd him Lord of Fontenaye,
> Of Lutterward and Scrivelbaye,
> Of Tamworth tower and town.
>   (*Scott*, Marmion, *c. 1, XII*)

The places mentioned here, Fontenay-le-Marmion (Normandy), Lutterworth (Leics), Scrivelsby (Lincs) and Tamworth, were all in the possession of the Marmion family in the twelfth and thirteenth centuries

A knowledge of the descent of land and an interest in genealogy went together. Such men as the Bassets lose little in comparison with Jane Austen's

> Sir Walter Elliot, of Kellynch Hall, in Somersetshire, . . . a man who, for his own amusement, never took up any book but the Baronetage; there he found occupation for an idle hour, and consolation in a distressed one . . . there, if every other leaf were powerless, he could read his own history with an interest which never failed.

That families of the thirteenth and fourteenth centuries felt it necessary to take their tenure back to the Conquest was not just a matter of family pride. A man who wished to prove his right to a piece of land had to come into the king's court, and detail its descent from generation to generation. In a case from Bedfordshire in 1203, Walter son of Maurice claimed from Ralph son of William six virgates of land in Cople:[7]

> Ralph came and defended his right, and admitted that they were both of one stock, namely that of Robert *Armiger*, who came at the Conquest of England. He begat two sons, Hugh and Gervase. Hugh was the ancestor of Walter; Gervase was the ancestor of Ralph. Robert *Armiger* gave Gervase the six virgates of land, to hold of the chief lord of the fee. He held them throughout his life, and after him his son William and after him Ralph son of William, who now holds.

In another case, from 1224, one Geoffrey of Roding in Essex claimed a virgate of land, 'of which his ancestors had been seized since the Conquest of England'. It turned out otherwise, for the land belonged to the local church, and Geoffrey himself admitted that he was a villein of the earl of Warenne. The peasants had the same attitudes to land holding as had their lords.

It is to these ideas that we should relate a good deal of the thirteenth-century interest in genealogy and heraldry. The first major collection of arms is to be found in the works of Matthew Paris, the St Albans chronicler, and dates from between 1244 and 1259. Most of the 130 shields in Matthew Paris predate the mid-1250s collection of arms in Glover's Roll, 'armes of the Nobilitye in Kyng Henry the 3 tyme taken out of a very Auncient Rolle in parchment written in the same tyme as appareth by the hand.' Matthew Paris was a great collector of information, but his heraldry cannot consequently be dismissed as the medieval equivalent of stamp-collecting. The shields of the great men are marginal to his text (see plate 4b) but not marginal to his story; for the interest was growing at the same time as the political opposition to Henry III, which Matthew chronicled in detail. Matthew's interest in genealogy is matched by many family chronicles found in the records of religious houses; the history of the Mandevilles in a document from Walden, and that of the Mortimers in the Wigmore chronicle. The arms of local lords are found both in Peterborough Abbey and in the neighbouring manor-house at Longthorpe; and similar heraldry survives on the walls of dozens of parish churches.

Coats of arms were a condensation of past history which when expanded established a man's position in the world. They stood for stability, and for independence. They were designed for display. Thus the first bequest of Lady Alice West in 1395, in one of the earliest wills to be written in English, was 'to Thomas my sone, a bed of tapicers werk, with alle the tapites of sute, red of colour, ypouthered with chapes and scochons, in the corners, of myn Auncestres armes'. And in 1431 William Fitz-Harry of London, ordained that 'on my body be laide a faire stone of Marble with my creste, myn armes, my vanturs, in blewe, reede, and white, and my worde "mercy and ioie", to which worde I take me fully for euermore'. The Lollards were never so radical as when they ordained that they should be buried under a plain slab, such as the 'flat playne stone, saue my name ygraued tharin' specified by Thomas Broke in 1417.[8] To renounce your arms was to renounce your sense of identity.

Men's conception of society and politics was governed by other ideas than those which came from the tenure of land, ideas less tangible but no less real. They can possibly be grasped most easily by examining the paintings which survive, unfortunately often in fragments and much restored, in many medieval churches and secular buildings. On all types of building, in the church paintings designed for the common people, and in the murals designed for the houses of the landowners, there are the same ornaments and the same moral tales. The ideas come from Christianity and from feudal lordship, and in a few buildings the scheme of decoration is complete enough to show their interrelationship.

In the great chamber of Longthorpe Tower just west of Peterborough there is a remarkable series of wall paintings, which probably date from the 1330s. The ideas of family are prominent. The Thorpe arms appear on the south wall, accompanied by the shields of the other tenants of Peterborough barony. On top of these there are two enthroned figures bearing larger shields with royal leopards, which must stand for either Edward II or Edward III, and for Edmund of Woodstock, earl of Kent, who was executed for treason in 1330. The decoration on this wall establishes the Thorpes' place in feudal society. The other three walls have a quite different scheme of decoration. Among the more striking paintings are series which show the Seven Ages of Man, the Three Living and the Three Dead, the Wheel of the Five Senses, the Labours of the Months, and a celestial orchestra which has become rather unbalanced with the passage of the years. Secular occupations are more than equalled by tales warning of the dangers of becoming preoccupied with them. These contrasts, the sense of guilt and the impermanence of so much of life's concerns, would threaten the sanity of most modern people if they were called upon to live in this room. For a succession of Roberts of Thorpe, however, it provided all the consolation of a familiar landscape, as restful as a day watching cricket or an early evening drink at the pub.

Each of the scenes here is developed in the literature of the period. The story of the three quick and the three dead tells of three kings or princes who go hunting in fine array and encounter three corpses. In the Arundel Psalter they converse. The living say: 'I am afeard'; 'lo what I see'; 'me thinketh it be devils three.' And the dead reply: 'I was well fair'; 'such shalt thou be'; 'for God's love be warned by me.' This encounter must have been a familiar one; twenty-seven other paintings of it are recorded from the fourteenth-century alone. A particularly fine painting in the Longthorpe series shows the Wheel of the Five Senses: a monkey, a vulture, a spider's web, a boar and a cock stand respectively for taste, smell, touch, hearing and sight (see plate 5). The moral was that men should not rely overmuch on the senses which are controlled by Reason—Reason being represented by the kingly figure standing behind the wheel—for even the animals can surpass us in this respect. The path of virtue, as has always been the case, is the less easy to represent pictorially as it is the more difficult to follow. But there is a fine nativity scene, with the Virgin suckling the Child and Joseph shown as an old man. There is a series of the apostles, each of them uttering a sentence from the Apostles' Creed, which supposedly had been given to each of them as his particular text at the time of Pentecost. Here they are again at Longthorpe Tower, all gathered together in one room.

When the painter of the Wheel of the Five Senses showed each of them as represented by an animal he was proceeding by means of allegory. As C. S. Lewis puts the matter in his famous book *The Allegory of Love*: 'it is of the very nature of thought and language to represent what is immaterial in picturable terms.' What started as a necessary aid to the imagination became the dominant and a constricting form in literature, preaching and all other aspects of communication. This is seen particularly clearly if we go back from painting to the written word, to the wealth of information that survives about medieval sermons. Thus Master Rypon of Durham dealt with the gospel story of the five loaves and two fishes. 'By the five loaves doctors understood the five books of Moses which are aptly compared to a barley loaf'; aptly because of the purity of the flour and because 'within they are full of moral senses and doctrines, useful alike to the preacher and to his audience'. And then the two fishes: 'by the two fishes are signified the Prophets and Psalms', and also, seemingly, 'the Gospels and the Canonical Epistles of Paul; for as fishes lie hid in the waters, so the moral senses lurk hidden in these books'.[9] Very little chance was given for any kind of moral to lie hidden within the confines of the gospels. The moral was underlined, but often at the expense of the sense of the scriptural passages used. The method of medieval preaching would horrify any modern theologian, who would wish to see the gospels preached as the word of the living God.

The point is worth developing further, for allegory was the dominant method of exposition, and the thought patterns that it encouraged influenced men's attitudes both to history and to current affairs. A favourite allegorical figure was that of the Castle or Fortress. For the preacher John Bromyard the Castle stood for each individual soul. The foundation of this castle was Faith; its outer wall was Charity; its keep was Hope; the inner defences were manned by the other virtues; its gates were the Five Senses; its constable was reason. In contrast there was the devil's castle, 'which has many castellans and many more hastening thereto', and as we found with the paintings at Longthorpe the picture here is much more vividly drawn. The office of justiciar of the devil's castle is held by Anger; the treasurer is Greed; Gluttony is in charge of the kitchens; 'and he is an excellent cook, because he poisons many; more die from his food than by the sword, through eating "late suppers" and other irregularities of this kind'; Lust holds his court here, and the chamberlain is the sin of sloth, who 'makes priests say Mass after midday, fearing more to give offence to their lords than to God'.

The virtues and vices came to life in this way, and it was then only a short step to paint them and give them a life of their own, and Langland in *Piers Plowman* has a set of the seven deadly sins:

Thenne awakede Wrathe, with two whyte eyes
and with a nivilynge nose, nippynge his lippes. . . .

Thus beggares and barones at debat aren ofte
Til I, Wrathe, wexe an hey and walke with hem bothe. . . .

They occur painted in twenty-one fourteenth-century versions; often they appear as a tree, with the various sins growing from it, and the devil presiding over the whole. The detail is usually of the simplest: thus Avarice will be a figure with money bags, or a series of figures sitting round a chest. There is usually a good supply of devils: at Hoxne in Suffolk they are sawing through the Tree's trunk, which is about then to fall into the mouth of hell.

The virtues, the saints in heaven and the characters of the gospels themselves came down from the walls and from out the pages of books, and they lived and walked amongst men. The characters from the gospels were inserted into a feudal world, and given their appropriate rank. Job became a 'gentleman' and a 'noble householder', a member of the gentry not the aristocracy. 'Sir Judas' and 'Sir Pilate' also appear, with no distinction made between them. The levelling was not just a matter of rank. Individuals were reduced to a single idea, which could then be drawn from the life. Men could understand 'why Paul has a sword, and Peter has the keys of Heaven', or Lawrence had a griddle; and more complicated iconography, 'the pot and the lily set between Our Lady and the angel Gabriel' in the standard Annunciation scene became comprehensible also. Of all the saints in the church's calendar, St Christopher was the most popular, since the sight of him was supposed to give a day's insurance against sudden death. By the side of an image of such obvious utility, the vices and others had to take a back seat; there are nearly a hundred surviving examples, many of them placed on the wall opposite the porch, so that they would be seen the moment an individual entered the church.

If the saints in this way became a part of men's world, there was a particular force and immediacy in the shrines of saints scattered

through the land, the points at which the local communities inter-
locked with this powerful visual and imaginative tradition, while the
most important of them were at the same time national centres of
some importance. Pilgrimage, from the journeys to Jerusalem,
Compostella and Rome, to a trip to the shrine of a local saint, was an
important facet of medieval religion. It worked because particular
saints, the intermediaries between God and man, could be tracked
down to a particular spot. Shrines of the Virgin there were a plenty;
the countess of Warwick's will made in 1439 gave a crown of gold to
'our lady of Caversham', a jewelled image to 'our lady of Walsingham', a large wax image to 'our lady of Worcester'; her finest gowns
went to the abbey at Tewkesbury, save one which 'I will St Winifred
have'. The saints were the most immediate contact with this vividly
imagined world.

   We see here something of the stock of ideas which men brought to
an understanding of their society, and to their dealings with individuals. We have to rely in large part on chronicle sources for our
understanding of the motivation of individuals. If we feel that very
often we are presented with paste-board figures in these chronicles,
then we must remember that the exemplars from the scriptures and
from romance presented people in just these terms. The moral was
the more clearly pointed by their having paste-board saints and
paste-board villains. If now we wish to say that we deal reasonably
with those whom we meet, we might use the phrase that we 'take
people as we find them'. So would our ancestors have done in the
fourteenth century; but they knew exactly what they expected to
find. What they were presented with was a series of stereotypes;
living individuals, but men who had one side to them only. The
writing was on the wall. It showed the saved, and the damned; the
virtues and the vices. The story of man's redemption was that of a
conflict between right and wrong. There could be no accommodation here. Everything was black or white; the fine shades of grey of
everyday life; the compromises of politicians; the good and the bad
sides of the one individual—it is the rarest of things to find in the
medieval period a description of the political life or of individuals in
these terms.

   Men on this earth, like the saints in heaven, could properly be
reduced to a single idea. 'Ha, good Lord', said one preacher, 'where is
the faith of Abraham, the good hope of Isaac, the prudence of Jacob;
where is the chastity of Joseph, the patience of Moses, and the great
zeal of Phineas?' In just the same way the author of *The Life of Edward*

II judged the king by means of stereotypes in evoking the ghosts of his ancestors:

> May he follow the industry of King Henry II, the well-known valour of King Richard, may he reach the age of King Henry, revive the wisdom of King Edward, and remind us of the physical strength and good looks of his father.

But, as he was to argue more than once, the simple virtues provided no guarantee of political stability:[10]

> see how often and abruptly great men change their sides. Those whom we regard as faithless in the north we find just the opposite in the south. The love of the magnates is as a game of dice, and the desires of the rich like feathers.

He is not the only one since to have been similarly exasperated by the political changes of the reign; but we should note his final judgment. It is not a throwaway line, but one that colours his whole attitude.

The political life of the later middle ages took place against this background of literature, portraiture and preaching. That 'the days are evil' was a frequent pulpit text; it was not just the transitoriness of men's concerns that was drawn to their attention, but the positive evil inherent in so much of them. The survey and criticism of the complete social order was part of the preacher's stock in trade. No man, and no orator, was beyond criticism from the pulpit. The reproach to the gossips of Winston, Suffolk, remains in a wall painting to this day. The vices of the clergy, as in all ages, were retailed with particular relish. The Dominican preacher John Bromyard described the way that greed caused clerics to heap up church livings; they were never satisfied (see note 9):

> the greedy think to extinguish their greed, when they say—'If only I had one church or prebend, I should never want any more'. But when they have got it, they start complaining that the place is in a bad atmosphere, or too near the high-road which brings them too many guests, or too far away from a good town, or else because there is no pasture or wood or fish there.

And so they need a second prebend; and then a third; and then a fourth, for 'they must have another prebend in their own district.' That this is reported speech that we are given here is clear not just from the logic of the way many pluralities were built up, but from the letters of the clerks themselves. Those of William of York from the first half of the thirteenth century show him writing in just the tone which Bromyard caricatures, seeking service near his prebends: the wine in his house in London, the quiet comforts of his estates in Lincolnshire, were his refuges in a busy life. Pluralism had some form of logic in the life of individuals. But each new increase in wealth, each fresh concern, was a new occasion of sin. The higher clergy were arrayed with the trappings of the prostitute; they were given over to gluttony; and so the work of the gospel was left on one side, 'evil priests make the people to sleep in their sins.'

The unjust lord, the unchaste priest, the wicked bailiff, the worldly prelate—there were a whole series of stereotypes. Just as the virtues and vices become more animated, so living men become less so, and all alike were reduced to the same level. But there is nothing here to threaten the social order. The insurgents in 1381 were not in their own minds threatening the state or reacting against religion when they captured Archbishop Sudbury and led him to his death. He was a type, or rather a series of types; for he was both an evil counsellor and a corrupt cleric. The very fact of their rising served to prove that they were oppressed. The devil raised rebellion, and yet it was a part of God's justice; for it sprang from the vices of the rulers, and served to recall them to their duty. Rebellion, like everything else in this world, pointed a clear moral.

The friars were preaching to men converted not just to the doctrines of the Christian religion but to this social analysis. There is no more radical criticism of the wickedness of lords and the sinfulness of man's estate than *The Book of Holy Medicines*, written by one of the greatest of the lords, Henry of Grosmont, Duke of Lancaster. It is a devotional treatise, written in French, and 'begun and completed', as the author records with some satisfaction, in the year 1354. The book is carefully structured. It described the seven wounds which afflict the author's soul, the poison inserted therein by the seven deadly sins, and the cures to be prescribed for each of them. The figures taken are conventional ones. His body is described as a castle, its treasure-chamber is the soul, and the world of evil attacks on all fronts. The seven deadly sins proceed from his own mouth: pride in his physical strength, covetousness which leads to unfair tax-gathering and un-just decisions in his court, the lewdness of love-songs which entice him to sin, and inevitably gluttony and sloth which cut short his religious duties. In every case the allegorical figures are developed in great detail. The book is long, and somewhat tedious. There is little originality to be found. But as with a woman's preaching, in Dr

Johnson's phrase, so with a rich layman writing homilies, the wonder is not that it is well done but that it is done at all. For Henry of Grosmont was in every respect a normal member of a military aristocracy. He was the nephew of Thomas of Lancaster, executed in 1322, and the uncle of Henry Bolingbroke, who seized the crown in 1399. The book was written between service on two French campaigns. It provides further evidence, from an indisputably 'secular' environment, that we are dealing with a culture common to the whole of society.

Men did not spend all their time working the land, or in church listening to sermons and gazing intently upon the wall. They sat by the fireside listening to the tales of the deeds of their ancestors, of the legendary heroes of antiquity, and of the outlaws of more recent history. The contents of these different types of fable merged with one another. There is no doubt of the moral content of the stories of Arthur and his court and of Robin Hood, which are still used by parents to amuse and edify the young. But do they reinforce, or do they undermine, the arguments for a common culture that have been presented above? The outlaws in particular seem to be subversive characters. It is tempting to argue that they were developing what we would now call an alternative society. And there would seem to be, in the later middle ages, more than one ideological attack on the exercise of lordship, both lay and ecclesiastical. There were in England gangs of armed knights roaming the countryside without fear of arrest; there were peasant rebellions affecting much of the country, in common with many other parts of Europe; and there was religious heresy also, an attack on the institutional framework of the medieval church. Were not Robin Hood, Wat Tyler and Wyclif, in the areas of life and thought that their names conjure up, destructive of many of the ideas of community whose structure and moral force have been outlined?

The fusion of legend and history, common to all ballads, is well shown in the story of Fulk Fitz-Warin.[11] It was current both in an Anglo-Norman French and in an English version, which shows that it reached both an aristocratic and a popular audience. Fact and legend, and simple historical confusion, were from the very beginning intermingled.

In the time of April and May, when the meadows and the grass grow green again, and every living thing regains its power, beauty and strength . . . we ought to recollect the adventures and doughty deeds of our ancestors who took pains to seek honour in loyalty, and should speak of such things as may be profitable to many.

   Lords, you have heard before now that William Bastard, Duke of Normandy, came with a great army and people without number into England, and by force conquered all the land and slew King Harold, and caused himself to be crowned at London, and established peace and laws at his pleasure, and gave lands to many of those who came with him.

At this point we are introduced to the Welsh marches in the Conqueror's day. There was Owain Gwynedd, who was in fact the ruler of Gwynedd in the mid-twelfth century; there was Roger of Belesme, and his sons, who were disinherited by King Henry I 'for they were disorderly people, and very cowards, and conducted themselves very ill toward their lord'; there was Joce de Dinan, who was lord of Ludlow in King Stephen's reign; and finally there was Payn Peverel, who was settled at Whittington in Shropshire, who died at his castle of the Peak in Derbyshire, and was succeeded by his son William Peverel.

   The author established his main characters in the first act, in the approved fashion, and the script said very clearly that the first act took place in the Conqueror's reign. The chronology is confused, and more rarely the genealogy also, but as he moves through the twelfth century the author becomes a little more secure. The Peverel lands came into the inheritance of Warin de Meez, who gained by knightly prowess in the tournament field the beautiful Mellette, daughter of William Peverel. The Fulk of the story was the grandson of this Warin. He was a friend of King Richard's but had been an enemy of John's from childhood days, for John had never forgiven the whipping he had received for breaking a chessboard over Fulk's head. When John came to the throne, Fulk was forthwith disinherited, and his lands given to Morys fitz Roger. The king refused him justice:

> Then said Sir Fulk to the king: 'Sire king, you are my liege lord, and I have become bound to you by fealty since I have been in your service, and because I hold lands from you. You ought to afford me reasonable support, and you fail me both at reason and common law. Never yet did good king deny law in his court to his free tenants; therefore I give you back our homages'.

This is the feudal *diffidatio*, the renunciation of homage, such as was offered to John on behalf of the whole community in 1215. This done, in flight from the king's anger and in search of adventure, Fulk went on a tour of the known world. He killed a dragon at Carthage; he rescued a damsel in distress from the attentions of seven robber chiefs in the Orkneys; he found protection at the courts of Llewellyn prince of Wales and Philip Augustus of France. He married Maud de Caux, with the connivance of Hubert Walter and against the king's wishes. The lot of the wife of an outlaw was clearly not a happy one. She had three children. The first was delivered in the sanctuary of Canterbury Cathedral, the second in Salisbury Cathedral, and the third 'was born upon a mountain in Wales, and was baptised in a stream'; this child, a boy, survived perfectly well, despite being born two months premature and in less than ideal circumstances.

It was in the forest, however, that Fulk and other medieval outlaws found their true individuality in a freedom from lordship, and the scope for their characteristic escapades. It is important to remember that in this story King John was a wicked man, who denied his men justice; in short, though the word is not used here, he was a tyrant. It was against John that Fulk and his companions directed their efforts: 'much mischief they did everywhere to the king, and to none other, excepting those persons who were openly their enemies.' On one occasion Fulk dressed up as a charcoal-burner, led the king into the thickest part of Windsor Forest, and held him until he promised to restore his inheritance. For most of the time, however, Fulk and his companions pursued their vendetta against the king at several removes. Wealthy townsmen, purveying goods to the king, were obviously fair game:

> Sir Fulk and his company came to the forest of Braydon, and there they remained privately; they dared not do so openly for fear of the king. There came thither more than ten burgesses, merchants, who had purchased with the money of the king of England the richest cloths, furs, spices and dresses for the personal use of the king and queen of England.

The outlaws were told that the loss would fall upon the king. The merchants were given a good dinner and sent on their way: 'then Fulk measured the rich cloth and the costly fur with his lance, and he clothed all who were with him, little and big, in this rich cloth, and to each he gave according to his degree.'

A similar story, protesting the same concern that innocent men should not suffer loss, is told later in the *Lyttel Geste of Robin Hood*, in which the cellarer of St Mary's Abbey, York, was relieved of more than £800. The forest offers freedom from the king's law, indeed it serves as a symbol of that freedom. On one occasion Fulk and his companions were surrounded by a large company of knights and men at arms; after fighting manfully, they had to retreat:

> Fulk and his companions struck their horses with their spurs and fled. The people everywhere raised the country upon them, and pursued them with the populace everywhere. At length they entered into a wood and saw only one man raising the country with a horn. One man shot him through the body with a bolt from a cross-bow. Then he left off crying for the people.

The machinery of constraint in this society is that of the hue and cry of the township and village; in practical terms the freedom of the forest is a freedom from the world of lordship.

If the record evidence is set against the ballads, it presents a much less romantic picture, of murder and rape, of protection rackets and con men, of local societies in which the surest justice came from self-help. There was nothing poetic about the lives of most medieval outlaws. And yet they worked on the boundaries of legality in more than one sense. Walter Musard was a gang leader in Worcestershire in the early fourteenth century. He was often paid a fee to take seisin of land for a client, a legal procedure provided that the client had a proper title. He was hired by an evicted rector to break into the rectory of Weston Subedge; but his men stole grain and goods, and they fought off resistance from the neighbouring manor house. On other occasions they were indicted for poaching from magnates' lands. This was an ordinary gang, in that its operations were strictly local. The Coterel gang from Derbyshire obtained more notoriety, because it operated on a rather larger scale. They were outlawed in March 1331, wandered from place to place in the Peak District and northern Nottinghamshire. At times they did work similar to that of the Musard gang. They were employed by the canons of Lichfield to eject the vicar of Bakewell from his church, and to collect the tithes and generally watch over the interests of the chapter in the Peak District. In an area in which lordship was weak, the Coterels were on one level a part of the machinery of lordship.

Other levels of these operations were, however, criminal by any standard. In 1327 Eustace de Folville, the leader of another famous gang, stood accused of three or four murders, one rape, and three robberies. He was the second of seven sons of a Leicestershire squire. The eldest brother inherited, and became a keeper of the peace. The other brothers made a career out of breaking it. In 1326 they murdered Roger Bellers, a neighbouring landowner and a baron of the Exchequer. The murder of so senior an official was unusual, and captured the public imagination. The man sent to bring them to justice was Sir Richard Willoughby; he was captured by both the Folvilles and Coterels acting in concert in 1332, and had to pay a ransom of nearly £1,000. Willoughby was an unpopular figure, and he was later charged 'by clamour of the people' with 'selling the laws like cows'.

The exercise of authority depended upon popular support. This can be seen very clearly in a case from Ipswich in 1344, when John of Holtby was murdered, according to the official record, 'for the reason that he busied himself about the king's business'. The bailiffs who should have arrested the culprits took refuge in the church, while the rest of the town made common cause with the murderers, giving them 'food and drink, and gold and silver, and singing so many songs of rejoicing in their honour that it was as if God himself had come down from heaven'. Worse still, when the justices sent to investigate the crime had left town, a pack of ruffians went into the courthouse and ordered the senior justice to appear before them under penalty of £100 'in mockery of the king's justices and ministers in his service'. The lack of public order is clear in this episode, but so also is the acceptance of royal justice.[12] The wrongdoers rationalised their crimes by appealing to the ill-repute of individual justices. This is a common theme. There are good justices as well as bad in the thirteenth-century *Song of Trailbaston*:

> Martyne and Knoville are pious men,
> And pray for the poor, that they may live in security.
> Spigurnel and Belfour are cruel men;
> If they were in my power there would be no help for them.

In 1381 also the armed bands had their short-list of unpopular justices.

The 1320s were a decade of ineffective government and localised anarchy. The 1330s, the beginning of Edward III's personal rule, put an end to the careers of some of the best known criminals. Several members of the Folville and Coterel gangs obtained pardons in return for agreeing to serve in the king's army in Scotland. It seems to have been the common pattern, that individuals moved from out-lawry to royal favour fairly rapidly. The idea of outlawry made this possible. The outlaws were associated with the forest, and the forest was a symbol both of their freedom and of the law's force. Outlawry satisfied the honour of both parties, the individual and the com-munity. Outlaws like Walter Musard rode about bearing arms and pennons. They were part of the world of lordship, and not in any sense an alternative society.

The nearest offered to an alternative society came as an alternative to the lordship of the church, not the state. The ideas of the Lollards, taking up and giving a measure of intellectual coherence to criticisms of the church that we have seen to have been widely current, offered the clearest threat to the structure of lordship in medieval England. The lordship was that of the church. It was not just that the ideas of the church were part of the network of order, but the structure of church government, the organisation of the church down to the parish level, was part of the network of order also. Archdeacon and sheriff were colleagues in a common enterprise. And the discipline of the church, even in the large dioceses of medieval England, was a good deal more immediate and more effective than that which the royal power could conjure up from Westminster. It was as well for the church that this should be so, for there was considerable resis-tance to church discipline both on a theoretical and a practical level. The paragraphs which follow will look at where the Lollards' ideas came from, and where they flourished.

Just as one of the symptoms of the weak government of the 1320s can be seen in the armed gangs that roamed the countryside, so in the 1370s the 'second childhood' of Edward III and the minority of Richard II produced severe tensions. The Peasants' Revolt of 1381, though put down relatively speedily, was only possible in an atmosphere of widespread political disillusion. The ideas of the Lollards took root at the same time, and they proved a lot more difficult to eradicate. It was an English university clerk, John Wyclif of Oxford, whose ideas provided the focus for this new sect. Wyclif was one of a group found in any age, the anticlerical cleric. He had an orthodox career as a teacher and royal servant; in 1374 he was presented to the living of Lutterworth in Leicestershire; and he seemed destined for high office. But anticlerical sentiments that found wide support in the Good Parliament of 1376 were developed in a series of highly influential writings, starting with the treatise on *Civil Lordship,* into firm anti-sacerdotalism. In his decade at Lutterworth—he died on the last day of 1384—he developed a direct and sustained attack on the medieval church.

In Wyclif's theology it was the Bible and not the church that mediated between God and Man. The imperfections of the church were not like the imperfections of individuals, they demonstrated that the church had no right to exist. If the structure of the church could be dismissed, the very existence of the priesthood was circumscribed: priests were to be judged by the sanctity of their lives, and by their zeal in preaching the word of God. The pope and the hierarchy became Antichrist, the body not of the faithful but of the damned. Damnation came from the exercise of lordship, and from what it involved: patronage, and concern with promotion; litigation and the exercise of church penalties, such as excommunication for the non-payment of tithes; the simony involved in the taking of first fruits for a benefice. It was the duty of secular lordship to curb the pretensions of ecclesiastical lordship. The king was Christ's vicar, and he had sovereign power within his dominions. From 1377 onwards, a growing list of Wyclif's ideas were condemned by the church. In his latter years he lost much of his support; his eucharistic doctrines alienated the friars, and he lost his pulpit in being banned from Oxford in the Council of 1382. His own career makes very clear the limits set upon the power of a university teacher in politics.

Wyclif's ideas, however, needed little modification to secure a large following, for they came from the church's own tradition of self-criticism, from the accepted themes of satire, and from the normal friction between clergy and laity over matters such as tithes. The earliest Lollards came from Leicester, where a group of clerics founded a school at a chapel attached to a deserted leper hospital outside the town walls. There came there men like William Swinderby, 'William the hermit', who had spent some time as a recluse in the local woodland but who clearly had no real vocation to the contemplative life. He was most at home on preaching tours in the surrounding villages and market towns—Melton Mowbray, Hallaton, Market Harborough and Loughborough were among the places mentioned when he came to trial. In 1382 the bishop of Lincoln moved against Swinderby and his colleagues. The charges then made against him are the first official record of popular Lollardy. Swinderby was found guilty of maintaining that a defaulting debtor should go unpunished; that tithes need not be paid to an immoral priest; and that a priest could not minister the sacraments if in a state of sin. He recanted any such beliefs, and survived to preach for another decade. It was another bishop who prosecuted him in 1391, for a much wider series of beliefs, for to the above was added a renunciation of oral confession, a rejection of papal indulgences, and a condemnation of the worshipping of 'the image of Him that was done on the cross'. Swinderby retreated into the Welsh marches, and was lost to view. The threat in these doctrines to the whole sacramental discipline of the medieval church was very clear, a threat in particular to the regular, public confession and communion laid down by the Lateran Council of 1215.

It is not just the doctrines of Lollardy that are of interest, but the areas in which it flourished. Leicester and Northampton, then later Coventry, the main towns of the midlands, were important centres. The area between Melton Mowbray and Market Harborough, the district of Swinderby's preaching expeditions, was precisely that of the Folville gang half a century earlier. Further back, if we trace out the area that the earls of Chester and Leicester were concerned to discipline in their agreement of the late 1140s, we find we are dealing with many of the same places. This was an area of weak lordship, where the accidents of Norman feudalism and ecclesiastical administration meant the absence of strong, local authority. There were many areas of a similar kind.

Royal justice, organised around the shire and its subdivisions, could often be avoided by crossing county boundaries. The Folvilles captured Willoughby in Lincolnshire, and then immediately transported him into Leicestershire. One of their favourite haunts was the castle at Rockingham, set at the boundaries of three counties, Northamptonshire, Leicestershire and Rutland. Some of the Lollards seem very like clerical outlaws. Swinderby is recorded as having celebrated mass in a chapel in a park near Leintwardine in Herefordshire; and on another occasion 'in a chapel not hallowed but a cursed shepherd's hut within a desert wood clept Derwald's Wood'. Even in rural Herefordshire, ecclesiastical discipline could effectively keep such men from churches and churchyards. Yet this is only one side of Lollardy. Others—a greater number—seem rather the recusants of a later age, the domestic chaplains of local gentry not accepting the doctrines of the established church. What gave Lollardy its strength was the protection that it enjoyed from lay lords, from men of gentle birth. In Northamptonshire, Sir Thomas Latimer's two manors of Braybrooke and Chipping Warden were centres of the heresy; it was at Braybrooke that two visiting Czech scholars copied a manuscript of Wyclif's *On Civil Lordship*; and a preaching chaplain made numerous converts around Chipping Warden in the south-west of the county.

What might have been threats to a common culture seem in short, upon examination, rather to reinforce it. Nothing has been said so far of the Peasants' Revolt, for while all the sections on social order need a political context to be fully understood, in the case of the revolt a knowledge of the political context is essential for any analysis at all. The ideas developed in the revolt are a mixture of moral precept, social comment, and political analysis. The revolt could only spread because the experiences and the mental attitudes of men in different parts of the country were the same. It is the argument of the chapters which follow that there developed a single political nation, of which the Peasants' Revolt is but one, well-documented manifestation. The achievement of that unity was in part a matter of administration. The country was compact, the distances were not great, and the links between shire and Exchequer, between the courts of the lords and those of the king, were kept in good repair. This was all necessary. 'When', according to Machiavelli, 'territories are acquired in regions where there are differences in language, customs and laws, then great good fortune and much hard work are required to hold them.' In late medieval England there was a unity of language and of custom. And behind that unity, there was a unity of ideas, supplied by Christianity and feudal lordship. Common experience was one thing, and could be manufactured, but it was these ideas which ensured that men's experiences were subject to the same construction. The community of England was founded on a community of ideas.

Chapter 6

Government and Society to 1272

The political community in the late twelfth century was a small one. The form that politics took was determined by the structure of feudal society. Political involvement was a condition of tenure, and its form was determined by tenure. The king held a court for his greater vassals, the barons, the men who owed their allegiance directly to him for their estates. This court gave judgments in lawsuits between members of the baronage. It also served as a court for ceremonial and political purposes. Some of the barons held hereditary offices in the king's household, as stewards, as marshals and as constables. Such offices embody a belief that the king's chief officials should be magnates of the first rank, and not professional administrators of humble birth. In Edward I's reign the hereditary constable and marshal of England led the opposition to his military plans by reason of their offices. While increasing bureaucracy may have taken much of the work of government out of baronial hands, none the less it was still generally assumed during the thirteenth century that the baronage stood at the head of the royal administration.

The king's court was the centre of the nation's politics. Three times a year, at the crown wearings at Christmas, Easter and Whitsuntide, the royal court would blossom forth in a display designed not only to exalt kingship but also to emphasise the position of the magnate class. Cases concerning the tenure of land would come up, for the descent of property of the great men who were the major forces in politics was a matter of primary political importance. So too were the formation of general rules concerning the descent and alienation of land, and the regulation of the services that were part of the obligations of lordship. So too was the king's court in its national aspect, regulating and approving the succession, and dealing with foreign powers. During the thirteenth century these full meetings of the king's court became known as parliaments; but they did not change in their function. They dealt with legal matters; they dealt also with what modern historians are insisting that we call high politics. They broaden somewhat in their composition, and the steps by which they did so will be traced in the following chapters; but the king and the magnates retain their predominant role.

It is these general considerations that determine the concerns of the chapter which follows. Of necessity, it will largely deal with 'the king' and 'the barons'. Monarchy was the pivot of the nation's political life. The characters of individual kings were important, for in this small community of people with real power, personal relationships could in the short and medium term dominate political development. So, for instance, with Magna Carta: we cannot be so preoccupied with the broad forces which might seem to be involved in social history as to ignore the fact that we are dealing with men of political and military weight confronted with a king they could not trust. So also with all the major crises of the period, which culminated in the depositions and murders of the fourteenth century. The contemporary *Life of Edward II*, a rare example of a chronicle written by a secular clerk, shows this small range of high politics very clearly. 'Give us peace in our time, O Lord, and may the king be at one with the barons': right through our period, this was what domestic peace involved. At the same time, we are dealing with a network of ideas, both monarchical and baronial, regarding the proper ordering of society. These provide the background to political development. As has been seen, one of the areas where these ideas impinged on day-to-day politics was in the counsel offered by the baronage—how was this general principle to be translated into practice? What were the matters that should be left to executive action? What were matters which required counsel? These are problems in any society whose politics are held to involve a measure of consent by the governed. In the later middle ages they were translated into disagreements as to whether the king should govern through his household rather than through the traditional—and aristocratic—officers of state. The history of the household seen purely as administrative history holds out little of interest. If, however, this is thought of as an increase in the power of the civil service, it becomes a problem whose implications and whose importance may more readily be appreciated by a twentieth-century audience. Politicians in the 1970s, whether they should be regarded as more sceptical than before or simply as more naïve, have brought the question of the control and the accountability of the civil service much closer to the centre of political and constitutional debate.

The late twelfth century saw at its greatest height the involvement of England in a political community controlled by men of French ancestry and comprising the greater—and the western—part of modern-day France. Yet it also revealed the limitations of this Leviathan. Administratively it was very difficult to control; politically it was undermined by the French kings. In the years around 1200 the Angevin Empire fell apart. In the mid-thirteenth century a treaty between England and France recognised the facts of a situation which left only Gascony in the hands of English kings. At the end of the century a war with France over Gascony started, and continued spasmodically throughout the fourteenth century. From 1334 to 1450 the Hundred Years' War overshadowed English politics, and in several decades dominated it. The loss of Gascony, in the mid-fifteenth century, removed the last French involvement of any substance.

Henry II and Richard I were the peripatetic rulers of a vast empire. Henry acquired first his father's conquest of Normandy, then his father's inheritance of Anjou, then Gascony in right of his wife Eleanor of Aquitaine—all before he conquered England, his grandfather's kingdom, in 1153, and succeeded Stephen a year later. Of his 35 year reign, only 154 months were spent in England, 176 months in Normandy, and 84 months in Anjou and Gascony. His son Richard spent only 15 months in England, and was on the continent from May 1194 to April 1199, when he died. These two, father and son, are buried at Fontevrault, in the very heart of Anjou.

The size of the Angevin Empire posed many problems of administration and government. The social changes which had taken place since 1066 permitted their resolution. The period from 1154 to 1215 saw the bureaucratisation of English government, and a tighter central control of the work of local government. Extra strength was given to monarchy thereby, while at the same time it became possible for the government to work effectively in the king's absence. This last point is a central one. The legal records of the early part of Henry II's reign are full of the journeyings of plaintiffs to the furthest parts of the Angevin Empire. The case of Richard of Anstey is well documented. He started out in 1158. A royal writ was necessary to initiate proceedings, and one of his men was sent over to Normandy to get it. This was in 1158. By the following year the case had ground to a halt; and Richard needed a further writ to get it restarted. This time he had to seek the king out in person, much further afield. He found him at Auvillar in Gascony, on his way to besiege Toulouse. Those less persistent, or more tied to English affairs, would await news of the king's return to the country. When the king landed at Southampton in January 1163, one of the Norman chroniclers tells us that most of the English baronage was on the sea-shore. Richard of Anstey was there as well. This vivid image shows a style of government that was passing away, one in which the king was the sole source of executive authority.

The administrative work of the early Angevin period went a long way towards clearing the bottleneck. Justiciars were invested with royal power over a wide area of administrative routine. In particular they could issue the writs which instigated new procedures and offered the protection of the king's court to all freeholders. From 1170 there was a session of the king's court which met at Westminster—the beginning of the development of the capital city as the legal centre of the nation, the end of the travels, at least on routine matters, of men like Richard of Anstey. Particularly urgent matters would still need to be referred to the king; but the bulk of the business which was now being attracted to the king's court was routine. That the availability of the king's court for the routine of land pleas was a service that was widely appreciated is clear from clause 17 of Magna Carta, which insists that a court stay at Westminster. The practice had been discontinued, because the court could not be staffed, during the clerical strike involved in the Interdict of 1208 to 1214. More and more disputes concerning land came from the feudal courts to the royal courts. This increase of business was only made possible by the streamlining of procedure, and by the removal of such business from any direct royal supervision. The work of feudal and ecclesiastical courts was not stopped in this way, but they were increasingly circumscribed. A survey of the legal measures of Henry II's reign shows on a number of occasions a minor royal official sent to sit in the back row of a subordinate court, 'to see how the matter is conducted there'. It would be less and less likely that he approved of what he saw. More and more, cases involving freehold land were transferred to the royal courts. The procedure was systematic, and streamlined. In 1249 the royal justices visiting Wiltshire handled 1,155 cases in less than two months. Such legal productivity was produced by reducing cases to their essentials, and by leaving little scope for advocacy. It was justice by computer.

It is clear from Magna Carta that the development of royal justice met with little opposition from the baronage. It was not only that the justice provided was cheap, and efficient, but also that the social changes of the previous century, in fragmenting the units of lordship that carried with them judicial rights, had made centralisation inevitable. These changes, the growth of central government in the later twelfth century, largely through the use of the crown's judicial authority, were not unique to England. The same process can be seen in the growth of papal government; the same process with the Capetians in France. The legal strength of the Capetians was the foundation of their power in the long struggle to remove English lordship from France. Spasmodic campaigns could not affect this position. The social changes of the twelfth century worked towards territorial monarchy, and within these nations for territorial lordship. The Angevins gained within England; by the same token, for the same reasons, they lost within France.

John succeeded his brother Richard in 1199. To secure the integrity of his inheritance in France, he had to make major juridical concessions. He appeared in the French court to have his right to succeed his brother recognised; he had to pay a heavy relief, the clearest possible sign of dependent tenure, to the French king. Two years later he was summoned to the French court to answer a case brought against him by his own tenants in Gascony. When he refused to attend, his French fiefs were declared forfeit; and he was unable to muster enough force on French soil to defend so large an area. Normandy and Anjou fell to the French in 1204. For ten years John tried to muster the forces for their recapture, but at Bouvines in 1214 his cause suffered a defeat which proved irreversible. The constituent parts of the Angevin Empire, kept together by 'an unholy combination of princely greed and genealogical accident',[1] resumed their separate identities. The links between Anjou and either Normandy or Aquitaine had never been very strong. The links between England and Normandy, forged by conquest and tempered by the political experience of the period up to 1154, had also lost much of their force. Different branches of the old Anglo-Norman families had largely split up their Norman and their English lands, and it was these cross-channel estates that had provided the real links between England and the continent. Only Gascony, with a comparatively weak central administration and with strong economic links with England, remained under Angevin control. For the Empire to survive—and this is true of any Empire in any age—men needed to believe in it, and to have something tangible to lose by its dissolution. By the end of the twelfth century, neither condition applied.

The loss of Normandy thus resulted as much from a failure of political will on the part of the Anglo-Norman baronage as from any brilliant military campaign. And this in turn proceeded not just from a lack of interest but from a growing opposition to John and his government of England. Financial concerns, inevitably, were high on the list of matters that came to be in dispute. The increased bureaucracy probably paid for itself only in part. Richard's Crusade had to be paid for; and at the end of it a ransom of £100,000 to the Emperor. Finally the loss of Normandy removed the indigenous support, which had never been very considerable, to its own defence. The pressures on the taxpayers were increasing just at the time when monarchy was gaining a notable increase in its pressure over individuals. The pressures are clear enough, though it was far from inevitable that they should have issued in political crisis, and certainly not in a crisis of the gravity of that of 1213 to 1216.

Henry II was severe but even-handed with the baronage, and their pockets probably suffered less than their pride. William of Newburgh praised Henry for his restraint in direct taxation: 'he never imposed any heavy tax either on England or his continental lands, until the recent tithe for the Holy Land.' The latter was taken in 1185, as a tax of 10 per cent on all revenues and movable goods. Small enough by modern standards perhaps, but the whole principle of non-feudal taxation was new, and the amount raised was double that of the old Danegeld, the tax which the Normans had inherited from Anglo-Saxon England. In 1188 the experiment was repeated in the 'Saladin Tithe' taken for Richard's Crusade; then, in 1193, a ransom of £100,000 was needed to redeem the king's person. This tax was far more severe than any raised in John's reign; the money was there, and the payment was customary. It was only in John's reign that non-feudal taxation became regular and severe. The thirteenth of 1207 yielded £60,000; along with it there went tallages, scutages, aids and demands for direct military service in practically every year.

Royal financial pressure, however, provides only a part of the story of the build up to Magna Carta. For these pressures, in terms of their novelty, were probably at their greatest in Richard's reign. In 1193 John revolted when he heard that his brother was in captivity. He met with no general support. The government was carried on, and the opposition to John was mustered by the civil service. There was no threat from such men of any innovation, of measures that might be taken to involve a reformulation of the barons' relationship with the monarchy. In such circumstances, ostensibly much more favourable to revolt than either 1173 or 1215, the king's government carried general support. This point is an important one when we come to consider the build-up of the baronial opposition to King John.

It is possible to argue that Magna Carta occurred because John inherited the pressures that would lead to a baronial revolt; that this revolt was in some way a commentary upon a whole 'system' of government. It is true that in John's reign, as before, kings dealt arbitrarily with individuals. In 1209 the king went in pursuit of debts long owed to him by William de Briouze: the king took hostages, confiscated castles, and mustered an army against him. William resented the direct exercise of royal power in his land, as did several other marcher lords in the west country and the north of England. William had backed a loser: he fled to Normandy, and his wife and child were imprisoned at Winchester, where they died. The case obtained a good deal of publicity. William's discomfiture was not of itself remarkable; but what seems to have happened as the reign wore on was that the number of those who felt threatened by royal government grew to the point at which they ceased to be isolated and embittered men with a grievance, but formed into groups of men with a cause. They felt insecure, a point remarkable in itself, considering their landed power, and the relative weakness of government. And they felt insecure, not because of any 'system' but because of their deep distrust of the king.

It was distrust that led to civil war, and prolonged the war until the king was dead. It had been clear since 1213 that John was threatened. He responded by calling off his struggle with the papacy, which had led to Interdict, and by making concessions to the baronage. He was happy to issue a charter, as earlier kings had done, which probably would not have been too dissimilar to Magna Carta as it finally appeared. But the barons wanted sanctions, some guarantee of the king's good faith. This the king would not offer until he was forced to do so. Magna Carta finally provided for a group of twenty-five barons to supervise the king's behaviour and report breaches of the agreement. When the text reached the pope, the king was absolved from his oath, as having been forced to accept a settlement that was demeaning and detracted from the royal dignity. A king could not be constrained in this way. In contemporary theory this was true, and the barons knew it all along. That they still went ahead is a measure of their distrust of the king, and of their despair of reaching a less formal settlement with him. There was civil war in 1215 not because of the accumulated pressures of Angevin government, but because the barons were dealing with a man they could not trust.

In the context of the social history of England in the thirteenth and fourteenth centuries, Magna Carta was an important document. It showed that a largely united baronage could extract permanent concessions from monarchy. For the rest of the thirteenth century, it provided a text around which political debate revolved; and for the rest of the middle ages it remained an episode in baronial folk-lore. It is also a text that shows very clearly the range of a new monarchy, the number of issues on which monarchy and baronage, if they sought to define their relationship, had to come to terms. It was on the old issues, old in the sense that they were specified in Henry I's charter of 1100, that the baronage made their permanent gains. Reliefs paid by knights and barons on entering their holdings were fixed at £5 a fee and £100 a barony respectively, removing the crown's rights to take heavy and arbitrary fines at this point. Scutages (payments in lieu of military service) and aids were to be 'reasonable' and 'taken by the common counsel of the realm'. The crown's rights of wardship and marriage were restricted. The early clauses of the charter, taken together, constrained the king in his dealings with the tenants-in-chief. There were a further series of clauses which, as has been seen, accepted the development of Angevin justice. Here again the concern was that the king should not act in arbitrary fashion: he had to proceed according to law, and he had to make justice available to all. These were the most important clauses of the attenuated version of the Great Charter which passed into law in 1225. They spelt out the basic philosophy of baronial attitudes, that the king should act in a reasonable way and according to custom, and that in his dealings with individuals he should be bound by his own law.

The kings of England, however, were not simply feudal lords; they had prerogative powers as kings, whose exercise the baronage found it difficult, and ultimately impossible, to restrain. The clauses concerned with the royal household, with foreign mercenaries, and asking for local sheriffs to hold office for traditional payments only, were omitted in the reissue of 1216, as being 'weighty and doubtful', and thus consigned to oblivion. A suggestion that certain important royal castles should be surrendered into the hands of custodians, an echo of the peace settlement of 1153, never even reached the Runnymede text. In one important area of the prerogative the king was restrained, and that was in the forest. Only a small area of land was actually removed from forest jurisdiction, but the worst excesses of the previous administration were avoided; one clause of the 1217 Forest Charter provided that 'no man should lose life and limb for the forest'. There were no precedents for the barons intervening in the king's regulation of his own household, or in his control over his own officials. Here no ground was gained by the baronage in 1215, but such ground was vital, and in the thirteenth and fourteenth centuries a good deal of effort was put into trying to take it. We can think on to the famous retort of Richard II that he would not dismiss even a scullion from his kitchen to meet the barons' wishes. A reluctance to make even trivial concessions is hardly the mark of a good politician: the king's rights were clear, but so also was the barons' insistence that they were part of the household. These were indeed 'weighty and difficult' matters.

Much of the difficulty and indeed a good deal of the weight went out of English politics when John died at Newark on 19 October 1216. Henry, John's eldest son, was crowned king. He was then aged 9. This was the first time since the Conquest that the crowned ruler had been under age. William the Marshal was made regent of England, and all the functions of kingship were vested in him. The choice of William was an interesting one. He was an aged and above all a romantic figure. A younger son, he had made his reputation in the tournament fields of France, and had acquired wealth by marriage into the family of Clare. In 1216 he served to remind people of the age of tournaments and chivalry; men could forget the sordid history of the previous three years. Louis, the son of Philip Augustus of France, had been invited to England by some barons, and secured control of London and the south of England. After John's death, the loyalties were less confused. In May 1217 the earl Marshal rode into Lincoln and defeated the French and their allies. Louis was sent back to France with 10,000 marks for his pains. The Marshal was advised by a council, the nucleus of which was provided by the seven magnates and five churchmen named by John as his executors. The aristocracy now proceeded to re-establish those royal rights and privileges so recently under attack. For ten years they effectively governed England in the king's name; and in 1225 they handed over to the king his regalian rights intact. The minority of Henry III is a highly significant episode. It provides a counter-balance, as it was intended to do, to a period of open hostility between the English monarchy and its subjects. In the minority the baronage made common purpose with the crown. It was no effort for them to do so. There was political tension between individuals, but there was nothing to activate larger groupings—the king was under age, and the claims in France lay moribund.

Magna Carta had circumscribed the king's ability to raise money by exploiting his rights as a feudal lord. If the king wanted to raise money, but not levy a feudal tax, he could do so in two ways. He could exploit the royal demesne, the crown lands, the towns and the Jews; and he could investigate royal rights, check royal franchises and supervise the activity of his officials. The first involved self-sufficiency; the second closer control, and a process of definition of rights previously undefined. Each of these developments had important political consequences. In the 1230s the monarchy developed a system of administration based on the royal household. The king's wardrobe became a financial department: at first it operated alongside the Exchequer but potentially, since the king had sole central control over the direction of his revenues, it represented a rival to it. By 1230 the king had a small private seal of his own, and thus could transact business away from the great seal at Westminster. The royal revenues were drastically overhauled. In 1232–3 Peter des Rivaux was treasurer of the household and sheriff of twenty-one shires, an unprecedented centralisation of power in the hands of a single royal servant. The baronial offices of state, the treasurership, chancellorship and justiciarship all atrophied to some degree, and the sheriffs also were more closely controlled. The new king and his advisers adopted a pattern of government suited to the needs of the day: the loss of Normandy made the justiciar less important; the growth of business inevitably increased the bureaucratic element at court; but undoubtedly also the king and his advisers were reacting against Magna Carta, and the baronial control during the minority.

The pattern of government was royalist; and for a number of reasons the baronage reacted strongly against it. Both the judiciary and the council became more professional, more specialised; as this happened, so it was felt that their actions became more difficult to check by the general body of their peers. Further, after the king's marriage to Eleanor of Provence in 1236, the Provençal element in the council became marked; not only was the council more remote, but it was run by foreigners to boot. The frustrations created during the first ten years of Henry III's personal rule appear in the political crisis of 1238. It was then proposed that there should be added to the king's council four baronial nominees, who were to act as 'conservators of liberties'; these men were to appoint five of the judges, and were to have control over expenditure. The leader of this revolt was the king's brother, Richard of Cornwall, and he had wide support. Yet the revolt subsided; Richard was bought off, and the baronage was left leaderless. Up to 1258 the king was never so badly off for money that he had to place himself in the baronage's power.

Henry III, like most medieval kings, would stand and fall by the success or failure of his foreign policy. His early efforts to recapture the lost parts of the Angevin Empire were distinctly low key. In 1229–30 a Breton rebellion offered him a foothold in western France, and a cause to fight. The French king, Louis IX, was under age. But there was no force, and no direction; the great men, according to Roger of Wendover, behaved as though they were at a Christmas party. In 1242 a second expedition was tried, this time trying to build on a rebellion in Poitou. It was no more cohesive or successful. Many of the English barons refused service, and the French king easily drove off the first attack. The legacy of these campaigns was a highly efficient scutage in 1242, collected on the basis of the most comprehensive set of feudal records that survive from the thirteenth century. It also left the king with the reputation of being ineffectual, a man of words not of action. Henry's brother-in-law, Simon de Montfort, cursed him as an incompetent in 1242, and said that he should be locked up like Charles the Simple. It is interesting that a man whom we have sought to make so traditionally English, was French by birth, and it was the traditions of the French monarchy that provided him with his exemplars.

In 1259, in the Treaty of Paris, Henry III surrendered his claim to Normandy, Maine, Anjou and Poitou; and in return the French offered recognition of his rights over Gascony. This acceptance of the *status quo* lost Henry little by way of prestige, and was to offer him solid gains. The links with the French court were kept up; King Louis, after all, was Henry III's brother-in-law. Henry must have found much to admire in France, and much that he was tempted to emulate. France was the wealthier country. In 1202–3 the French king's income had been £73,000, while John's income was about £30,000. With the increase in French territory, the gap had widened. These resources offered the French king a large measure of independence from feudal constraint; and all the western monarchies, the papacy among them, were developing their theories of royal power at the same time as their control over their kingdoms was consolidated.[2] There are some elements here, at least in the language used, of the divine right monarchy of a later age. In 1242 the king intervened in a case concerning the church at Lincoln: 'the All

Highest has constituted us defender of the church which, His grace allowing, we will and must defend.' These theories had secular and highly practical implications. The king's relations, it was claimed, were placing him on a pinnacle on which he could ignore 'the common practices of the kingdom . . . they damnably whispered to him that a prince was not subject to laws.' These fears were widely held, and they explain the opposition to the king's expansion of his rights. He claimed the need for those who exercised subordinate jurisdiction to have a specific royal grant. To conservative men of a suspicious nature the trend of all these developments was clear. This was a monarchical world, and likely to become more so. At the same time, the king was a man of ideas and enthusiasms, not of action. One of these ideas foundered, and nearly ruined him; and in the process it not only allowed the baronage to formulate their own ideas but also for a number of years to put them into effect.

In 1254 Henry had accepted from the pope, Innocent IV, the offer of the crown of Sicily for his second son, Edmund. This was one of the more ridiculous stratagems in the papacy's long fight against the union of Germany and Sicily, which surrounded and threatened to stifle its interests in central Italy. The pope offered to find the army to recapture Sicily, if the English king would pay for it. Henry accepted the proffered terms: he had to find nearly £100,000, failing which he was threatened with excommunication and interdict. The scheme was quite impracticable—Richard of Cornwall commented that he could as easily fly to the moon—and the king had nothing to show for a scheme which reduced him to penury, and forced him for the time being to accept whatever terms the baronage offered him. In May 1258 the king 'put himself in the counsel of his barons': if the king would reform the state of the realm then the barons undertook to ask 'the community of the realm' to grant an aid. There followed a period of intense political activity. From then until December 1266—a period of eight and a half years—the royal and baronial factions, groups of men frequently changing in their composition, fought for power on a series of battlefields and round a series of conference tables.

This was the most sustained political crisis of the later middle ages. It discussed at length, though like all the others it left unresolved, the problems involved in making an increasingly specialised royal government responsive and responsible to both public opinion, and the particular opinions of the barons. A concern for popular feeling, as well as an understanding of the value of popular support, lay behind the clear desire of the baronage between 1256 and 1260 to reform not only royal but also baronial administration. The barons' particular concern was to secure a permanent control over the administration. The Provisions of Oxford of 1258 established a Council of fifteen which was to be in permanent session at court, and claimed the power to advise the king in all matters touching the king and kingdom. The Council had two years of power: in the Provisions of Westminster of 1259 it made permanent reforms in the administration of justice, in particular concerning procedure, and the rights of mesne tenants. We can see in all these documents the interaction of complaints and legislation, and the detailed negotiation of legislative and administrative reform. And we can see why this exceptionally painstaking reform movement ultimately failed.

It failed because the baronage were not a homogeneous group. The initial 'baronial' committee contained men of widely different wealth and opinions. And as the Council of fifteen went about its work, some of the most conservative of its initial supporters lost sympathy and fell away. Men could be on the same side in 1258, and yet be at odds in 1260. In the first flush of enthusiasm, loyalty to the latest plan of reform might hold. In 1259, Matthew Paris says that the earl of Gloucester was told by the nobles not to quarrel with Simon de Montfort, and to follow the 1258 programme himself: 'this frightened the said earl, who sent his steward Herwin throughout his territories, with orders to see that justice was observed according to the statutes.' But the shock was temporary. Much would depend on the attitude of the king. Individuals could be picked off by means of threats and promises. Henry III had a good deal of skill in so doing. In 1252, says Matthew Paris, 'the king, having become possessed with a most greedy thirst for money, resorted to his usual cunning and deceit, and sought to bend to his will, one by one, those who united he could not break.' He sought out the bishop of Ely, but for his pains got only a long sermon on the liberties of the church. 'Do I need to mention that glorious martyr, the blessed Thomas?' Probably not, but the bishop did. More often, the king succeeded. The nobility had their own interests, and their private quarrels. All the initiative lay with the king. As circumstances changed, so did men's allegiances. It is misleading to think, in modern terms, of any 'constitutional opposition' to royal government. There were no parties, no 'right-wingers' or 'left-wingers'. Every text became dated, even that of Magna Carta itself.

The baronage could never permanently take the initiative from the king. Oaths could always be claimed as having been taken under duress; and rightly, for no king would surrender his power save under duress. In April 1261, giving this as his reason, Pope Alexander IV absolved Henry from his oath to abide by the Provisions: its formality, for 'the king himself had been present, and had held a candle in his hand', availed them nothing. In 1263 the king was forced to swear a new oath; and then in 1264 the dispute went to the arbitration of the French king, who found in favour of his English counterpart on every point. The barons could not win a paper war, for pieces of paper could not constrain the royal prerogative: 'the king shall have full power and free authority in his kingdom and in all that pertains to it.'[3] War followed. The king and Richard of Cornwall were captured at Lewes in May 1264; but Simon de Montfort gained no real initiative thereby, and forfeited much support. His death on the battlefield at Evesham in 1265 settled the issue as between the protagonists, but left an awkward mopping up operation, as do most civil wars. The re-establishment of the prerogative was a patient, diplomatic affair. Part of the patience was born of necessity, for peace did not improve the king's credit, and in 1272—the year of the king's death—his council was to insist, as the reformers had earlier done, that all revenues were to be paid direct to the exchequer. Part also was born of piety, which gave a reputable excuse for neglecting the more secular aspects of government. The new church of Westminster Abbey, in building for a generation, was consecrated in 1269. Matthew Paris in one of his books drew portraits of Henry III and his predecessors, each of them sitting in state and clutching as it were a model of one of their religious foundations (see Plate 4a). In addition to Henry III and Westminster they show Henry II with Waltham Abbey in Essex, Richard I with the church of St Thomas at Acre in the Holy Land, and John with Beaulieu Abbey in Hampshire.

It may be useful here, having given a brief outline of a century of political change, to examine the social changes of the same period, and the relationship of these changes to the politics of the age. The context within which both the gentry and the baronage normally operated altered in this period. It altered both because of social change, and because of the external pressures of government. It is facile to suggest that during the reform period the gentry were 'educated' to fill a new and more responsible position in the community. Experience is always useful; but there was little that the gentry had to learn.

Changes in estate management may be considered first of all. From the 1170s on most of the larger estates landowners reclaimed manors from the gentry, who had 'farmed' them for fixed sums much as the sheriffs had 'farmed' their shires, and exploited their lands directly. The lives of all those involved were altered considerably thereby. The peasantry, as has been seen, found their services redefined and their obligations to labour on the lord's estate reasserted. The gentry had to rely more on their own inherited properties, which probably had been directly managed all along. The baronage became increasingly preoccupied with estate management. A type of modern English landowner—careful with the accounts, devoted to hunting, and good with the tenants—can first be distinguished in the thirteenth century. Then it was a new role, and required new support: the estate administration was equipped with writs, tallies and letters patent, with private exchequers and with private councils. There were direct parallels here between royal and feudal government. Each was becoming more professional. In 1182 Abbot Samson of Bury St Edmunds announced that he could manage without his feudal officers, the steward, the constable and the rest: 'the monks marvelled, the knights were angry, condemning his arrogance and speaking evil of him in the king's court, saying that he refused to follow the advice of his free men.'[4] There is a clear tension here between new needs, and an accepted climate of ideas.

The county courts were the meeting places for the local gentry, the knightly class. There the local community met with the demands of the king. It was not just a place of business, but also a forum of ideas. Much of the business was commonplace: the sheriff empanelled juries to appear before the justices itinerant; knights were required for the Grand Assize, for enquiries and for a multitude of business. In summer 1258 the new council nominated four knights who were to enquire concerning abuses in each of the thirty-eight counties of England. Knights occur frequently in Glanvill as having an integral part in the working of the Angevin machinery of justice. Every forty days the county court met in full session to do the royal business. The records of these courts show that the gentry who gave judgment had very clear ideas both on the detail of business and on the general principles. A case comes from Lincolnshire in 1226.[5] The sheriff had held his pleas from dawn to dusk. When he adjourned the shire court to the next day the knights refused to serve, claiming that one day was the ration. The sheriff countered by summoning a meeting of the wapentake court, which equally the knights were bound to attend. A spokesman, Theobald Hautein, replied that the business could only be dealt with in the county court, and further that the wapentake court should be held only twice a year. What was more, he had just returned from the royal court, where he had spoken to the Lord Archbishop, the earl of Chester and other magnates, and he could report that a writ would shortly come from the king putting an end to such sharp practices. After further altercations, the knights' spokesman finished up by swearing volubly. Not only was he sure of his ground, but his information was correct; in 1234 the meetings of hundred and wapentake courts were indeed fixed at twice a year. A large section of the Provisions of Westminster in 1259 was concerned with problems of a similar kind. Theobald Hautein was a man secure in his base; he and his ancestors had been settled in the county for generations. The family was probably of English descent, the original name 'Haldein' having been progressively changed, to 'Haltein' and thence to 'Hautein', in the course of the twelfth century.

There was nothing new in the county court being an important local meeting place. It must have been so since its establishment in the twelfth century. Yet the increase in its business, and also of its contacts with Westminster, left their mark. In John's reign the county and local communities dealt with the king in purchasing privileges, among them the removal of areas of land from forest jurisdiction. The knights and freeholders of the soke of Peterborough were responsible for purchasing the disafforestation of the soke for almost £1,000. Four knights and a clerk surveyed the woodland, to work out how the fine should be apportioned. Six knights sealed a letter acknowledging the debt to the king, as representatives of the local community. Had they not done so, the document would have been as crowded with seals as an agreement made shortly thereafter between the earl of Chester and the men of Frieston and Butterwick in Lincolnshire (see plate 6).

The political awareness of the gentry came not just from their involvement in local government, and the exercise of responsibilities placed on them by the king. It is men's day-to-day concerns that are the chief source of their ideas, and for the gentry this meant the running of their own estates and the estates of others. Some records of thirteenth-century lay estates survive, and provide a key to these ideas; they may help a modern reader to understand the development of the political community in the thirteenth century. The estate book of Henry de Bray, a Northamptonshire landowner, was considered in the previous chapter. The book is self-conscious, being designed to establish Henry's position in the world. The gentry, no less than the aristocracy, had their liberties. Theobald Hautein and his colleagues appealed to Magna Carta, saying that the sheriff's actions were 'contrary to the liberty which they ought to have by the charter of the lord king'. A less forceful witness is Richard Hotot of Clopton, who wrote an estate book in the 1240s similar to that of Henry de Bray. His family history was taken back to a grant by Turold, the first Norman abbot of Peterborough. His book was mainly concerned with estate business. Bound in the middle of it, however, and obviously copied out for him, were copies of Magna Carta, the Charter of the Forest, and two other official but quite irrelevant records to make up the weight. There was nothing superfluous in the book. Magna Carta served as a guarantee of Richard Hotot's position in the world.

Henry III received many sermons on the virtues of Magna Carta. He was apt to reply, according to Matthew Paris, that the magnates should look to it themselves: 'Why do not these bishops and nobles of my kingdom observe to those subject to them, this charter about which they make such outcry and complaint?' As the text of Magna Carta was copied, and as it was more frequently confirmed, so it became more difficult for them not to do so. The local investigations of the 1250s were in this sense inevitable, and they proved divisive, as Henry III realised very well. The gentry were important in the confident years 1258 and 1259, and it is tempting to suggest that here again they were discharging responsibilities given to them by their social superiors, in this case by the magnates. Such an attitude would be mistaken. There is no need for any 'descending' theory of government in the thirteenth century, which sees authority as being handed down from above. The gentry were established landowners, and it was they who had local authority. What was new about the gentry in the thirteenth century was first their clear sense of their position, and second the closer identity of their concerns with those of other members of the landowning class in England, including the king. They knew their place.

Members of gentry families provided the senior staff, in particular they acted as stewards, for the ambitious estate management of the magnates. The stewards had agricultural responsibilities, but most particularly they were administrators, holding courts and checking accounts. It was for these men that the many treatises were written, such as Walter of Henley's *Husbandry* and the *Seneschaucy*, which gave details of the routine of farming practice, and the chief matters to be checked in the accounts. The number of copies made of these books was considerable; over eighty copies of Walter of Henley survive, the last of them made in Welsh in 1800. They survive characteristically as a part of groups of legal treatises, the working memoranda of lawyers and administrators. This was a professional class, and a large one, for quantitatively the greater landowners did far more of the work of governing England than did the king.

The period covered by this chapter saw the establishment of the courts of law in a structure which was to serve until the nineteenth century, and the establishment of a legal profession. The law played an important part in men's lives. This was not new. Law was an instrument of order, and an instrument of social control. It was also an instrument of government. Social relationships, which in the modern period would in themselves have no legal content, in the middle ages did have. Thus the Treasury is now in England an important department of state. There are Treasury solicitors, and Treasury counsel, but the Treasury is not a court of law. In the middle ages the Exchequer was both a department of state and a court. Men's rights were reduced to writing and put on the record, whether the record was Magna Carta, or the foot of a fine recording the transfer of land, or the entry to a two-acre holding in a manor court. Magna Carta was not just concerned with the technicalities of holding courts and supplying writs, but with the performance of services by tenants to their lords, and with having the king in turn deal with his men 'according to the judgement of their peers or by the law of the land'. All of it dealt, in one way or another, with the law. Much of this chapter has therefore involved the law and legal development. The law stood for the right ordering of society.

Government was a growth industry, and with growth there came specialisation. The network of courts which served through to the modern period had their origins in the century after 1170. The court was the king's court, and initially it could only do justice in the king's presence, *coram rege*. There grew from the court *coram rege* the court of king's bench which became, but only slowly, a regular court of law which sat apart from the king's person. The first sedentary court was the Exchequer, brought to rest by the weight of its records, a court presided over by the great justiciars. From the Exchequer there grew two courts of law, the Exchequer itself, and the common bench, or court of common pleas. The barons in Magna Carta asked that common pleas, actions between private individuals, should be held in some fixed place. The three courts were in regular session from 1234. Each of them, along with the chancery, the royal secretariat, can be looked upon as a department of state. Each had its professional civil servants, and lawyers, and its own records. It was in the court of common pleas that the common law of England was made, and the name, although it disappeared from the English system of justice in 1880, is still preserved in many American jurisdictions. The records would accumulate, and the fog would surround them; few will forget the beginnings of *Bleak House*, with fog everywhere over London, and 'hard by Temple Bar, in Lincoln's Inn Hall, at the very heart of the fog, sits the Lord High Chancellor in his High Court of Chancery.'

In the thirteenth century, by comparison at least, all was clarity and light. We may get a clearer picture of the work of the courts, and of the part which they played in the unification of the political nation, by looking at the work and the records of the lawyers themselves. The itinerant justices on their eyres did a whole range of the work of government, from civil and criminal pleas, to an audit of the sheriff's financial records, and the investigation of the rights of the crown. A set of letters survives, sent back to the chancellor in London by William of York, a royal clerk.[6] In August 1227 he wrote to the chancellor: 'My lord, I implore you to arrange that I do not have to go on eyre in Cumberland. It would mean a long journey, and the climate there disagrees with my constitution.' He went none the less. He protested at the expense and at the pace of work, for the senior justice was Martin of Patishall, who 'works from sunrise to nightfall, and has worn out all his fellows.' When the Carlisle eyre was over he none the less reported back with some satisfaction: 'we were there nine days, and obtained forty marks a day for the king, the total of the eyre being 360 marks or more.' The style was the man, a professional man, who worked hard and earned good rewards, in the shape of an expense account and a whole succession of church benefices, 'fat blessings' he called them, rather cynically, at one point. William of York was to serve as a justice both of common pleas and king's bench, and he became bishop of Salisbury in 1246.

By the 1230s, at the latest, there can be no question that England had a clearly established legal profession. The decisions of the great justices, the prodigious Patisall and William Ralegh, were being collected in the 1220s and 1230s, each collection having the more notable cases of the last term. Henry of Bracton's famous note book consisted of a number of such collections, and so also did the great collection, *On the Laws and Customs of England*, a work of vast erudition, which has come down under Bracton's name, though his authorship is now disputed. Bracton is ten times the length of Glanvill, the late twelfth-century treatise on the law, but it was less its length than its method that was important. The lawyer's concern for precedent, the detailed study of the judgments of the great justices and the minutiae of individual cases, can be seen clearly worked out in the text of Bracton. The book served a burgeoning profession. There grew up a class of professional pleaders, the barristers of a later age, as illustrated in Plate 2b from the early fourteenth century, lineal ancestors surely of the men whom Dickens found, 'groping knee-deep in technicalities, running their goat-hair and horse-hair warded heads against walls of words, and making a pretence of equity with serious faces, as players might'. And in the county towns and the countryside there were lawyers also, the solicitors of a later age. A collection of texts made for John of Longueville, a Northampton lawyer of the early fourteenth century, contained Bracton, copies of the statutes, including of course Magna Carta, and the forms of the standard writs. It also had texts on estate management, on the hold-ing of courts, and a treatise on letter writing. There were the specialists and the general practitioners, all making a good living and all, spread through the land, drawing on common records and com-mon experiences.

'For God's sake,' wrote William of York, 'don't forget to tell me how things go with you and the court.' At the apex of the courts of law, and of the political nation, there stood parliament. Parliament was a court in the broadest sense, both a court of law and a political assembly. The developments from the three crown-wearings of the post-Conquest period to the Provisions of Oxford in 1258 was a logical progression: 'Let it be remembered that there are to be three parliaments a year; the first at the Octave of Michaelmas [6 October], the second on the morrow of Candlemas [3 February], and the third on the first day of June.' To establish regular parliaments was central to the work of reform. Both in William Rufus's time and in Henry III's time, there were great courts held, in which the king and his immediate entourage were joined by the magnates. A wide range of business could be done on these occasions. In 1236 for instance, since this has been taken as the first official use of the word parliament, there was legislation concerning the royal forests, a perennial subject of discussion, and some detailed tinkering with the forms of action at the common law. In the same assembly the king's demand for an aid was met by the grant of a thirteenth on movable property, given in return for a further grant of the charters. A minor case concerning the advowson of a church in Wiltshire came up to it; and doubtless there were many matters of like kind also referred for a final decision. Parliament was a meeting of the king's court, which changed its name at one stage of its development.

As government became more professional, with increasing rapidity from the late twelfth century, so did parliament. In particular, with the administration fragmented and with the creation of three courts of common law, the need for the oversight of a single tribunal was increased. It is possible to argue that this was the main function of parliament in Henry III's reign, that they dealt with the problems of government as they emerged in the departments and in the law courts. That it spent much of its time dealing with relatively trivial business is not in doubt. No one who has served on any broadly based body, which has executive powers over a wide range of business, will find such a conclusion surprising. At the same time, the anxiety of the reformers that there should be regular parliaments was not simply due to a passion for efficient administration. It was parliament that made the big decisions, parliament that granted taxation, parliament that might be made to carry through sweeping reforms or be made the instrument of a regular and detailed supervision of the work of royal government. This is all politics under one heading or another.

The knights and burgesses, who would become the commons at a later stage of parliament's evolution, had no place in the king's court and no part in the work of the earliest parliaments. Knights came to four of the thirty-four parliaments held between 1258 and 1272, and burgesses to only one of them. In 1254 two knights were elected by each shire court, able to agree on behalf of their communities to a grant in aid. In theory their assent was not required, but in practice, in a time of emergency, it was useful to have it, and in return for a further reissue of the charters the grant was made. The shire court was an important political centre, and the knights as a group had particular concerns. It is interesting, and far from anachronistic, to see here the beginnings of a process by which parliament would become the political forum of the whole nation.

Ideas of community were much discussed in the mid-thirteenth century. The idea of the 'community of the land' occurs frequently. In 1258 the Burton annalist wrote as follows:[7]

by the common counsel of the lord king and the community the following charters of the lord king were drawn up, written in

Latin, French, and English and sent to all shires throughout the kingdom of England, there to be read by the sheriffs and understood and for the future firmly observed intact by all.

But who were 'the community of the land'? Most often, when the phrase is used, it refers to the baronage. They had to give counsel to the king, and assist his court in giving judgment. They had a right to be consulted, and a duty to consent, when the king levied a scutage or required an aid. There developed from this the idea that the approval of the community was required for legislation, and that the magnates were the proper persons to speak on the community's behalf. The barons spoke for the political nation, but this does not mean that the idea of a wider community was a fiction. The Burton annalist was certainly thinking not just of the baronage, but of a wider community of the realm of England. The community was to be centred on parliament. Parliament gave publicity, and publicity was itself a part of due process. The king who died in 1272 would probably not have foreseen this development. His was a private view of history, and publicity was not one of his weapons. In 1257 he had been at St Albans, and while chatting after dinner he had named not for the first time, 'all the holy kings of England who had been canonised', and Matthew Paris wrote them all down. 'The king also enumerated and mentioned by name all the baronies of England which recurred to his memory, and he discovered them to amount to two hundred and fifty.' Every name told a story, and in those stories there was the history of England.

Chapter 7

The Nation Unified

At the end of Henry III's reign it was possible for the king and the magnates to argue their differences over the best part of a decade of civil strife. Time was on the monarchy's side. In the reigns of the first three Edwards, which are covered by this chapter, the pace changed. It changed because warfare, which up to the 1290s had been an occasional source of expenditure, now became a regular charge on the national community. In pursuit of royal ambitions, English armies went beyond boundaries of authority which had existed since the Angevins came to power and their baronage's view of custom had been formed. These armies had to be fed, and they had to be paid. Their payment, through taxation, led to a number of social and political changes of great importance for the future. On the surface, political life went on much as before. But it became more concentrated. The problems of warfare needed instant resolution, even though deliberation was built into procedure and habits of mind. Power came to those, both individuals and institutions, that could promise expedition. And more than ever before rested on the capacity of those individuals whose rights the nation was organised to pursue, the kings of England themselves. They had to make public their concerns, in order to draw upon the resources of the nation in their support.

The fourteenth century saw the establishment of a single political nation, a single community. Its focus was in the king's parliament, which became the sole source of taxation, and hence an essential instrument of the king's war aims. To parliament came the representatives of the communities of the land. They had no right to refuse the king taxation, provided the urgency of the king's need was made plain to them. But no more had the king the right to exploit his subjects, and so the grievances of the nation were also raised in parliament. Increasingly, as warfare strengthened the unity of what was still a military aristocracy, petitions for the redress of popular grievances would be left to the representatives of the shires and the towns. From this social change, there followed constitutional change. The commons, initially observers, became established as a separate estate within parliament. A chronicler writing of the 'Good Parliament' of 1376 referred to the *collegium* or 'house' of commons, and it was in the same parliament that the commons first elected a Speaker. By trial and error, by the pressure on resources and by the reaction to that pressure, the kings of England discovered what the communities of the land would bear. Much of the social history of England in the fourteenth century, in consequence, is written upon the rolls of parliament.

Edward I was aged 33 when he succeeded his father in 1272. While still in his teens, he had been made a major landowner in England, and he had been given whatever rights the English monarchy had in Ireland, Wales, the Channel Islands and Gascony. His concern with the lands that lay beyond the frontiers of England was a distinctive feature of his kingship. He had played a major part in a protracted civil war, first supporting Simon de Montfort, and then leading the army that defeated Simon at Evesham in 1265. He treated the Anglo-Norman families of Scotland and the Welsh chieftains in just the same terms as he did the English baronage—the rights of monarchy were to be clearly spelt out and equally clearly recognised. Already in 1272 he was a man set in his ways. He had seen demonstrated very clearly both the strengths and the weaknesses of the English monarchy. In the course of a reign of thirty-five years he was to stretch the potential of that monarchy to its limits.

Relations with Wales and Scotland did not suddenly become a force in English politics in the late thirteenth century. The Normans who conquered England in the eleventh century found no natural boundaries, or cohesive military force, to hold back their expansion into Wales and the Scottish lowlands. Both in Scotland and in Wales political power was fragmented. In Wales the lords of small regions were each kings, in that they had regalian rights, and any larger unit was the transient creation of forceful individuals. In Scotland there was a single monarchy, but the kingdom was not united until the mid-thirteenth century. The English kings sought the recognition of a feudal overlordship over the kings of Scotland and Wales. That they involved themselves in Wales and Scotland, and when they did so, resulted as much from a desire to control their own men as from the value of the subjection of other kings. For the lords of the British Isles shared common concerns, and their families intermarried. One approach to such relationships is to look at the foundation of religious houses. Of the thirteen Cistercian houses founded in Wales, seven were founded by Welsh and six by Anglo-Norman families. Wales and Scotland were a part of European feudal society.

Gerald of Wales, a writer descended from one of the Norman families of South Wales, described in his autobiography an occasion in the 1180s when the Lord Rhys ap Gruffydd came to Hereford to meet two envoys from the king of England. They met at the house of the bishop of Hereford, and while they sat at breakfast Gerald remarked 'in courteous jest' that the Welsh chief sat between two members of the great house of Clare, part of whose inheritance Rhys held. Later in the day they fell to talking of the descendants of Nesta, a Welsh princess, who had married a Norman and been the mistress of Henry I of England. The picture of a relaxed gathering of friends was drawn from the life. In similar vein, the Lord Rhys is credited with summoning the first Eisteddfod, at his Christmas feast of 1176. He invited competitors not only from Wales, but from England, Scotland and Ireland. Such relationships across both the Welsh and the Scottish borders were forces making for the unity of a larger area than England alone. The links between Scotland and England involved some of the same families. In 1240 Isobel de Clare, a daughter of William Marshal earl of Pembroke, married Robert Bruce of Annandale. This Robert Bruce, 'the competitor', was the fifth lord of Annandale in the Scottish lowlands. He had a long career at the court of Henry III of England, and in 1268 he became the first chief justice of the court of king's bench. He fought for Henry at the battle of Lewes, and at the age of 60 he went on crusade with the Lord Edmund, the king's younger son. He was the 'runner-up' for the succession to the throne of Scotland in 1292, when he was in his eighty-third year. The Scottish lord of Annandale was a more loyal follower of the English king than Earl Gilbert 'the Red', the English head of the house of Clare. On a less grand scale, there were many such careers, which followed naturally from the tenure of land in both countries.

The fragmentation of power in Scotland and Wales, and the loyalties and feuds of individual families, kept boundaries imprecise and relationships close. The English civil war of the 1260s, when combined with changes in Wales and Scotland at the same time, were to threaten this equilibrium. It was on the frontiers of his lordship that Edward was to find most difficult the re-establishment of the situation as before the civil war. Llewellyn the Last supported Simon de Montfort in the civil war. Simon lost but Llewellyn gained, and his position as prince of Wales was confirmed. Llewellyn had an authority in Wales that had not been enjoyed by any one man since the Norman Conquest. The Scottish monarchy, starting from a stronger base, similarly made gains at this time. The Norse defeat at Largs in 1263 greatly increased the range of Alexander III's authority. It made him the effective ruler of the whole of Scotland, highlands and lowlands, and the islands also. And while the native rulers of Scotland and Wales became stronger, the marcher lords, by the same token and for the same reasons, became more independent. When royal officials came to analyse the results of the *quo warranto* commissions, they made a special list of the royal rights abrogated by the earl of Clare, and in 1279 and 1280 they pushed a vigorous attack on his franchises. Just as there was no clear frontier, so there is no distinction to be drawn between Edward's works in England, and those in Scotland and Wales.

Edward's dealings with Wales show his attitudes and techniques at their more straightforward and successful. Llewellyn refused Edward homage when it was required of him. The result was a defeat, the halving of his lands, and the attempt to institutionalise English lordship. Edward transported a group of civil servants to Wales who were to introduce an administration on the English model. English justice was to be applied, through a system of shires. Deviations were not to be tolerated: the archbishop of Canterbury was shocked to find that most of the Welsh clergy had one wife, while most of the laity had two. For the first time, the inhabitants of central and northern Wales were to be governed by the monarchy of lowland England, and made subject to English law and custom in the name of order and civilisation. The new programme was resented, but in 1282 Llewellyn was killed. The Welsh revolt collapsed, and Edward set out to establish his rule all the more firmly. In 1284 the Statute of Wales declared confidently: 'divine favour has now totally transferred to our ownership the land of Wales and its inhabitants, formerly subject to us by feudal right, and has annexed it to the crown of England as part of the same body.'[1] Edward claimed to be not the feudal overlord of Wales but its ruler. He stopped short of complete administrative integration. The exchequer was kept distinct, as was the actual machinery of justice. The construction of the castles at Conway, Caernarvon, Beaumaris and elsewhere was tacit recognition that not all Welshmen might agree with his philosophy. It was to be left to Henry VIII, in 1536, to make England and

Wales a single political unit. But in Welsh historiography this is 'the Conquest' of Wales.

Edward dealt in similar fashion with the baronage of England. An important element of his policy was the scrutiny of existing privileges. *Quo warranto* proceedings, which lasted from 1278 to 1294, required all those who claimed special jurisdictions or privileges of any kind, to justify the claim by producing their title. Privileges ranged from the all but total autonomy of the bishop within the palatinate of Durham, to the greater aristocracy's rights to have their own officers execute royal commands, to rights to hunt in his own woodland which any landowner might claim. In theory—as theory was being developed by royalist lawyers—all such rights were vested in the king, and could be reclaimed from subjects. In fact earlier kings had not interfered with customs which were sanctified by tradition, and few barons had charters to support their claims. Hundreds of proceedings on *quo warranto* writs were instituted before the justices: the operation failed as much because of its scale as because of baronial opposition. But the terms in which the baronage explained their opposition are revealing. According to Walter of Guisborough, when the aged earl of Warenne appeared before the king's justices he brandished an old and rusty sword.[2]

> Here, my lords, here is my warrant. My ancestors came with William the Bastard and conquered their lands with the sword. I shall defend them with the sword against anyone who tries to usurp them. The king did not conquer and subject the land by himself, but our forefathers were partners and co-workers with him.

Whether apocryphal or not these words reflect an attitude of mind that was widely shared.

Neither the king nor the baronage made substantial gains as a result of this struggle for the definition of royal rights. There was a wide area of agreement on matters of policy, and in legislation much of real substance was achieved. Both king and barons agreed that the incidents of feudal tenure were becoming more difficult to enforce, and that the ease with which land could be alienated caused landlords administrative difficulty and financial loss. The feudal system had to be maintained as a source of profit for landlords. The preambles to statutes naturally put matters rather differently.[3] In 1279 the statute of Mortmain prohibited gifts of land held by laymen to the 'dead hand' of the church: ecclesiastical tenants were not liable to wardship and marriage, and they did not pay reliefs. Thus there was the loss of services, 'which from the beginning had provided for the defence of the realm.' In 1290 the statute of *Quia Emptores* prohibited all subinfeudation of land, the lengthening of the tenurial chain: 'Lords were losing wardship, escheats and marriages because of the machinations of their tenants, which seemed to the lords to be very hard and difficult, since it amounted in fact to their clear disinheritance.' The crown continued to license alienations in mortmain. Subinfeudation was prohibited, but there remained many other ways of transferring land. The purpose of Edward I's property legislation was to ensure that social change did not operate to the prejudice of the landlords.

The nation of Scotland, only recently united, faced in the 1280s a real crisis. Alexander III died in 1286, and left as his heir his granddaughter Margaret, the daughter of the king of Norway. In 1290 Edward I negotiated the marriage of Margaret with his son Edward of Caernarvon. It was established that the heir of this marriage would rule the two kingdoms jointly. But Margaret died in the same year. The Scots then faced a situation without precedent in western European history. Their royal dynasty had failed. The Scots barons feared civil war, and they feared in particular the intervention of the king of Norway. They looked naturally to the English king as the arbitrator in their 'great cause'. Fourteen persons entered a claim to the throne. In 1292 judgment was given at Berwick for John Balliol, and Edward was recognised as 'superior lord' of Scotland. The phrase had been used before, but Edward's interpretation of it was new, and the Scots particularly sensitive. The English king started to hear appeals from Scotland in his court. In 1294 he asked for the personal service in Gascony of the Scots king, ten earls and sixteen barons. He sought to deal with Scotland as though, like Wales, it had been 'annexed to the crown of England'. The result was a series of revolts in Scotland which, when combined with warfare in Gascony, stretched Edward well beyond the limits of his patience and his resources. Edward's position in Scotland was not in essence different from the French king's position in Gascony. What Edward would term French aggression in Gascony was in his own eyes when he dealt with Scotland no more than the defence of established rights. A developing theory of sovereignty led the western monarchies to assert the full range of their monarchical rights beyond the frontiers of their effective lordship.

Edward's first Scottish campaign in 1296 offered no hint of his later difficulties. He took Berwick and left scarcely a soul alive. The main Scottish army was defeated at Dunbar. The earl of Warenne was made guardian of Scotland. The stone of Scone, the inauguration seat of the Scots kings, was removed to Westminster. Direct administration on the Welsh pattern proved a focus for discontent. In 1297 William Wallace descended from the hills and won a famous victory at Stirling Bridge. In the same year Edward had to face opposition from the English baronage headed by the earls of Norfolk and Hereford. They objected to royal plans to send a feudal army to Gascony while the king went to Flanders. They objected further when the king obtained a grant of taxation reportedly 'from the people standing around in his chamber'. The king was forced not only to confirm the charters but to add concessions to them, among them that he would not tax 'save with the common assent of the whole kingdom'. That the king only did this, and the phrase was vague enough, with a bad grace and in clear military and financial need, must have been obvious to all. He promised disafforestation, but in 1299 he omitted no less than five clauses in the forest charter. When the text of the new statute (de finibus levatis) was read in St Paul's there was an uproar. Shortly after this, a mandate went out 'to arrest, try and punish persons congregating by day and night, and speaking ill of the king and his subjects'. The episode shows that the Londoners had a high level of political understanding, one that might be expected in a capital city, but which is sometimes ignored. The London populace knew the text of the charters very well.

Edward was to die at Burgh-in-the-Sands on the Solway Firth in July 1307 with the Scottish problem, which was largely of his own making, unresolved. The crisis of the 1290s, and the difficulties of his later years, were the result of a conventional though very capable man struggling to make the government of England run at a new pace. Not only was the pace new, but the demands were new, their effects were unpredictable, and the king's tone was peremptory. Up to the 1290s his direct taxes were few, and his main innovation was the export duty on wool, first levied in 1275. After 1294 his regular income, raised through aids, tallages and taxes on trade, came to around £75,000 a year. The sum was roughly double that which had served him in his early years, which in turn was well above the level of the previous century. The scale of taxation provoked a reaction; the maltote or bad tax comes down already glossed by contemporaries, and to the king's tax-collectors there were added those of the papacy. The maltote was bad not just because it was severe but because it led to a fall in prices; the price of wool fell during the years 1294–7 by about 24 per cent. This fall was not looked for, any more than any government intervention in the economy was planned. But wool was the main cash crop, and so a fall in the price of wool affected landlords' incomes directly. In 1294–5 taxation took 29 per cent of the net revenue of Bolton Priory in Yorkshire, and at St Mary's, York, the monks' bread ration was reduced. Taxation was immediate, and revenues were inflexible. The needs of war, possibly for the first time in English history, brought a fall in the living standards of individuals.

It was as well, granted that the effect of taxation was unpredictable, that Edward himself was the most predictable of medieval kings. He maintained popular support for his politics, and a grudging respect for his personal capacity. A ballad written within a year of his death ran as follows:[4]

> listen lords to a song on the death of a brave king, who by his loyalty withstood a very great encounter. Of his realm he lost nothing. Of England was he lord and king, who well knew the art of war. In no book can we read of a king who maintained his land better. All that he wished to do he brought wisely to a conclusion.

The precise terms in which this encomium is couched are worth careful study. To those who would have criticised Edward I for unfinished business within Scotland, the author would presumably have replied that success here was only a matter of time. He left a considerable debt, of around £200,000, but nothing resembling a financial crisis. He 'maintained his land well': the judgment is unequivocal. There is a temptation for historians to judge men in terms of a few high spots, the great campaigns, the public quarrels. Yet contemporaries judged men, as we do ourselves, on the balance of day to day affairs, and by the standards of competence and application appropriate to their rank. It would be a mistake to regard Edward as a man whose force of character narrowly saved him from the fate reserved for his son. Warfare strengthened monarchy, but brought it more than ever into the public gaze. Just as the rewards were to be greater than before, so also were to be the penalties of failure.

One of the last acts of the old king had been to banish from England, for leaving his army in Scotland without permission, a Gascon household knight called Piers Gaveston. It was the first act of Edward II to recall Gaveston and create him earl of Cornwall. Less than a year after Edward II's accession a group of magnates appeared in parliament to demand and secure the new earl's removal. What was wrong, according to the valuable chronicle *Life of Edward II* was that

> though of old it has been desirable for all men to find favour in the eyes of kings, Piers alone received a gracious welcome from the king; and enjoyed his favour to such an extent that if an earl or baron entered the king's chamber to speak with the king, the king would address no-one in his presence.

Royal patronage of a favourite could be tolerated, and was indeed expected, but for the favourite to monopolise that patronage was insupportable. It was the king's treatment of Gaveston, and later of the Despensers, that precipitated the crises of the reign, and brought the baronage together as a group. Their rights to give counsel, and their hereditary position as members of the king's household, were threatened as much by the tone of the new regime as by its actions.

A good deal of interest attaches to the theories of government and society which the conflicts of the reign produced. In April 1308 the baronage declared that the allegiance they owed was to the crown, and not to the person of the king. What lay behind the statement was less a threat to the king's person, than the idea that there was an estate of the crown, which existed for the benefit of the community and which the community was bound to sustain. It was Gaveston's crime to waste the crown's estate. The Ordinances of 1311, which dominated a decade of English politics in which estate management was particularly difficult, were a treatise on good stewardship. Its ideas were those of Walter of Henley and the *Seneschaucy*, which were examined earlier in the book. The king's own person and his management of his household were circumscribed. He was not to leave the country, or go to war, without the consent of the baronage in parliament. All revenue was to pass through the Exchequer. Parliament was to meet once or twice a year. The king indeed was made so dependent that it would have to do so, for the king's bankers were banished, royal powers of purveyance were curtailed, and new customs and maltotes, made since the coronation of Edward I, were abolished. It was a long but coherent document. It was to be published in every county, 'there publicly proclaimed and commanded to be observed by all'. One chronicler wrote as follows: 'ordinances were made by common consent for the custody of the household of the lord king, so that he should live more wisely, and avoid tallages and oppression of the people.' This was the popular view of a popular document.

A king limited in resources of character was thus very early in his reign shackled with a document which made his limitations clear, and which was widely publicised. Gaveston this time was gone less than a month; by Christmas 1311 he was back at the king's side. He was captured at Scarborough, and brought south for trial. The earls of Lancaster and Warwick held their own court, and sentenced him to death on the authority of the earlier ordinances. 'Thomas Earl of Lancaster', says the chronicle, 'took upon himself the peril of the business.'[5] Ten years later Lancaster would lose his own life for this action. 1312–22 was to be a decade that he was to dominate but not master. Another chronicler reported that 'perpetual hatred grew up between the king and the earls.' It was not a happy base from which to build and to do business. Business there was in plenty; yet when Edward should have been campaigning against Robert Bruce, he was rumoured to be trying to secure a safe haven in Scotland for his friend Gaveston. Not until May 1314 did Edward lead a major expedition north, and it was to be a disaster. He led an army of 20,000 men, but at Bannockburn by Stirling the Scottish infantry routed them. Lancaster was able to claim that failure was due to a lack of regard for the ordinances; he took over the administration, and set out to put the 1311 reforms into action. A stalemate between his own household and that of the king made for chaos. In addition, the government had to cope with a succession of bad harvests in 1315, 1316 and 1317 which drove grain prices to the highest in living memory. In Northumberland, where misery was compounded by Scottish raids and civil disorder, the dearth was reported as especially bad, and dogs and horses were eaten for want of anything else. Ideas of good lordship were stood on their head in those years, and the country had no focus.

Edward's love of hedging and ditching was well reported. The author of the *Life*, who wrote with no knowledge of the king's fate, is one of numerous contemporary witnesses. 'If only he had given to arms the labour that he expended in rustic pursuits, he would have raised England aloft, his name would have resounded throughout the land.' What in fact was heard in the land were the dull echoes of incompetence, cheerfully embroidered. One July morning in 1314, shortly after the disaster at Bannockburn, a royal messenger stopped at his native village of Newington in Kent for a chat with the local bailiff. He was asked, as possibly he expected to be, whether he had any news of the king. He said that he had, and that it was bad news, for the lord king was coming back from Scotland after a heavy defeat. When the bailiff marvelled at this, the messenger said that it was not at all surprising, for the lord king only went to mass with great reluctance. The bailiff then asked what the king did when he should have been at mass, and the messenger said that he lazed around, and occupied himself in hedging and ditching, and other unseemly activities. The story got to the ears of the king's court, and the parties were summoned to explain themselves. This is in itself another sign of how small and politically integrated English society had become.

In 1322 the parliament at York repealed the Ordinances, saying that the royal power had been restricted and that whenever in the past 'provisions had been made by subjects concerning the royal power of the ancestors of our lord the king' there had been nothing but trouble. The view of royal power was based, just as was the barons', on a view of past history. The king's deposition five years later, which was to add a striking episode to that history, came as the result of a struggle at court. 'See how rapidly the great men change their sides': the chroniclers took as their keys to the struggle the antipathy of the queen, Isabella of France, to Hugh Despenser the younger, and her liaison with Roger Mortimer of Wigmore. She went to France on official business in 1325; she returned in 1326, set on the removal of the Despensers, with a very great deal to lose. The king was forced to flee London. The Despensers were captured, and were tried and sentenced to death 'by notoriety'. The elder Despenser had been made earl of Winchester, and it was to Winchester that his head was sent after his execution. His son's head was put on London Bridge, 'with much tumult and the sound of horns in the presence of the mayor and community'. These somewhat macabre details may serve to emphasise the popular feeling which not only supported, but provided a large measure of the force behind, the revolutionary acts of 1326 and 1327.

It was one thing to execute the Despensers, quite another to depose the king. There were no precedents for such an action. It had to be done, in some sense, by the whole community, and so it had to involve parliament. In the depths of winter, the Londoners kept the temperature high. The bishop of Hereford preached from the text, 'A foolish king shall ruin his people.' The baronage, in this revolutionary situation, had no wish at all to speak for the community of the land. A deputation composed of the different estates waited upon the king to announce his deposition. William Trussell, 'on behalf of the whole kingdom', renounced the nation's homage. A document known as the deposition articles, which probably dates from after the king's death, lists the charges made against him. They stated that he was incompetent to govern, unwilling to listen to counsel. He had destroyed the church and the noble men of his realm. He had lost Scotland, Ireland and Gascony. He had broken his coronation oath to do justice to all, had stripped his realm, and by his cruelty and weakness had shown himself quite incorrigible. Some of this was far-fetched: the destruction of the church and the loss of Gascony need more than qualification to become acceptable, and his regard for the property rights of his subjects had been at least as well developed as had been his father's. But that he was incompetent, and incorrigible; that he would not listen, and that he would not learn—these were the charges made against him, and in this case the charges and the cause of downfall were one and the same. In terms of competence Edward I and his son represent the zenith and the nadir of medieval English monarchy. Many qualifications can be made, but only by moving the judgments away from the general standards of competence and good stewardship which were obviously paramount in contemporary ideas of kingship.

The ability to take counsel remained a touchstone, and Edward's treatment of his favourites meant that he was consistently found wanting. Contemporary texts reveal something of the historical attitudes that were being developed to justify the barons' position. The tract upon the office of steward is one of two important texts drawn up in 1321, and connected with the removal of the Despensers in the parliament of that year, the other being the *Modus Tenendi Parliamentum*, the procedure for holding a parliament. The stewardship tract claimed that the steward had a duty 'to supervise and regulate, under and immediately after the king, the whole realm of England'. The steward should intervene against evil counsellors, and if necessary remove them from the king's side by force. So it had been with Godwin earl of Kent in the Confessor's time, and with Hubert de Burgh in the minority of Henry III, 'who for his evil deeds and other suchlike counsels of his was taken by the steward and other magnates, and adjudged to lose the same earldom by consideration of the whole parliament.' The document is a speculative venture in self-justification on Lancaster's part; and within a few months he was dead. The ideas remained current in Lancastrian circles, and in Richard II's reign they would return with renewed force.

More importance attaches to the *Modus*, a treatise on the holding of parliament, because its ideas were more widely disseminated. It began as follows:[6]

> Here is described the way in which the parliament of the king of England and of his English was held in the time of king Edward the son of king Ethelred: which way was recited by the wiser men of the realm in front of William duke of Normandy, conqueror and king of England, on the conqueror's own orders, was approved by him, and was the customary way in his times and also in the times of his successors the kings of England.

The idea of the Conqueror listening patiently to what follows is a pleasant one, and the scene may be compared with that given in figure 10. Most of the *Modus* is concerned with procedure; it is the medieval equivalent of Erskine May. Whereas before the baronage had spoken for the community of the nation, now it was the commons that did so: 'it is to be understood that the two knights who come to parliament for the shire carry more weight in parliament in granting and refusing than the greatest earl of England.' So radical did such a view appear that the authenticity of the text was long called into question. But what the above extract says is simply that the representatives carry more weight than those who speak only for themselves, and it was only in parliament that the nation could grant an aid. In 1360 the king summoned representatives of the shires to five centres, London, Worcester, Taunton, Lincoln and Leicester, but the writs accepted that really 'the whole community of the nation' could not be in five places at once. Once it was established that aids could only be granted by a full parliament, then the position of the commons was secure. The commons in parliament assented to laws, granted taxes, and presented the grievances of their communities in turn. The views of all parties were noted by the clerks. The idea of the community of the realm of England became a matter of record.

Edward III was crowned on 1 February 1327, at the age of 14. The dominance of Mortimer and Isabella offered no prospect of permanence, nor any great popular support, to the new regime. Henry of Lancaster was made the chief of a regency council, and regained the greater part of his father's inheritance. Mortimer was able to devote his chief energies to his own aggrandisement. The new council could not delay a decision upon Scotland. Robert Bruce had been treating for peace, on his own terms, for several years. A treaty was made in March 1328. The Scottish king was to pay £20,000 and to marry his son to Edward's sister, Joan of the Tower. In return

Edward renounced all claims to suzerainty over Scotland. There are signs that Edward himself was not happy with the advice he got, and the peace was certainly unpopular. The Londoners, always a good indicator of public opinion, refused to allow the stone of Scone to be returned to the Scots, as the treaty had promised. The £20,000 got no further than Isabella's own wardrobe. Yet for all this the peace recognised the realities of Scottish independence, and withdrew the necessity of an expensive Scottish war from the inherited obligations of the young king. It was a timely compromise. By 1329 Bruce was dead, and in 1329 and 1330 the English regency council fell apart, largely because it lacked any common purpose. Mortimer was executed. Isabella was given £3,000 a year and complete freedom of action. She lived on until 1358, and the inventory of her possessions made after her death shows an interesting list of reading matter. On the one hand there were the works of popular culture, romances, stories of Charlemagne, of King Arthur and of the Trojan war; on the other hand works of popular piety, a book of homilies, a gradual and an ordinal.

As kings came to be more circumscribed in their domestic policies, they were almost inevitably forced towards their strongest ground, that of being leaders of their nations in war. Warfare gave the king a common cause with the aristocracy, and a common cause also with the rest of the populace; and it gave him legitimate and quite un-equivocal rights over their persons and over their goods. In the 1330s each of these themes was clearly worked out. Edward III allied himself with the aristocracy in his war with France, and parliament, carefully managed, gave him the resources to prosecute his claims. The death of Charles IV in 1328 left France to his cousin Philip VI, but it also left a claim to his nephew, the English king. There was no solid reason why this claim should have been pressed, but it did serve to complicate the conflict once the two parties had decided on it. For what Edward had inherited in his blood was less a claim to France than a desire, shared by all men of rank, for military exercise, and to perform deeds of arms which would rival the exploits of the heroes of old. It was in order to emulate Arthur and his Round Table that Edward decided to inaugurate the Order of the Garter in 1348. The Round Table that now hangs in the great hall at Winchester was probably made during the 1330s. Edward I had been a great Arthurian enthusiast; the Garter ceremonial introduced by his grand-son bound together in a fellowship similar to Arthur's twenty-six knights, among them the greatest in the land. The king's castle at

Windsor, his birthplace, was the new Camelot and the Garter stalls in St George's chapel reveal most clearly the aspirations of Edward III and his fellow knights.

Warfare and a balanced approach to patronage offered him the support of the nobility, but he none the less needed allies and money on an unprecedented scale, and thus needed wider support. On problems of logistics, of constructing a sound basis for national taxation, his schemes for glory nearly foundered in the early years. He used the wool export trade to raise vast loans, nearly £100,000 from Italian and English creditors in 1336 and 1337 alone. And he made a whole series of concessions to parliamentary opinion. The chief of them, in October 1339, was the abolition of purveyance, because of its capacity to ruin individuals. This was only one of the prerogative rights of the crown, so stubbornly defended through the thirteenth century, that came under fire in the war parliaments of Edward's early years. The right to sell the chattels of felons, or the right to take scutage: these were rights that meant little in the four-teenth century, but it was still a major step that during the course of his reign all grants of extraordinary taxation became confined to parliament. In 1374–5 the annual revenue of the Exchequer was £112,000. £22,000 of this came from the hereditary revenues of the crown; £82,000 from direct and indirect taxes; and the balance from borrowing. Anyone concerned with the development of English society must be struck by the limitation of these prerogative rights, however attenuated they had become. Each party could negotiate from a position of strength. The king had the right to be supported but parliament had the right to scrutinise his need. Parliament was becoming the political centre of the nation. The required demonstra-tion of need was an opportunity as well as an obligation. The war propaganda of Edward III provided a final, crucial stage in the development of a national political consciousness.

When the first check to Edward's plans came in 1340–1, which in terms of resources committed and hopes generated was the most serious reverse to monarchy during our period, it passed off in a paper war of heat but little violence to individuals. Archbishop Stratford, as chief minister responsible for levying money for the war effort, had to defend himself against charges stopping little short of treachery. He did so not merely by reference to the liberties of the church, and the rights of magnates to judgment by their peers, but by appealing to history, by claiming to stand in the main line of the English political tradition. On Becket's feast day, 29 December 1340, he treated a doubtless appreciative congregation to a long sermon on the state of the nation, in which the punishment of kings for their transgressions bulked large. The loss of Henry's overseas dominions was a just consequence of his treatment of Becket; perhaps even Bannockburn was connected with the way that Edward I and Edward II had treated the church. Elsewhere he offered a long homily on the necessity for wise counsel, which started with the prophets but which soon came to Edward II, 'your excellent father', who had been led astray, 'and what happened to him in that cause you sir know well'.[7] Edward seems to have recognised the force of the public opinion that Stratford marshalled against him with such skill. The charges against the archbishop were left on the file. Both the past, and the logic of a common enterprise, counselled caution. Yet in the end it was Edward's own judgment, and not necessity, which led to his acceptance of this advice.

Edward made a fresh start to the war in 1340. His claim to France was now actively pursued, for it alone gave him a base in northern France, the empire of his twelfth-century predecessors, on which the great battles of the war would be fought. He promised to re-establish 'the good laws and customs which were in force in the time of his progenitor king Louis'. This represented more than a conventional promise. England from the twelfth century at the latest was a unified political unit: in France a tradition of provincial separatism remained a powerful political force, to which Edward could refer as it suited him. It suited him very well in the 1340s, not least because it took attention away from Gascony to fertile regions such as Normandy. His armies were promised and found 'great towns that have not been walled, from which your men shall have such great gain that they shall be the richer for twenty years.' The 1340s seemed to confirm the prediction. At Crécy in Normandy in 1346 Edward defeated the French in a battle which, paradoxically in the great age of chivalry, showed that cavalry stood little chance against well-equipped archers who were able to occupy a defensive position of their own choice. And Crécy was but the most convincing victory of many at this time. The Scots were defeated at Neville's Cross, and King David II of Scotland was captured. Calais was taken after a year's siege, and was to provide the English with a foothold on the continent for more than two centuries. In little over a year Edward was established as a national hero. When he returned to England in 1346 the rolls of parliament record that 'all thanked God for the victory he had granted to their liege lord . . . and said that all the money they had given him had been well spent.' For the commons this was generous praise, and fully justified Edward's diplomacy in his early dealings with them.[8]

It was in the years around the Black Death, when the crisis of the plague might have been expected to cause social tension on a dangerous scale, that the monarchy, aristocracy and commons came together to produce a single, cohesive political society. The crisis of 1340 had seen the commons as an independent political force; and the decade which followed showed how much they could influence a monarchy well aware of the importance of public opinion. In theory the commons' power was limited. They could petition the crown for the redress of grievances, and they had the acknowledged right to assent to taxation; but they had no right to withhold taxation until their grievances were met. In many parliaments, as in 1346 and 1348, the commons were only invited to mention their grievances after they had granted a tax. The crown's rights made ciphers of the commons, but the practice of parliament was more flexible. The crown would negotiate on all that it regarded as inessentials; and in war years all that was essential was money. Particularly inessential were the prerogative rights of the crown, on which a century earlier so much had been held to depend. In 1344 the commons granted taxation on condition they were relieved of the 'aids and charges', such as purveyance, military service, and the feudal aids, which had been put upon them hitherto. Such also were judicial fines, on individuals and communities, which were intended to supply the war. In a time of war the king's rights over individuals were extensive; and so it became the commons' objective to sanction their exercise within parliament, and wherever possible to bargain for their abolition in return for straight money grants. What was a convenience for the king was at the same time a victory for the commons, that the king should treat with his subjects only through parliament. A king concerned only with the assertion of his rights would reckon himself the loser by such a procedure; one conscious of his obligations to rule in accord with the common good would not. Discussion was kept away from principles, as it usually can be when men are working together amicably.

Purveyance was the issue which brought the war home most immediately to the local communities—bows and arrows for the Black Prince's expedition of 1355 and 1357, victuals for the troops guarding the coast. With the supply of Calais, which became a permanent charge, the picture was different. Merchants operating under royal licence, offering ready cash, met the crown's needs speedily and with no local resistance. By the 1350s the prerogative right of purveyance had vanished from the centre of the stage. Even the crown's rights to take troops for the defence of the realm, in our eyes a basic necessity, could be circumscribed by statute to make the practice more acceptable to the local communities. Troops mustered for service overseas were to receive the king's wages from the point of crossing the county boundary; those defending the north were to be paid from the point of muster at either Newcastle or Carlisle. Here as in later centuries it was the local communities, and not the poor individuals who were pressed into service, that had to be wooed. In a society that policed itself, even a small village in revolt offered a challenge that could embarrass authority. This point became very clear during the Peasants' Revolt. The crown in the middle years of the fourteenth century seems concerned both to placate the lords who dominated the villages and the general body of village opinion. The most remarkable feature of these years was how little a society that was organised for war was in fact changed by warfare. The commons insisted that the needs of war never became so pressing that established rights could be overridden at will. The rhythm of campaigns took second place to the routine of the countryside. The war did not suspend political discussion; rather it made it more concentrated, more intensive.

One area of continuing discussion concerned the authority in administering justice that was to be given to the representatives of the local communities, rather than to justices sent out from Westminster. In the twelfth and thirteenth centuries royal authority in the localities was vested in the sheriff, and his activities were supervised centrally by the Exchequer. In the fourteenth century the general eyre was to atrophy, and with it the sheriff's main powers in criminal matters. Authority in minor crimes, felonies and trespasses, was vested in the keepers, later to be the justices, of the peace. The keepers were one of the many experiments of the 1260s. It came to result in an office which was to have a long history, that of justice of the peace. The job of the keepers in Edward II's time was to enforce the provisions for local order contained in the statute of Winchester of 1285. They were appointed by the crown, and initially they had no judicial powers. The commons in the fourteenth century sought both to control their appointment via parliament, and to give them such powers. Magna Carta had asked that sheriffs should be local men, and the idea that local affairs should be handled by local men was not a new one in

1215. The extension of this idea marked a shift of responsibility from the centre, from men like William of York to men like Theobald Hautein.

The commons made some ground in the early stages of the Hundred Years' War. On the eve of the king's departure from England in 1338, the keepers were given powers to determine cases, and hence for a time made justices. In 1348 they argued the case for local nominations, 'since those who live in the shire are better and more often able to punish felons and trespassers, and with greater advantage and less grievance to the people than foreign justices.' Not all believed this argument. The keepers and justices had no formal legal training, and from 1344 it became customary to add a number of lawyers to each commission. The men of law were mindful that the knightly gangs came from the same families as the justices of the peace. In the 1380s local men were reckoned not strong enough to deal with the threat of insurrection, and the formidable justices of trialbaston, whose powers were so resented, were sent out from Westminster. But still the local men won the day. The justices' powers were effectively recognised in 1350, in the aftermath of the Black Death. For much of the 1350s there were separately established justices of labourers, whose work will be considered in the chapter which follows. In the late fourteenth century the commission for the peace met four times a year, and each commission had about eight members. Responsibility for the preservation of local order rested firmly in their hands. It is significant that the first signs of the justices' ultimate victory came in the late 1330s, when it was thought the king's absence would inevitably lead to a weakening of public order, and the government was concerned to learn some lessons from the history of earlier wars with France. The king's own letters show that there were some fears of a general insurrection at this time. The developments of the next half-century show the power of the commons. But they are also a reminder that political stability depended on the king's person, and on general support for government policy.

The peace of Brétigny in 1360 offered Edward the prospect of peace and some self-indulgence in his declining years, and his subjects a lessening of the burden of taxation. The king still needed resources, but now lacked the plea of the necessity of war; his tone became even more conciliatory. It was set by the presentation of a number of detailed accounts to parliament, designed to show that the king's commitment to defending the frontiers of his land (much extended by the success of the previous decade) and the general expenses of government, made the grant of taxation essential. The deficit was shown at 40,000 marks annually, that was the sum needed for defence and the costs of peacetime diplomacy; and the same sum, as it turned out, could be raised by doubling the rate of the wool subsidy. These figures were designed to conceal the fact that the deficit was caused not by the needs of defence but by the demands of the crown. The king set set to work refurnishing his residences: £11,000 was spent on this work in 1365–6 alone. He also built new castles, and improved the accommodation at his hunting lodges. The years of peace show that the commons paid for the war, but that the profits of war went to the king, and—to a lesser extent—to his war captains. In the 1360s at least £200,000 and possibly nearer £250,000 was paid in ransom money for the French king. This money went straight into the king's pocket. Some of the profits were ploughed back into war, particularly in money spent to establish the Black Prince in Gascony. But much also went into stone, and into more transient display. Just as the wealth of England after the Norman Conquest had gone to rebuilding the churches of Normandy, so exactly three centuries later the wealth of France was devoted to Edward's more secular tastes. The commons were deceived, but for the moment they had no quarrels to find with the king's display. The opportunities for negotiation offered by peace enabled them to consolidate the gains of the previous decade. In 1362 it was the turn of purveyance to be closely defined, a measure that followed hard on a revisitation of the plague in 1361. When Edward in the 1360s is compared with Edward in the 1330s, the consistency of his policy is clearly shown. If his measures were designed to exploit, they never became predatory, at least not upon his subjects in England. How fragile a plant public confidence was, however, the latter years of Edward III were to show.

The 1370s have been described as 'a disastrous decade', and those around the old king and his young successor were to stand hostages for a government that slowly lost public esteem and sympathy. Much was staked on the king's ability, and on the control of parliament. In 1372 Edward III was 60, an old man by the standards of the day. The political nation became increasingly uneasy, increasingly afraid for the future. The war was going badly, yet taxation was just as high as it had been in the 1340s. The king was becoming senile, and the Black Prince was obviously dying. Which Edward would survive the other? Either way, there would shortly be a minority, and minorities were dangerous, both politically and militarily. The civil service machine could cope very well without the king, but political stability could not be assured by sound administration alone. The great magnates jockeyed for position. The Speaker in the Good Parliament of 1376, the first Speaker of the commons, was to be Peter de la Mare, the steward of the earl of March. More than procedure was involved in his exchanges with John of Gaunt, who took the king's place in parliament. March, in the person of his infant son, had a strong interest in the succession to the throne should the young Richard of Bordeaux, the future Richard II, die childless. Anything could happen, for there was no law of succession to the English crown. These uncertainties were made worse by the favour shown to the king's mistress, Alice Perrers, and the smell of corruption that attached to the king's financial dealings.

All these forces, and all these fears found an outlet in the Good Parliament.[9] A knight from the south of England voiced a general complaint, that the royal revenues had been appropriated without the king's knowledge. He named no names, but others were more bold. Lord Latimer, the royal chamberlain, and Richard Lyons, a London merchant, were singled out for impeachment, a process which would bring yet more power to parliament. Parliament in effect refused to grant taxation: the wool subsidy was granted for three months, but then was not to be taken for a further three years. This striking refusal to accept their clear obligations came from a complete lack of sympathy with the tenor of government policy. In 1375 an expedition to Brittany had been abandoned, and a form of concordat made with the pope which allowed the papacy to tax the clergy on a scale without recent parallel. All this was done in the interests of peace, but it was peace at a price that the laity, left to finance an unsuccessful war on its own, could not support. A further plague in 1375 had visited a country dominated by immorality and corruption, whose great war leaders were now in physical decay, and in which the trends of successful policy had been reversed. The signs of divine disapproval were there for all to see. The Good Parliament had the extra force of self-righteousness.

Once parliament was dissolved, then the old court party reformed. It was soon able to establish a basis for the parliament of February 1377, the Bad Parliament, which would undo the work of the Good. The main discussion turned on how the king's needs might be met by taxation. There was a long debate. Some men favoured the grant of tenths and fifteenths, some a mark on the wool customs, some a hearth tax and some a new tax at fourpence a head. In the end they agreed on a tax of fourpence a head from all those over the age of fourteen. The grant of the first of the ill-fated poll taxes, against which the people were to rise four years later, is an event of some interest. The circumstances of the first grant prove that what was achieved was what was intended, the shifting of the burden of taxation from the knights of the shire to the more prosperous of the peasantry. This novel taxation proved an unfortunate legacy for the young Richard II, who succeeded his grandfather in June 1377.

The central years of Edward III's reign provided a model of harmonious government, concentrated upon the king's campaigns in France. The 1370s had shown the limits to the unity thus achieved. There remained both the divisions between the different classes and the factionalism of the magnates themselves. The reign of Richard II was one of successive crises. While the king was still a child, he faced a major social crisis in the Peasants' Revolt of 1381. When he achieved manhood, he was to preside over quarrels among the aristocracy which were to lead to a political crisis between 1397 and 1399, and his own deposition and murder. The political and social crises cannot be entirely separated. The peasants had a political programme as well as an economic one, while it was only the weakness of magnate leadership which allowed the rebellion to progress as far as it did. Similarly, at the end of the reign, Richard's dealings with the communities of the land need to be considered as well as his relationship with the earls. Each crisis focuses upon the person of the king. It is appropriate that the most famous of Shakespeare's history plays, *Richard II*, should start with the quarrel between the two earls, and with the king presiding in his court over their dispute. In the play, those who stand by, and watch the crisis unfold, range from the king's uncle, John of Gaunt, to the gardeners who watch as the king is led to his death, and John of Gaunt's son succeeds him. They utter the same warnings, of bad stewardship and bad husbandry. At the beginning of the reign it was the gardeners, and common folk, who held the centre of the stage.

On London Bridge, late in June 1381, a visitor would have found the heads of Simon Sudbury the archbishop of Canterbury, the treasurer Sir Robert Hales, prior of the order of Knights Hospitallers, John Legge a royal serjeant-at-arms, and a friar named William Appleton, physician to the duke of Lancaster. The sight of each might have seemed symbolic to those who passed by: Sudbury and Hales were the chief officers of the council responsible for advising the young king; Legge was known in Kent, whence many crossing the bridge would have come, as an unscrupulous tax-collector, while the physician was a reminder of the Londoners' long vendetta against Lancaster, and that of the community at large. At the same time at Bury St Edmunds, in the heart of East Anglia, a traveller might have seen the heads of the prior of the church and of one of the monks, and of Sir John Cavendish the chief justice of the king's bench. It was a particularly sad end for a prior, mourned in his community, who 'excelled Orpheus the Thracian, Nero the Roman and Belgabred of Britain in the sweetness of his voice and his musical skill.' In the centre of government, and in important centres of feudal lordship, those in authority had been briefly in the power of the common folk. Though few had suffered decapitation, the penalty of treason, all had been severely shaken by the experience.

On 30 May 1381 one of the special commissioners appointed to reassess the poll-tax granted by parliament the previous November came to the village of Brentwood in Essex. The villagers resisted; a hundred of them, it was said, but anyway more than enough for one justice of the peace, two policemen and three clerks. The majesty of the law was then sent, in the person of Robert Belknap, chief justice of the common pleas, but he had little more resources, and he too was despatched home, having been made to swear that he would never again hold such a session. It is interesting, and shows how 'political' the revolt was from the beginning, that it started in Essex. The poll-tax had been given by parliament in support of one named expedition, then wintering in Brittany in expectation of a spring campaign. But the situation changed, and the expedition never set off. By April Buckingham its leader was back home, and many of his followers—a good few of them from Essex—would by May have been reporting to their fellow villagers on the latest triumph of English arms. When the commissioners came to Essex to collect a new tax for an abortive campaign, they had picked the wrong area, and the wrong time. The rebels demanded that they be taxed only by the fifteenths that they knew of old, and the poll-tax was not taken again.

The men of Essex, between their two visitations, had established links via London and across the estuary with the men of Kent. They moved in concert, but it was Kent that provided the leaders. Their captain was Wat Tyler, who joined the Kentish mob at Maidstone, their chaplain John Ball, whom they released from the archbishop's prison when they got to Canterbury. On 13 June the south bank party crossed London Bridge, which was not held against them, and moved westwards through the city. They opened the Fleet prison; burned lawyers' rolls in the New Temple; beheaded lawyers, Flemings and others on Cheapside; they attacked the priory of St John in Clerkenwell, the headquarters of the Hospitallers; and with the Londoners' aid burned John of Gaunt's palace at the Savoy. Anarchy reigned in the capital, and the king and his council had to make peace as best they could. The following day, Friday 14 June, the king met the rebels at Mile End, and was received with enthusiasm. He received a list of demands that would shortly echo through the countryside—that he would hand over 'the traitors', would guarantee the abolition of villeinage, that labour services be performed on the basis of free contract, and that land should be rented at 4d an acre. Finally, they asked for a general amnesty for their actions up to that point. Thirty clerks set to work to issue charters granting freedom and an amnesty for all who came to claim it.

The king's actions at Mile End determined the later history of the revolt. As he bargained, Sudbury, Hales and others were meeting their end. Many of the rebels forthwith went home. It was only a militant rump that met the king the following day at Smithfield, when Tyler was killed. The Essex rebels were given an armed escort through London, rather as a football crowd is shepherded from the ground to the station. As they moved on, the word of the concessions at Mile End spread through the countryside. The townsmen of Cambridge rose in revolt on the Saturday that Tyler died; their targets were their lords, the university and Barnwell Priory. When the townspeople attacked the priory on Monday 17 June they were led by the mayor, who was called to account the following month. He protested that he had acted under constraint, and moreover that 'he was in doubt as to the attitude of the king'. The community of Cambridge, he said, knew that the commons of Kent, Essex, Hertfordshire and London had risen with no treasonable purpose but with the consent and knowledge of the king. A crowd of a thousand had gathered, and had issued him with an ultimatum:

> you are the mayor of our town and the governor of our community; if you will not carry out our will and command in all things enjoined on behalf of the king and his faithful commons you shall straightway be beheaded.

It is clear from this and from many similar passages that the commons kept their petty anarchy going by claiming to be acting on the king's behalf against his corrupt advisers. They claimed for themselves, and there can be no doubt that they believed that they had, the moral authority of properly constituted government.

The authority of the rebels came from a highly conservative reading of the contemporary political scene. In hunting the traitors they felt themselves part of one 'great society'. In the Cambridgeshire countryside the first attack was on a manor of the Knights Hospitallers at Chippenham, and Adam Clymme rode up and down, 'commanding all men whether bond or free as they valued their heads to cease the performance of any service or custom due to their lords, except as he might inform them on behalf of the great society.' He also proclaimed that all lawyers should be executed. The same law was to execute him a few months later. But there were others who spoke for this 'great society', among them George of Dunsby in Lincolnshire, who appeared at Bury St Edmunds and 'counselled men of the town to rise up against the lord king'. He too was executed. To the concept of a 'great society' all could attach their different aspirations. At Dunstable the chief malefactor Thomas Hobbes claimed to have come from the lord king.

> And when the lord prior enquired about the lord king's will, the said Thomas Hobbes with a fierce and menacing look replied: 'the lord king orders and requires you to give a charter of liberties to his burgesses of Dunstable like they had in the time of King Henry I.'

The prior was at first tempted to refuse, but thought of what had happened in London and St Albans and gave way. The charter, of course, 'though written in a solemn style and sealed with a great quantity of wax' did not last for long. It was cancelled when the king came to St Albans in July.

At Dunstable, Bury St Edmunds, St Albans and Peterborough, all centres of revolt, the local lords were Benedictine monks, with whom the townspeople had long been in conflict. St Albans was near enough to London for a group of townsmen to return the same night from Mile End to tell their fellows that the king had abolished serfdom and all manorial rights. They sang a few songs and went to bed. The next day they drained the abbot's fishpond, killed his game, forced him to burn his charters and to issue a charter emancipating the townsmen. Later another charter was required, which spelt out their rights of self-government. Towns of this kind, closely supervised by resident and highly conservative lords, had obtained but a fraction of the rights granted to townsmen elsewhere. They still paid fines for entry to town houses and they had to pay to grind their corn at the lord's mill. In 1318 at St Albans the townsmen tore up the mill-stones which paved the abbot's parlour, 'a witness and a memorial of an ancient plea between the villeins and the monastery', by which in 1274 the townsmen had been forced to grind their corn at the lord's mill. Their subjection was indeed a part of the fabric. In 1461 the Peterborough court leet concluded with a generalised complaint:[1]

> also we present and complain of the grievous toll that the bailiff takes of men and tenants of Peterborough in the town dwelling and in the parish, of carts and carriages, the which we think and desire by the freedom that my lord has should be free and pardoned. And thereof we pray and beseech my lord that it may be so, for we cannot think but if it be contrary it will be full ill paid; whereof we put this matter to my lord, he to be good lord to us all.

The complaint must have been echoed in several towns in the later middle ages whose residents like those of Peterborough, could only grumble and make general appeals to the concept of good lordship. There was no quarrel with that idea, but it could be interpreted in more than one way.

The revolt of 1381 spread beyond Kent, London and East Anglia. Bridgwater in Somerset, Scarborough and Beverley in Yorkshire were each originally excluded from the pardon of the November 1381 parliament. But it is the south-east which shows most clearly the geographical and ideological links between townsmen and peasants, freemen and villeins. The key to the whole episode is the excitement and confusion of the crowd which surrounded the king at Mile End. The crowd had arrived with two main ideas, that all men should be free, and that 'the traitors' should be arrested. Mile End gave them a cause. They could march under a royal banner; when shown the royal charter they could reckon themselves to be 'gentlemen of royal descent'. The world was being turned upside down. Anarchy was rife. Sir Charles Oman wrote spiritedly of events in London while the king was at Mile End: 'every form of villainy was in full swing on that dreadful Friday, from open murder down to the extortion of shillings, by dreadful threats, from clergymen and old ladies.'[2] But the political purpose was there also, for the crowd had a short list of villains, headed by the chancellor, the treasurer and John of Gaunt. All over the country the manors of the Hospitallers went up in flames, and Gaunt's local agents were singled out. That the peasantry felt themselves to be part of the political nation is clear throughout the course of the revolt.

The peasants' political aims can easily be missed. Their social objectives on the other hand, and in particular their desire for the freedom from the restraints of villeinage, have never been in doubt. It was on the outward signs of lordship, on the abbot's fish and game, that the men of St Albans vented their spleen. It was lawyers and the documents they drafted that were most in danger in the summer of 1381. Villeinage as a social system was resented, but it was the lawyers who enforced the machinery of constraint. The law which was most resented was that which regulated the movement of agricultural labourers and the wages they could take. The Black Death marked an end to an era of cheap labour in England, and necessitated adjustment in estate management. The first reaction of individual lords, natural in a time of crisis, was to carry on as before. The labour legislation which they introduced was prompt and wide-ranging. By an ordinance of 1349 and a statute of 1351, the Statute of Labourers, the government had attempted to fix wage-rates at the levels which had applied before the Black Death. All able-bodied men of under 60, with no visible means of support, would be made to work. Annual rates of pay were fixed for each different type of agricultural worker, and daily rates of pay for the different building trades. Those who had lived in one village during the winter were not to be allowed to move to another during the summer months. Men were to be kept to their occupations; and their rates of pay were to be fixed. A sweeping solution to the problem of labour supply was offered in the most conservative terms.

The legislation applied to all working men, whatever their social condition, while villeinage as such applied only to a small and dwindling number of them. An examination of some of the cases brought before justices of the peace in Suffolk, an important centre of the revolt, will help to explain the particular resentment which the statute had caused. They show the range of offences which were possible under the statute. There is a particular emphasis in these rolls on the idea of 'office', that a man was tied to his calling and should not depart from it.[3]

Nicholas atte Cros webbe has been active in enticing workmen to leave the village in autumn.

They present that John Wlnard carpenter of Cratfield refuses to work at his craft in his own village and has worked for the prioress of Flixton taking 2d and his supper each day in winter-time. He swore to keep the king's statute, but has utterly broken it.

They present that Robert le Goos labourer went to other labourers and warned and counselled them that none of them should take less than 3d and his supper for a day's work, since he himself would not take less.

They present that John Nobelot of Culpho ploughman refuses to serve in the office of ploughman because of the greater profit to be gained by working by the day.

They present that Richard Longe a good ploughman and carter has abandoned his office, and taken from William Cok of Woodbridge 20s a year and his board for weaving towels.

They say that Stephen the Ray on the Saturday before the feast of St John the Baptist in the king's 37th year took from Avicia Short for mowing three acres of meadow land 30d, 10d per acre, against the statute, where he was accustomed to take 5d an acre.

They present that Richard Sherwynd of Combs removed Simon Voysey the son of Augustine Voysey from the service of the said Augustine in the 31st year of the present king. And he did the same with several men, whom he took out of the county.

They present that Alexander Thatcher of Westleton made an agreement with the Friars Minor of Dunwich to serve them in the office of thatcher in the 37th year of the lord king, taking 15d a week and his supper, against the statute.

Item Richard Williemessore procured Robert of the fen to be a fisherman in the sea when previously he had been a ploughman, because of his cupidity for excessive reward, and thus he utterly refuses his office.

Item that John Cok of Higham was a common sawyer, and now he does not wish to serve anyone other than himself.

The cases date from between 1361 and 1364. One of the justices before whom they were heard was Reginald de Eccles. In February 1362 while carrying out his duties in Clippesby in Norfolk, he had been set upon and robbed by an armed gang, who 'threatened him with strung bows and arrows drawn to heads with instant death if he resisted.' This episode he survived, but not the Peasants' Revolt. He was seized at his lodgings on 17 June 1381 by Thomas Aslak cordwainer of Norwich and Adam Purler of Higham, dragged to the pillory, stabbed in the abdomen with a dagger and finally beheaded. Considering how many of the gentry were involved in applying the labour laws, it is surprising that as a group they fared no worse. This legislation supplied the fuel for a general rising in a way that no other issue could.

The records of the justices of labourers show the points of tension in the English countryside. It was in the autumn, when the need for hands was at its greatest and the work would not wait, that labourers could exert most pressure to secure higher wages. There are also clues as to the type of employer vulnerable to such pressure. Many of those who seem not just to be paying high wages but actually cheated were women; and minor religious houses seem to have been vulnerable also. Craftsmen, of necessity more individual than labourers, seem to have done particularly well. It would be interesting to know who was responsible for bringing most of these cases to court. With labourers it was presumably the employers, though the employing class was a large one, and did not consist simply of lords. The abbot of Meaux in Yorkshire is shown in the abbey chronicle removing labourers, who were his villeins, from the service of some wealthy peasants in Wawne, but it then appears that the wealthy peasants were his villeins also. It may not just have been the lords who protested about the craftsmen, however; the whole community would have been affected if the blacksmith put up his charges, or might have come to rely on a local craftsman who suddenly went to sea, or was enticed away to weaving in another village.

Many of those presented before the justices were 'outsiders' of various kinds, vagrants and others regarded with distaste by their peers. One such was surely John Hogyn of Stubbington in Hampshire, presented to the justices at Winchester in March 1371, who

> insulted a certain William Maistre and beat him and wounded him and did him ill against the peace of the lord king, and he is a common perturber of the peace and every day he threatens John the abbot of Titchfield and all the tenants of the abbot in their life and limbs and with burning down of their houses, and he wanders through the countryside and refuses to take employment, and he sleeps by day and is awake by night when he is at the tavern playing at the board, namely prickpenny, and where his money comes from none of his neighbours knows.

Then there were the Welshmen who appeared in the Marches. The bailiff of the Cistercian abbey of Hailes was presented in 1396 for retaining Ievan ap Gruffyn and 100 Welshmen at Evesham, Matthew Walshman and 17 others at Wormington, and Griffin ap Howell and 23 others at Hailes, Celtic combine harvesters whom the locals clearly resented being paid 8d a day for three weeks. The village blacksmith, however, can hardly be counted an outsider, and it would be wrong to think that it was only misfits and cranks who were constrained by this legislation. It bore on all men, and it gave them a common cause.

Resentment of the statute merged with a general resentment of the burdens of villeinage. In 1356 at Ware in Hertfordshire a vicar and a hermit were indicted for preaching that the statute of labourers was wicked, and that there was nothing to prevent labourers from taking what wages they pleased. Much could doubtless be made of the hermit, but the pulpit had its uses also. Shortly before the revolt John Godfray of Wiltshire made himself an adviser to various bondmen of the county, and had made for them certain extracts from Domesday Book showing that they ought to be free, 'to the serious injury of the lords and magnates of the shire and a bad example to the bondmen and other tenants in villeinage'. Petitions that came before Richard II's first parliament in 1377 mentioned such enterprise and the danger it might cause. The lords were not just fighting to retain the services of their tenants, they were fighting for their minds. In a time of pestilence and of weak government, when the manorial system was so clearly in decay, the tide was running against them. Most clearly was this shown with labour services, for unpaid service on the lord's land was the clearest sign to contemporaries of a man's servile tenure. The leasing of the demesnes, as has been shown, was far advanced by the 1370s.

In these circumstances it became more than ever important for the lords, and more than ever difficult, to keep the residual control over villeins which would keep them tied to the manor and dependent on the land. The labour legislation, framed by the lords, was seen by them as crucial to the preservation of dependent tenure and hence to a stable society as they knew it. If feeling ran high on the peasants' side, so also it did on the lords'. In the early years of labour legislation, which combined with a period of great activity in the French war, there was a strong feeling that a mobile peasantry were ducking out of obligations that all the rest of the community shared. Fines under the labour laws went towards the community's obligations towards the subsidy. In the late 1370s, in a time of peace, this interdependence could no longer be appealed to. The conflict of interest could not be disguised. With their economic demands, as with their political, the communities of the land attacked the central issues, and they chose their targets with care. The court rolls of St Albans, of Waltham Abbey in Essex, of Broomholm, Binham and Carrow priories in Norfolk, of Mettingham castle and dozens of lay estates, were burnt. So were the books of the Inner Temple, and the muniments of the university of Cambridge—'away with the learning of clerks, away with it', shouted a woman in the crowd, unaware of how little learning is to be found in most official university documents. So were the archdeacon's records at St Albans, and those of dozens of local justices. Writing was seen as an instrument of subjection; it stood for the record of services due, or of fines to be paid. The learning of clerks, of course, was needed in due season. If court rolls were burnt, charters of liberty were required, and the rebels at Mile End had to queue for pardons, written in a language they did not understand by the very class they most distrusted.

A knight from Suffolk, Sir Richard Waldegrave, was the speaker at the parliament of November 1381. In warning of the extravagance of the court and the weakness of the executive, he took up the themes of the previous decade. But he also warned of the exactions of local officials, and of the danger of renewed insurrection if remedy was not found for the people's grievances. Most of his colleagues, however, were less reflective, and more concerned to make sure that the charters granted at Mile End were made null. They complained that the king had no right to enfranchise the villeins of others, and 'they would never consent to it of their own free will, even if they all had to live and die in one day.' The king indeed was still willing to free the serfs of his kingdom when parliament met. The royal courts had started to show some sympathy with the tenants of customary land. There seems to have been a distinction here between the king on the one hand and the magnates and gentry who enjoyed lordship on the other. The royal manors, farmed from the earliest days of royal lordship, were not dependent upon servile tenure. It may well be that the division in society on the matter of villeinage went deeper than the solid front presented in parliament implied. As manors were leased out to tenants, the rights over labour went to the farmer, but the rights of justice were retained by the lord, and with them the rights to the sundry services to which the villeins were liable. The interest of the farmer in efficiency, and those of the lord in control, might pull in different ways. This divergence of interest added to the tension in the fourteenth-century countryside.

No villein gained from the events of 1381, but no lord forgot them either. The Cambridge parliament of 1388 returned to the labour legislation with renewed vigour. Higher wages were authorised in some cases, but they sought a much tighter restriction upon the movement of individuals. No servant or labourer was to be allowed to leave his village 'unless he bring a letter patent under the king's seal, which shows the cause of his going and the time of his return.' Around half a dozen of the seals made for this purpose still survive, giving the name of the county and the hundred—a couple of these are shown in Figure 12. The commons mentioned that many itinerant villeins claimed on being apprehended that they were pilgrims, and so many were the shrines that most roads could be held to lead to one of these. Pilgrimage is yet another social bond between the different regions of England. In September and October 1381 a number of men planned to rise against the king and replace him by the duke of Lancaster. They did so apparently because they had heard from pilgrims from the north of England that the duke had been liberal in granting exemptions from servile dues to his northern tenants. We cannot be sure from this report that Lancaster had taken his un- doubted unpopularity to heart, but here is yet another example that England was a single political community.

According to the French chronicler Froissart, it was the teaching of John Ball that incited the peasantry to revolt. He harangued the people in the churchyards after Mass.[4]

Figure 12 Official passes were introduced in 1388 to try to control the movement of labourers about the countryside. Their seals had to show the name of the county round the edge, and that of the hundred in the centre. Those illustrated are for South Erpingham hundred in Norfolk, and Staploe hundred in Cambridgeshire (actual size). Other such seals survive from Middlesex, Lincolnshire, Suffolk and Huntingdonshire

'Good people, things cannot go right in England and never will until goods are held in common and there are no more villeins and gentlefolk, but we are all one and the same. In what way are those whom we call lords greater masters than ourselves? How have they deserved it? Why do they hold us in bondage? If we all spring from a single father and mother, Adam and Eve, how can they claim or prove that they are lords more than us, except by making us produce and grow the wealth that they spend?'. . . Many of the common people agreed with him. Some, who were up to no good, said 'he's right', and out in the fields, or walking from one village to another, they whispered and repeated among themselves: 'that's what John Ball says, and he's right.'

He found so responsive an audience, it is clear, because he preached what had been the commonplaces of the pulpit for generations. The *Book of Sermons* of the Dominican friar John Bromyard takes the death of the rich and the vainglorious, as one of its standard themes. The rich, like the pig, were of profit only in their death.

Go, ye rich men [said another preacher], weep and howl for your miseries that shall come upon you . . . behold the hire of the labourers who have reaped down your field, which you have kept back by fraud, crieth out; and the cries of them which have reaped are entered into the ears of the lord of Sabaoth.

These men were not preaching revolt: as the last of these sermons concludes, 'be ye patient, therefore, brethren, unto the coming of the Lord.' These men were just as much conditioned to the lawfulness of earthly authority as they were accustomed to the unworthiness of many of those who exercised it. In 1381 the moral authority of the government was weak, largely as a result of the military disasters and financial scandals of the previous decade. The fate of Sudbury and Hales is clear evidence that the people thought they were agents of a tyranny. Sir John Fortescue defined later medieval ideas about tyranny when he glossed Aquinas almost a century later: 'As St Thomas says, when a king rules his realm only to his own profit and not to the good of his subjects, he is a tyrant.' Tyranny was a familiar theme in medieval political philosophy.

The Peasants' Revolt brings into a single focus many of the images of society and politics that have been shown earlier in this book. The growth of trade, the needs of warfare, and the extension of royal authority into the shires, had each in different ways integrated the communities of the land, and in so doing had broken down the natural barriers against open revolt. The crisis was a general social crisis, political as well as economic. The communities had their local grievances, strongly felt, but also general views on lordship and good government. They marched on London, for London was the centre of the court, the only place where their grievances could be heard. And the news of their doings travelled out from London, to reach the farthest parts of the land. The common people were a part of the political nation: the revolt demonstrates this point, though it had been implicit throughout the fourteenth century.

Richard II was 11 when he inherited the crown, and 33 when he was deposed, the same age that Edward I had been on his accession. Neither the king nor the secular aristocracy served any guaranteed apprenticeship in government. Clergy from aristocratic families could expect swift promotion. William Courtenay and Thomas Arundel, successive archbishops of Canterbury in Richard II's reign, were given their first dioceses when aged 28 and 21 respectively. Few reigns show more clearly than Richard II's the limitations of primogeniture. Thomas Arundel was a capable man, but his elder brother, Richard, an important political figure throughout the reign, was a boor. Around the person of the new king in the 1380s clustered a group of individuals jockeying for power. It was a young man's world, and it degenerated into vendetta and chaos. The 1390s were calmer. Richard struggled for the kind of mastery in years of peace that his predecessor had enjoyed in time of war. The control which he sought, he waited for patiently and only narrowly failed to achieve. Like Henry III, the only other boy king since the conquest, he was a man more concerned with theories of power than with practical strength. If fate was less kind to Richard than to Henry, it was because in the century between Henry's death and Richard's accession kingship had become a bigger job, and both the rewards of success and the penalties of failure had been increased.

By 1384, when the king was 18, it is possible to form a first impression of the nature of his rule. Parliamentary petitions concentrated upon the power of the royal household. They sought economy in the household, and complained of the extension of the authority of the household courts, and of the increasing use of the signet seal. The king's main advisers, Aubrey de Vere the chamberlain and Simon Burley the under-chamberlain, were attacked. There was much to remind men both of the personalities and the policies of Edward II's early years. By 1384 several magnates were suspicious of the king, and the king's volatility increased their suspicions. In the parliament of that year Arundel made a personal attack on the king, saying that his realm lacked good government. Then, according to Thomas Walsingham, a Carmelite friar reported that Gaunt was plotting the king's death. It was the friar, almost certainly mad, who suffered from the accusation. There is less evidence of Gaunt's disloyalty than of jealousy of his position. He was the richest magnate in England. He was, in English eyes, *iure uxoris* the king of Spain. A separate throne was set aside for him in parliaments, at the king's right hand. There was disagreement as to how his claim to the Spanish throne should be prosecuted. From 1380 he had been looking for Richard's support for this venture, and in 1386 he got it. Uncertainty of magnate policy was combined with popular distrust of government. Early in 1385 the archbishop of Canterbury complained that the royal court was a centre of intrigue, and that those responsible for it were threatening 'the laws and customs of the kingdom'. In Courtenay's view, the weakness of the court was a threat to the whole community.

Between 1386 and 1388, as Courtenay had feared, the instability of the court came to threaten the political stability of the whole nation. In 1386 the earl of Gloucester and Bishop Arundel spoke for the whole parliament in criticising the king and his entourage. The themes were the familiar ones, but now their talk had a cutting edge to it. Evil counsellors were held to be responsible for the miseries of a land reduced to poverty by heavy taxation, and 'by ancient statute and recent precedent the commons had a remedy.' The king was barely out of his teens when the threat of deposition was made against him. He had a further council set over him, similar to those which had governed him in his early years, and it was told to seek out 'the defaults and offences of the household officers, whereby the profit of the crown has been diminished or the law disturbed'. Reform of the household became the issue of the hour, and the new council was given a year in which to accomplish the task. It was part of the strength of the household, however, that it was mobile. The king's reaction to a threat which went to the heart of his own power was to take to the country, and while away from London and the parliament to build up his resources and reassert his prerogative.

But how strong were the foundations on which he sought to build? London may have been a difficult environment, but it was the capital city and the centre of royal power, and in turning his back on it at a time of crisis, Richard was turning his back also on several centuries of political development. He sought instead to build up his authority in Chester and in North Wales. In 1387 he was able to recruit a large army from the resources of the earldom. But it was in a sense a private army. In seeking to establish an army in Chester, he was behaving like a magnate, and a parvenu at that. When Chester was captured in 1399, he had no other base from which to fight:

> Your uncle York is joined with Bolingbroke;
> And all your northern castles yielded up,
> And all your southern gentlemen in arms,
> Upon his party.

Scroop had said enough; as individuals fell away, so did the castles, and the regions which they controlled. All that was in the future in 1387. The king was building castles in the air. He sent for the justices, and asked for a legal definition of his power. He got one, in response to the famous 'questions' which he put to the justices at Shrewsbury and Nottingham in August. The first question elicited the answer that the statute appointing the last council, the commission council, 'derogated from the regality and prerogative of the lord king'. It was further established that all those responsible for the statute were liable to death, and that those who had forced the king to accept it were liable to the penalties of treason. A more general series of questions defined royal rights over the business of parliament, that it met at the king's will, did the king's business, and had no rights over the king's ministers. The royal tone in 1387 was uncompromising; it too had a cutting edge. More than this, in his insistence both on the landed and the theoretical bases of his power, Richard sought to map out a new political landscape. And yet outside Chester in 1387, so the sheriffs reported to the king, the common people supported the barons. The monarchy could only be strong if it drew upon the resources and the support of the communities of the land.

The crisis turned, though only briefly, to civil war. In November the nucleus of what was to be the appellant party, the duke of Gloucester and the earls of Arundel and Warwick, had faced the king. In December the earls of Derby and Nottingham joined them, and the five defeated de Vere at the battle of Radcot Bridge on 20 December 1387. It was as a military coalition, which had defeated the king's army with ease, that they came before parliament in February 1388 ready to throw the charge of treason back against their opponents. Eight men were executed, including the chief justice of the king's bench, Sir Simon Burley and three other chamber knights, while Pole and de Vere were condemned to death in their absence. The other justices who had been questioned by the king lost their lands and were banished to Ireland. Not only was the parliament 'merciless', however, it was highly confused. The case of Nicholas Brembre, mayor of London, was sent to a group of four magnates and eight barons who reported that they could find nothing in his record which merited the death penalty. The appellants were also divided over the execution of Burley; Derby, Nottingham and many lords demanding that he be spared. The commons insisted on his death, supported by the threat of a rising in Kent, where Burley had a landed base but none of the loyalty and support which might have gone with it. Parliament could be no stronger than the court, and in 1388 it was ruled by the arbitrary will of a small group of magnates.

In May 1389 at Westminster the king resumed his power. He stated that since his coronation he had been ruled by others, and the kingdom had been heavily taxed. The commons were happy to be convinced, and the court reasserted itself with some ease. The return of Gaunt in the autumn of 1389 was a further force making for stability, and his son Henry Bolingbroke betook himself to tournaments and to a modified version of the Grand Tour. If in the 1380s it had been the magnates who had taken the initiatives, in the 1390s it was to be the king. He sought first to reverse the work of 1388, and in this he succeeded; and also to go further, in which he failed. The early 1390s saw some accommodation on Richard's part, and little opposition to his domestic policy. There was peace with the French, largely due to Gaunt's statesmanship, and a successful military expedition to Ireland. The Irish expedition of 1394 quelled the opposition of the native chiefs, particularly of Leinster, to the Anglo-Irish within the pale. This was a rare success in the consolidation of Plantagenet lordship over the British Isles; the knighting of the chiefs provided both pageantry and a splendid propaganda exercise. Parliament was pleased: in 1395 it congratulated Richard, and provided him with a tenth and a fifteenth. Negotiations for a permanent peace with the French had been in progress since 1390, and a truce was finally agreed in March 1396, intended to last for twenty-eight years.

The reign ends in some confusion. A royalist coup at a council in 1397 led to the arrest of the three senior appellants, who were appealed in their turn by a group of eight lords, including their former colleague Thomas Mowbray. The sole charges against them related to events ten years before. If Richard did not want revenge, he certainly wanted to fight old battles; and the difference between these two propositions seems not to be very significant. Gloucester was murdered in Calais before the proceedings had begun against him in parliament. Arundel took his stand on his two earlier pardons, but they availed him nothing, and he was executed. Warwick broke down, confessed his guilt, and was exiled to the Isle of Man. From this conspicuous personal triumph for the king, two lines of argument will be followed—the first concerns the king's attitude to government, the second his treatment of the two remaining appellants. According to the chronicler Thomas Walsingham, who wrote at St Albans and who reflected baronial attitudes, it was in the summer of 1397 that Richard began to tyrannise his people. Seventeen out of the thirty-three deposition articles were concerned with events of the period 1396 to 1399. The force comes from their being taken together: individually there was little for which precedent could not have been found in the political history of the previous two centuries. The concern with past history became increasingly important as the fourteenth century progressed. The tyranny of Richard II was an exercise in antiquarianism.

The parliament of 1397 had granted a general pardon to all, 'except for fifty people whom the king would not name for the present'. The king was prepared to offer pardons to individuals, though they had of course no means of knowing whether or not they were on the king's 'little list'. Thomas Fitz Nicole paid £100 and then £50, 'for residing with Richard earl of Arundel', and Richard Crowe £13 because he had been retained by the earl, while a London mercer was brought to book for having ridden with the condemned lords. From such relationships alone might guilt have been presumed. Some were given the security of having their pardons entered on the Patent Rolls. The majority of the pardons, however, survive upon a couple of special pardon rolls, which record the granting of pardons to the astonishing number of 596 people between October 1397 and September 1398. The fines for pardon may have brought in around £30,000, and the money was certainly useful; but such sums were available from parliament following normal procedures. What Richard wanted was the control over individuals. He sought to add to this similar powers over whole communities. Seventeen counties were induced to seal the famous 'blank charters', which acknowledged treason and evil deeds against the king and submitted to his pleasure. One of the chroniclers reported the form of words in these charters as follows: 'because before your time we have grievously offended your majesty, we submit ourselves and all our goods to your will.'[5] The king felt it necessary to make special provision for the security of these rolls before he went to Ireland early in 1399. They had in some way become central to his kingship.

On any reading of previous English history, and by any standards of previous political competence, it would be difficult to exaggerate the ineptitude of such behaviour. John's reign showed fairly clearly that monarchs could pick off individual magnates, that the king's 'wrath and ill-will' could be exercised quite openly against a few. What he could not do was even to appear to threaten whole communities or the general interests of the lords. The point at which an individual feels that the next knock will be on his own door is the point at which, for him, the basic nature of politics changes. Procedures which offered security now threaten insecurity and danger. The long list of names shows this happening very clearly in the period 1397 to 1399; and this uncertainty, dominated by the king's will, men called tyranny. It was the more dangerous in being founded not on present relationships, which men can alter, but on the past, which they cannot. The battle of Radcot Bridge was a defeat that Richard could not exorcise. In the autumn of 1398 four thousand marks had been sent to Chester abbey to be distributed to the men of Chester who had fought at Radcot Bridge. For what Richard regarded as a criminal injury there was this local compensation board. The men of Chester could profit from reliving old times and rediscovering old scars: those of the rest of England could only be haunted by such memories. In the last few years of Richard II's reign there was a mixture of incompetence and morbid political imbalance which has something of the flavour of Watergate.

There was none the less no prospect of a spontaneous rising, of the kind that had taken place in 1381, against what for most people was a threat that could be redeemed by a fine. The political impetus of the later years of the reign is supplied by the king's relationship with the appellants. After 1397 there were two at large, Thomas Mowbray and Henry Bolingbroke. The quarrel between the two junior appellants, the beginning of Shakespeare's play, can now be seen as but the most striking example of the insecurity that so many in the realm shared. At parliament in 1398 Bolingbroke appeared and retailed a conversation he had had with Mowbray while riding from the village of Brentford to London.[6] 'We are all about to be undone', said Mowbray. 'Why?' said Bolingbroke. 'For what was done at Radcot Bridge', came the reply. There were many rumours, one of them of a plot against Gaunt. Bolingbroke told his father; his father told the king. The outcome was that Mowbray was banished for life, and Bolingbroke for ten years. Whatever the political sense of Richard's actions, these punishments were inflicted by due process. In February 1399, however, Gaunt died, and the question arose of whether the exiled Bolingbroke should inherit. The matter was settled, abruptly and quite improperly by altering the parliament roll, banishing Bolingbroke for life and declaring the whole estate forfeit to the crown. Whatever the position had been when he sailed, Bolingbroke now had a grievance, which he could not legally pursue in his own lifetime.

Kings had dealt arbitrarily with individuals before, and would do so again. The sequestration of the Lancastrian inheritance cannot be made into a horrific example of an arbitrary action standing against centuries of proper procedure. The king took a gamble. Could the new principality of Chester stand against the resources and the traditions of the house of Lancaster? The outcome was not long in doubt. Richard was in Ireland, re-visiting the scene of his early triumphs, when Bolingbroke landed at Ravenspur. Near Doncaster, in the heartland of the Lancastrian estate, he was joined by Henry Percy earl of Northumberland and his son Henry 'Hotspur'. Chester was occupied by the Lancastrian forces before Richard could get back. Hopelessly outnumbered and cut off at Conway, Richard was given terms. His crown, he was assured, was not in danger. All would be forgiven if Bolingbroke was restored to the Lancastrian inheritance, if parliament was summoned, and five members of the council were surrendered for trial. Northumberland swore on the host that Richard should retain his throne. They were all forsworn. Richard was ambushed before ever he reached Flint castle. He was taken in captivity to London. He resigned his throne under duress on 29 September; and on 30 September the commons and the estates renounced their fealty.

Though not the first deposition of the middle ages, let alone the first major revolt, the Lancastrian succession represents the first change of dynasty with which this book has been concerned. It is important to examine the terms on which it was effected, and the degree of discontinuity which was involved. If we are looking for development, we have to assess whether the development of kingship was affected in any way by the events of 1399.

Henry claimed the crown of England, which he had secured by

force, by right, as a direct descendant of Henry III through his younger son Edmund. A theory that Edmund had in fact been the elder brother of Edward I was rejected. The Lancastrians had long held an individual view of English history, but even in 1399 they could not make so transparent a falsehood stick. It all added to the confusion, which possibly was the intention. Bolingbroke claimed by Conquest also, 'through that right which God of his grace hath sent me with the help of my kin and my friends to recover it.' And he continued, by way of comment on the previous regime rather than to explain his conquest, that the realm 'was in point to be undone by default of governance and the undoing of the good laws.' The detail of this claim shows up what will be the problems of the early years. He had a strong landed base, which had given his ancestors Thomas of Lancaster and John of Gaunt a strength which none of their contemporaries could equal. From it his family and his friends had toppled Richard with surprising ease. He had to reward them, in the situation of a conquest, and yet not seem to threaten the 'good laws'. He had to choose the ground of action and inaction with care; 'default of governance', after all, was at best an incomplete comment on Richard II's last years.

By excepting from his general protection 'those persons that have been against the good purpose and common profit of the realm' he left to his first parliament, which met in October, considerable scope for punishment and retribution. The provisions of the parliament of 1397–8 were annulled; and the commons set out to discover the villains. Had they had the king's support, many could doubtless have been found. But the very confusion and distrust which gave him his opportunity might easily have become a threat to his own title. Henry was happy in the end to accept that William Scrope, Bussey and Green (the latter two already dead) had been 'responsible for all the ill that had come to the kingdom'. There was wisdom in having so selective a memory. The appellants of 1397 lost only their titles, not their lands, and remained to be judged by their future not their past actions. Within four months of Henry's accession, the first rising had been put down, Richard had been killed, and Henry returned to London in triumph. The heads of his opponents, carried in sacks or mounted on poles, preceded him for display in the city of London. Three of the earls had been lynched without judgment, in Cirencester and in Bristol. Even well away from the traditional centres of Lancastrian authority, popular opinion had no time for any plot which sought to release the old king. In that support may well have lain the difference between success and failure in the early months of Henry IV's reign.

Henry had however only got by with a little bit of help from his friends. Their aspirations were to prove a more serious and more enduring threat to his power. The three Percies were the most prominent of these: Henry Percy, earl of Northumberland, his son Henry 'Hotspur', and Thomas the earl's brother. All had military experience; the father indeed had been active in the field before Richard II had been born. They had held the wardenship of the Scottish marches all but continuously from 1383 to 1403. To this the new king added control over Cheshire and north Wales, thus giving the Percies control over the centres of Richard's old power. The two brothers were much at the king's side in the early years. In April 1402 the contract for the king's marriage was witnessed by one bishop, the earl of Somerset, and the three Percies. Neither their treatment, however, nor their northern base set them apart from their peers. Ralph earl of Westmorland, the head of the house of Neville, had a marcher authority which could rival the Percies' own. The Lancastrian estates, and the monarchy's popular support, stood as a powerful reserve.

The first Percy rising was in April 1403, when, according to Adam of Usk, 'on behalf of the crown of England, claimed for the earl of March . . . a deadly quarrel arose between the king and the house of Percy of Northumberland.' What had caused this break-down, so sudden and dramatic, is not clear. Contemporaries felt that the Percies, having seen the success of king-making, aimed to become kings in their turn. A chronicler reports that at the battle of Shrewsbury Hotspur's troops chanted 'Henry Percy King'. A good slogan, but Hotspur was killed that day, and his uncle captured and executed. The earl's life was spared by Henry, and he came to make his submission at York, where his son's head stood as a reproach and a warning on Micklegate bar. The earl's power base was attenuated, but not his ambition to overthrow the king. In 1405 he was implicated in another rising, this time led by Archbishop Scrope of York and involving a wide variety of the local clergy and laity. They conducted a paper war of some skill, as befitted their order. A manifesto was fixed to the doors of churches and posted about the town, much as election posters would be today. It complained first of the impossible burdens suffered by the clergy. It moved on to complain of the subjection and annihilation bearing upon the secular lords contrary to their rights of birth and their position in the country.

Finally, it complained of innumerable taxes and subsidies which burdened men of property, the merchants and the commons, and of too much government intervention. The phrase has a curiously modern ring to it, and marks a development in political debate. Yet what was most remarkable was the coherence of the programme, and in particular the idea that popular opinion might be mobilised through complaints that the government was attacking the propertied classes. In part this was because such ideas as 'the destruction of the lords' were traditional slogans not analytical concepts; but there was more to it than that. Medieval England was very far from being a classless society, but it had something very close to a classless politics.

Only in a major and a cathedral city could a clerical protest be made to stick, but its involvement with treason compromised it fatally. Scrope was executed just outside his city, though the lawyers would have spared his life. Henry probably felt particularly strongly that the moral authority of the clergy, once harnessed against him, offered a threat that could rapidly destroy his title to rule. The earl of Northumberland, implicated but not involved in the rising, lived to fight again; he was defeated at the battle of Bramham Moor in 1408. It was the events of 1405 that secured the position of Henry IV, and he owed much of his security to the support of Ralph Nevill, earl of Westmorland. And with the forfeitures of the early years, Henry's landed base was more than ever secure. In the north he could consolidate his family's landed base; to the west he continued his predecessor's policy of developing the Welsh marches as a centre of royal power. The period from the thirteenth to the early fifteenth century sees the rise and the fall of the Marcher dominance of English politics. A mixture of care with land and some generosity to individuals marked the early rebellions of Henry IV's reign with a distinctive stamp, which was clearly that of Henry himself. It has been said that he was too lenient for his own security. This is doubtful. He was successful. More than this, his policy was calculated, if only slowly, to remove much of the fear and recrimination from English political life. If leniency encouraged the Percies to hope for success, it lessened the desire of their peers to join in. The Percies stood for a continuation of the policies of the 1390s. They got little enough support. Politics is a matter of mood. Henry IV captured that mood very well.

It was a sign of general confidence, as well as of the commons' relief, that parliament was so generous with taxation in Henry IV's reign. This support was crucial, for political without financial stability would have been much more difficult to achieve. The commons continued to battle, tenaciously but not vindictively, over ground which had been in dispute for generations. The redress of grievances before supply was asked for by the commons in 1401 more in hope than in expectation. They could, however, look for some progress in supervising the collection and spending of the revenues they had granted, and in demanding a proper account. 'Kings were not wont to render account', said Henry, but tunnage and poundage was only voted in 1406 on condition that parliament audited the accounts for 1404. The king did not make an issue of the rare reverses of this kind. In the main he found the commons firm defenders of the royal estate, and anxious to avoid his displeasure. Not only the legacy of Richard's reign but also the commons' attitudes to monarchy can be seen in one of the petitions of 1401, in which they asked pardon, 'if they or any one of them had through ignorance or negligence done anything in word or deed against the royal estate which might in any way be displeasing to his royal person.' Henry IV's parliaments ran over familiar ground, and they judged issues not individuals. The memory of the past was both Henry's weakness and his strength.

From the 1370s an increased importance attached to the king's Council, as a body through which the community might seek to control the king. An Ordinance on the Council, dated 1390, had assumed that the Council would meet daily to conduct the routine business of government. It stated that no gift of land or revenue should be made without the Council's approval. In this way, through the Council, the political community sought to achieve a long-standing ambition, to control the king's use of patronage. The Council, though appointed by the king and answerable to him and not to parliament, achieved a measure of independence through its control over routine and through the commons' support. In the Long Parliament of 1406 they sought actually to transfer power to the Council: 'In all matters the king should govern through the advice of his councillors and trust them.' The Council was strong, and it was to grow still further in its strength, because it in a measure institutionalised the traditional taking of counsel by the king. With Henry IV's ill-health and his son's absences abroad, it was the Council which governed England. In 1406 it was established for the first time that all councillors were to be paid, a sure sign of professional standing.

When at the beginning of his reign Henry IV had met the request that he make no grants save with the advice of his Council, he had reserved his position with the phrase 'saving his liberty'. He spoke of his liberties, just as the baronage two centuries earlier had spoken of theirs, when in 1215 'the barons for their liberties came to the king'. The idea had not changed its content: a man's liberty was the complex of lands and rights, the whole position in the world, which he had inherited from his ancestors, and which he had in turn to pass on to his heirs. After the change of dynasty in 1399, the protection of the royal estate was Henry IV's main charge. After 1408, when the military threats against him had largely been removed, he still had to struggle for legitimacy. His ill-health reproached him with his sins, but there was no turning back, 'for my children will not suffer the regalia to go out of our lineage.' Much has been made of Henry IV's quarrels and reconciliation with his son, and Shakespeare no more than followed the tradition established by Henry V's contemporaries. The young Henry first appears as a royal councillor in 1408, and thereafter he was a leading figure in his father's court. The disagreements were within the Council, and over policy, in particular over policy in France. In 1412 rumours were current that he sought to depose his father, and rule in his stead. The community was divided over the conduct of the French war, and legend had already started to gather about the person of the young Henry. When he did succeed his father in March 1413, he had to ensure that legend and rumour would be his servant and not his master, and that the legitimacy of his dynasty should shine forth before the world.

Such considerations of policy, as well as his undoubted piety and military ardour, explain Henry V's preoccupations during his reign, with the maintenance of religious orthodoxy, and the prosecution of his rights within France. Each of these in different ways stressed his legitimacy, and his following of the traditions of the English monarchy. It was for military victory, and in particular for the great battle at Agincourt, that he is best remembered. But the unknown clerk, who wrote early in the reign of *The Deeds of Henry the Fifth*, started rather with Henry's treatment of the Lollards, and the rising of Sir John Oldcastle. John Oldcastle was a Herefordshire knight who had served in the Welsh wars in the forces of prince Henry. He had attained baronial rank through marriage, and an estate centred on Cooling Castle in Kent, in what was very far from being an area of weak lordship. Oldcastle's manifest heresy was referred to the new king in the early months of his reign, and only after a personal appeal from Henry was the archbishop of Canterbury given leave to act. Oldcastle was condemned as a heretic, escaped from custody, and set to work to organise a force which was to capture the king and establish a new government. A group of men disguised as mummers were to capture the king at Eltham in Kent, and supporters would come from the four quarters of the kingdom to take over London. Treason on such a scale could hardly be kept secret; the mummers did not get beyond London, and the forces from the shires were cut down as they approached St Giles's Fields. Around 70 men were captured and immediately executed. It was to be the autumn of 1417 before Oldcastle himself was captured and executed. The whole rising seems in retrospect a rather pathetic episode, but so also might the revolt of 1381 have appeared to have been, had it been met with equal vigour.

The king's concern for true religion was further publicly demonstrated by his foundation of two new religious houses, one Carthusian and the other Bridgettine, the last religious houses to be founded in medieval England. The Carthusian house was founded at the royal manor of Sheen, a favoured residence of Richard II, to whose memory Henry V was devoted, and whose bones he had transferred to Westminster Abbey. The Bridgettine house migrated in the same area, and came to reside on the site of what is now Syon House. Here, in what is still one of the pleasantest areas of west London, was the moral centre of Henry V's monarchy:

> Two chantries, where sad and solemn priests
> Sing still for Richard's soul.

By these foundations the Lancastrians also atoned for the execution of Archbishop Scrope, a penance enjoined on Henry IV when he was pardoned by the pope for this act in 1408. Henry V showed a general concern also for the health of the monastic order in England. In 1421 several hundred Benedictines were summoned to London to hear a sermon from the king on the original purity of the monastic life. His royal ancestors, the monks were told, had put their trust, as had the other founders of houses, in the value of prayers offered by men of austere life. Let them look to the past. Henry V here reflected a general interest, current in monastic circles for the previous century, in the origins of monasticism. It was all part of the general historical awareness in fourteenth century England. In a sense Henry V brought together the historical interests of the whole community, and harnessed them to his own ends.

Though he started with the king's protection of true religion, the author of *The Deeds of Henry the Fifth* rapidly moved on to war.[7] He had been with the king at Agincourt, 'sitting on a horse among the baggage at the rear of the battle'. Henry V was to spend five and a half years in France, as had his predecessor Richard I. Henry stressed from the time of his accession that he sought 'the peace and tranquillity of kingdoms, and especially (because they were more closely connected and associated) the peace and tranquillity of the two kingdoms of England and France'. But peace could only be secured with justice, and justice involved acceptance of the king's rights. An embassy sent in March 1415 required, with some modifications, the lands allowed by the treaty of Brétigny in 1360. Before this delegation set out, preparations for war were well advanced. The king crossed over to Normandy, 'in order first to recover his duchy of Normandy, which belongs to him entirely by a right dating from the time of William the first, the Conqueror'. He sought first to take Harfleur, off which the Norman dynasty had foundered in the White ship disaster of 1120. The siege of Harfleur occupied much of the summer of 1415. When it fell, Henry had the town muniments and all title-deeds to property burnt in the market-place; only English immigrants were allowed to inherit property, and the French became in effect tenants-at-will. Henry was a man much concerned with the keeping of proper records. He had a whole series of books made, of former treaties and of documents relating to title; and the chronicler wrote as though his readers would have access to these 'books of royal evidences and records'. The king fought a paper war of some skill, appealing to opinion in Europe, as well as to his own people, sending in English details of his progress to the Londoners.

He pressed on, even though winter was approaching, to march through Normandy to Calais. It was towards the end of this journey that he was intercepted by the French, and secured the engagement which probably he had looked for. The battle of Agincourt could not settle the war, but it more than amply justified Henry's policy, and established his title to rule. The English claimed that the battle was the third and a decisive divine judgment on the justice of the king's cause. The first had been the naval battle at Sluys (1340), 'in the time of the most famous king the last king Edward', the second Poitiers (1356), fought by 'the most famous prince Edward, his first-born son and heir', and the third was Agincourt. There was no mention of Crécy. It was the unfinished work of Edward III that Henry V sought to complete. All this had been done in less than three years from the king's accession:

no evidence is to be found in the chronicles or annals of kings of which our long history makes mention, that any king of England ever achieved so much in so short a time and returned home with so great and glorious a triumph.

The triumphal return to London will be considered shortly, but first it is necessary to consider the degree to which Henry was able to build upon military victory.

Between 1417 and 1419 Henry V conquered Normandy, starting from a base in the centre of the duchy and then moving first west and then east as so many of its earlier invaders had done. For the rest of the reign, the king was on the offensive within France. After the conquest, the English war captains took lands and titles in Normandy, as the Normans had done in reverse, three and a half centuries earlier, in the years after 1066. The sixty or so castles of Normandy were placed under English control. A military and a civil administration were established, on the basis of these castles and the Norman *baillages* (the administrative districts), and considerable reserves of manpower were needed for their maintenance. The English now had a second and more prosperous duchy, and a base from which they could advance on Paris. The French sued for peace. In 1420, by the Treaty of Troyes, a federation of England and France was envisaged, under the control of the house of Lancaster. Henry was made 'heir' to the kingdom of France. Each kingdom was to remain independent of the other, and to be governed by its own laws. But the French king's son, the dauphin, cut out of the succession, retained control over large parts of France. Henry was condemned to siege warfare, and at the siege of Meaux he contracted the illness from which he died. The dauphin was to rule France as Charles VII, 'the king of Bourges', and to drive the English out of France. The treaty of 1420, made at the time of Henry's greatest triumph, had yet recognised the existence of two nations. Though for a time Henry V recaptured much of the territory of the Angevin Empire that John had lost, the new regime lacked the Anglo-French personnel and the traditions which might have given it a meaning in the lives of those who would have to pay and to fight for its continuance.

When England in 1175 is compared with England in 1425, little enough seems to have changed on the surface. At both dates the English had a base in France, which they were to lose within the lifetimes of many of those who were then adult. The ways that Englishmen had made their living had not changed. Population

levels were the same, though in the intervening period they had
fluctuated markedly. The families of kings, and the greater aristocracy, pursued their private quarrels. England was led by her kings,
and governed by the great clerical officers of state. Hubert Walter,
started in 1175 on a career that would take him to Canterbury, and
Henry Chichele, who was his successor in 1425, were men in the
same mould. And yet they, and the kings who were set over them,
lived in two very different worlds. England in the intervening period
had become, from a land of small regions and of private rights, a
single community. Kings and government would ignore those
regions and those rights at their peril. But they came together,
through trade, through parliament and through the pursuit of war,
much more frequently than they had before. Ideas of representation
and community were current throughout the period; immediately
before it they are met rarely, and after it they are almost commonplace. It was the king who provoked much of the discussion. He
claimed authority over the whole kingdom, to legislate and to have
his orders obeyed. 'The king and his legitimate orders and instructions, must be fully obeyed by each and every man, great and small,
in the realm'—thus the Dictum of Kenilworth, the arbitration of a
group of magnates, in 1265. What was legitimate could be discussed,
but there the discussion ended. As government became more professional, and as shortly thereafter warfare became a regular charge
on the community, so those orders and instructions went out more
frequently. As the pace increased, and the community came together
more often, men looked increasingly, for security and for legitimacy,
to England's past history. There was a single political community,
overlying the other communities of the land, and like any community it needed its focus, and it had its moods. The focus was the
king.

Triumph and pageantry, the ritual of kingship, emphasised
monarchy as representing the community of the land. After Henry
V's victory at Agincourt the Londoners, at short notice, put on a
pageant of great magnificence.[8] The ideas, the themes of monarchy
and of national unity, came to them ready-made, and doubtless they
were rehearsed on many other less magnificent and less well-
recorded occasions. The king was met at Blackheath by the mayor
and aldermen and citizens, all of them wearing 'a richly fashioned
badge which conspicuously distinguished the crafts one from
another'. He was led over the bridge, welcomed by the giants which
defended the jurisdictions of the cities of northern Europe, and on

into the streets of London. The streets were sumptuously decked out, the figures and the characters finely arrayed. And the pageant was planned as a unity. Each group of figures had their texts. Each text pointed a moral. At Cornhill there were the arms of the royal house, and displayed prominently beneath them, 'the arms of St George, St Edward, St Edmund and of England'. A company of prophets, in tunicles and white capes, released sparrows and other small birds as the king passed by, and the birds, doubtless well schooled in their turn, descended on the king's breast and settled upon his shoulders. Thence to Cheapside, and more coats of arms:

> And under an awning were men of venerable old age in the garb and of the number of the apostles, having the names of the twelve apostles written in front of them, together with twelve kings of the English succession, martyrs and confessors, girt about the loins with golden belts, with sceptres in their hands, crowns upon their heads, and their emblems of sanctity plain for all to see, who, at the king's approach, in perfect time and in sweetly sounding chants, sang the psalm: 'Save us from those who afflict us, and confound our enemies.'

Further on, on his way to St Paul's, the king passed a tower in which various niches had been cunningly constructed, 'and in each one was a most exquisite young maiden', and these 'with gentlest breath, scarcely perceptible, puffed out round leaves of gold on the king's head as he passed by.' It was quite a show, and the city was packed to see it. In the city, with the clergy who welcomed the king at St Paul's and Westminster Abbey, with the great men and their ladies who watched the procession pass by, and with the gildsmen and the maidens with walk-on parts, each of them 'following their text', there was symbolised on that day not only the glory of kingship and the favour of God, but the unity under God and the king of the whole community of the land.

Appendix

The figures below show the movement of prices of wool and grain between 1209 and 1448, and the changes in the price of labour during the same period. The figures *for wool* are in shillings per stone; those *for wheat* are in shillings per quarter of grain; and those *for wages*, the product of a more complicated calculation, the rates in pence for threshing and winnowing three rased quarters of wheat, barley and oats on certain manors of the bishopric of Winchester.

Table 3

Year	Wool	Wheat	Year	Wages
1209–18	1.93	3.22	1210–19	2.96
1219–28	2.04	4.71	1220–9	3.51
1229–38	2.92	3.81	1230–9	3.13
1239–48	3.04	4.64	1240–9	3.25
1249–58	2.65	4.66	1250–9	3.30
1259–68	3.61	3.95	1260–9	3.37
1269–78	4.16	6.26	1270–9	3.45
1279–88	4.56	5.28	1280–9	3.62
1289–98	4.05	6.15	1290–9	3.57
1299–1308	4.73	4.94	1300–9	3.85
1309–18	4.79	8.60	1310–19	4.05
1319–28	5.51	6.40	1320–9	4.62
1329–38	3.85	5.41	1330–9	4.92
1339–48	3.53	4.90	1340–9	5.03
1349–58	2.96	6.77	1349–59	5.18
1359–68	3.58	6.78	1360–9	6.10

Year	Wool	Wheat	Year	Wages
1369–78	4.90	7.81	1370–9	7.00
1379–88	3.83	4.83	1380–9	7.22
1389–98	3.37	5.08	1390–9	7.23
1399–1408	3.92	5.70	1400–9	7.31
1409–18	3.99	6.27	1410–19	7.35
1419–28	3.21	4.98	1420–9	7.34
1429–38	3.72	6.17	1430–9	7.30
1439–48	3.36	5.89	1440–9	7.33

The figures given are for the average prices during decades stated, which differ by a year as between prices and wages.

Sources

For wool and wheat prices: T. H. Lloyd, *The Movement of Wool Prices in Medieval England* (*Economic History Review* supplement no. 6, 1973), Table 4, p. 50.

For wages: W. Beveridge, 'Wages in the Winchester Manors', *Economic History Review*, 7 (1936–7), pp. 22–43 (table on p. 38). For a guide to subsequent work on medieval wages, see the references and discussion in A. R. Bridbury, 'The Black Death', *Economic History Review*, 2:26 (1973), pp. 581–4.

Notes

CHAPTER 1 THE DEVELOPMENT OF ENGLISH SOCIETY

1 Printed in A. R. Myers (ed.), *English Historical Documents*, 4 (London, 1969), pp. 62–3.
2 W. W. Shirley (ed.), *Royal and other Historical Letters illustrative of the Reign of Henry III*, 1 (Rolls Series, 27, 1862), pp. 247–312, *passim*.
3 G. D. G. Hall (ed.), *The Treatise on the Laws and Customs of the Realm of England commonly called Glanvill* (London, 1965), p. 42.
4 H. Hall (ed.), *Red Book of the Exchequer*, 1 (Rolls Series, 99, 1896), pp. 230, 400.
5 H. E. Butler (ed.), *The Chronicle of Jocelin of Brakelond* (London, 1949), p. 12. The Bury election in King John's reign is described in R. M. Thomson (ed.), *The Chronicle of the Election of Hugh, Abbot of Bury St Edmunds and later Bishop of Ely* (Oxford, 1974).

CHAPTER 2 POPULATION AND SETTLEMENT

1 J. C. Russell, *British Medieval Population* (Albuquerque, 1948), pp. 180–5.
2 M. W. Beresford and J. G. Hurst, article on Wharram Percy in *Medieval Settlement*, ed. P. H. Sawyer (London, 1976).
3 H. E. Hallam, *The New Lands of Elloe* (Leicester University occasional papers in local history no. 6, 1954), p. 38.
4 H. E. Hallam, 'Population density in medieval fenland', *Economic History Review*, 2:14 (1961–2), pp. 71–81. Cf. Joan Thirsk, in *The Agrarian History of England and Wales, 1500–1640*, 4 (Cambridge, 1967), pp. 38–40.
5 J. Z. Titow, 'Some evidence of thirteenth century population increase', *Economic History Review*, 2:14 (1961–2), pp. 218–24; M. M. Postan and Titow, 'Heriots and prices on Winchester manors', in M. M. Postan, *Essays on Medieval Agriculture* (Cambridge, 1973), p. 172.

CHAPTER 3   LORDSHIP AND WEALTH

1 K. B. McFarlane, *The Nobility of Later Medieval England* (Oxford, 1973), p. 200.

2 E. A. Kosminsky, *Studies in the Agrarian History of England in the Thirteenth Century* (Oxford, 1956), pp. 203–6.

3 W. G. Hoskins, *The Midland Peasant* (London, 1957), p. 42.

4 C. Johnson (ed.), *Dialogus de Scaccario* (London, 1950), p. 30.

5 R. H. Hilton, 'Freedom and villeinage in England', *Past and Present*, 31 (1965), p. 13.

6 *Curia Regis Rolls*, 12, no. 1031.

7 P. D. A. Harvey, *A Medieval Oxfordshire Village. Cuxham 1240 to 1400* (Oxford, 1965), p. 72; the Cuxham records are printed in Harvey, *Manorial Records of Cuxham, Oxfordshire, circa 1200–1359* (Oxfordshire Record Society, 50, 1976).

8 Figures for the movement of prices will be found in the Appendix.

9 G. A. Holmes, *The Estates of the Higher Nobility in Fourteenth-Century England* (Cambridge, 1957), p. 117. The idea that servility was in the blood had been a familiar one in western Europe since at least 1300. There were two explanations, one biblical and the other racial, for the origins of 'nobility'. The biblical rested on an exegesis of the story of the three sons of Noah, and the racial derived from the supposed wanderings of the many sons of Priam of Troy.

CHAPTER 4   TRADE AND INDUSTRY

1 *Matthew Paris's English History*, trans. J. A. Giles, (London, 1835), 2, p. 412.

2 Dorothea Oschinsky, *Walter of Henley and Other Treatises on Estate Management and Accounting* (Oxford, 1971), p. 399.

3 Eileen Power, *The Wool Trade in English Medieval History* (Oxford, 1941), p. 79.

4 R. H. Tawney, *Business and Politics under James I* (Cambridge, 1958), p. 83.

5 Mary Bateson (ed.), *Records of the Borough of Leicester*, 1 (London, 1899), p. 89.

6 E. M. Carus-Wilson, 'Evidences of industrial growth on some fifteenth-century manors', *Economic History Review*, 2:12 (1959–60), p. 201.

7 *Victoria County History of Derbyshire*, 2, (London, 1907), p. 326.

The Wirksworth dish is still in the Moot Hall at Wirksworth. Made in 1512, it bears the legend: 'this dish to remayne in the Moote Hall at Wyrkysworth hanging by a cheyne so as the merchants or mynours may have resorte to the same at all tymes to make the trew measure.'

8 G. R. Lewis, *The Stannaries. A Study of the English Tin Miner* (Cambridge, Mass., 1924), p. 36.

9 Margery James, *Studies in the Medieval Wine Trade* (Oxford, 1971).

10 This table is taken from A. R. Bridbury, *Economic Growth: England in the later Middle Ages*, 2nd edn (Brighton, 1975), pp. 32–3, with the addition of the figures for cloth exports, which Dr. Bridbury has kindly supplied.

CHAPTER 5   THE COMMUNITY OF IDEAS

1 A. R. Myers (ed.), *English Historical Documents* (London, 1969), 4, pp. 62–3.

2 This diagram is taken from J. Z. Titow, 'Some differences between manors, and their effects on the condition of the peasant in the thirteenth century', *Agricultural History Review*, 10 (1962), p. 13; it shows the succession to the holding and the entry fine levied on each transfer.

3 R. S. Thomas, *Not That He Brought Flowers* (London, 1968), p. 33.

4 J. A. Raftis, *Tenure and Mobility* (Toronto, 1964), pp. 44–5.

5 G. C. Homans, *English Villagers of the Thirteenth Century* (Cambridge, Mass., 1941), pp. 137, (Damemalde), 217–18 (rules of family law).

6 British Museum manuscript, Sloane Rolls, 31:4.

7 *Curia Regis Rolls,* 2, pp. 301–2; the following case is *ibid.,* 11, no. 1755.

8 F. J. Furnival (ed.), *The Fifty Earliest English Wills* (Early English Text Society, 78, 1882), pp. 4, 27, 88.

9 The paragraphs which follow are much indebted to G. R. Owst, *Literature and Pulpit in Medieval England*, 2nd edn (Oxford, 1961); the main quotations are from pp. 58–9 (five loaves), 80–2 (castle), 145–6 (saints' symbols), 256 (pluralism).

10 N. Denholm-Young (ed.), *Vita Edwardi Secundi* (London, 1957), pp. 36–7, 7–8.

11 Quotations are from the translation by J. Stevenson in *Radulphi*

de Coggeshall Chronicon Anglicanum (Rolls Series, 66, 1875), pp. 275–415.

12 G. O. Sayles (ed.), *Select Cases in the Court of King's Bench,* 6 (Selden Society, 82, 1965), pp. 37–8. *The Song of Trailbaston* is printed in Isabel Aspin (ed.), *Anglo-Norman Political Songs* (Anglo-Norman Text Society, 11, 1953), pp. 67–78.

CHAPTER 6   GOVERNMENT AND SOCIETY TO 1272

1 J. C. Holt, 'The end of the Anglo-Norman realm', *Proceedings of the British Academy*, 61 (1975), pp. 239–40.

2 J. R. Strayer, *On the Medieval Origins of the Modern State* (Princeton, 1970); M. T. Clanchy, 'Did Henry III have a policy?', *History*, 53 (1968), pp. 203–16.

3 The documents of the reform period make a substantial volume: R. F. Treharne and I. J. Sanders (eds), *Documents of the Baronial Movement of Reform and Rebellion 1258–1267* (Oxford, 1973); the 'award' of the French king is on pp. 281–91.

4 *Jocelin of Brakelond*, ed. Butler, pp. 26–7. The idea that a lord should take counsel from his men did not apply just to the king.

5 *Curia Regis Rolls,* 12, nos. 2142, 2312; quoted in J. C. Holt, *Magna Carta* (Cambridge, 1965), pp. 280–1.

6 The letters are printed in C. A. F. Meekings, 'Six letters concerning the Eyres of 1226–8', *English Historical Review*, 65 (1950), pp. 492–504.

7 H. Rothwell (ed.), *English Historical Documents* (London, 1975), 3, p. 156.

CHAPTER 7   THE NATION UNIFIED

1 The statute is printed in *ibid.*, pp. 422–7, and the settlement is considered in R. R. Davies, 'ColonialWales', *Past and Present*, 65 (1974), pp. 3–23.

2 F. M. Powicke, *The Thirteenth Century* (Oxford, 1953), pp. 520–1; D. W. Sutherland, *Quo Warranto Proceedings in the Reign of Edward I* (Oxford, 1963), pp. 82–5.

3 T. F. T. Plucknett, *Legislation of Edward I* (Oxford, 1949), pp. 77–109.

4 The document is printed in Isabel Aspin (ed.), *Anglo-Norman Political Songs* (Anglo-Norman Text Society, 11, 1953), pp. 78–92; the translation is that of E. L. G. Stones, *Edward I,* Clarendon biographies no. 19 (Oxford, 1968).

5 N. Denholm-Young (ed.), *Vita Edwardi Secundi* (London, 1957), pp. 18, 28.

6 The *Modus* is printed in Rothwell, op. cit., pp. 924–34.

7 The whole document should be read. It is printed in A. R. Myers (ed.), *English Historical Documents,* 4 (London, 1969), pp. 72–3.

8 J. Le Patourel, 'Edward III and the Kingdom of France', *History*, 43 (1958), pp. 173–89; E. B. Fryde, 'Parliament and the French War, 1336–40', in E. B. Fryde and E. Miller (eds), *Historical Studies of the English Parliament* (Cambridge, 1970), 1, pp. 242–61.

9 The *Anonimalle Chronicle*'s account of the Good Parliament's proceedings is translated in A. R. Myers (ed.), op. cit., pp. 117–21, and there is a full study in G. Holmes, *The Good Parliament* (Oxford, 1975).

CHAPTER 8   CRISIS AND RECONSTRUCTION

1 Mary Bateson, 'The English and the Latin versions of a Peterborough court leet, 1461', *English Historical Review*, 19 (1904), pp. 526–8.

2 C. Oman, *The Great Revolt of 1381,* 2nd edn (Oxford, 1969), p. 70.

3 Bertha Putnam, *Proceedings before the Justices of the Peace in the Fourteenth and Fifteenth Centuries* (London, 1938), pp. 342–83.

4 Jean Froissart, *Chronicles*, ed. G. Brereton (Penguin classics edn, 1968), pp. 212–13.

5 Caroline Barron, 'The tyranny of Richard II', *Bulletin of the Institute of Historical Research*, 41 (1968), p. 11.

6 K. B. McFarlane, *Lancastrian Kings and Lollard Knights* (Oxford, 1972), p. 44.

7 Quotations from this chronicle are from the edition of F. Taylor and J. S. Roskell, *Gesta Henrici Quinti* (Oxford, 1975).

8 The pageant is fully described in *ibid.*, pp. 101–13.

Suggestions for
Further Reading

The main source material used has been indicated in the notes. The number of references there to the Nelson Medieval Texts, now continued as the Oxford Medieval Texts, will make it clear how much those studying medieval history are indebted to this excellent series. A substantial collection of documents will be found in two volumes in the English Historical Documents series, published in England by Eyre & Spottiswoode and in America by Oxford University Press; vol. 3, ed. H. Rothwell, covers the period 1189–1327, and vol. 4, ed. A. R. Myers, the period 1327–1485. The main secondary reference work is still the *Oxford History of England:* the relevant volumes are by A. L. Poole (1087–1216), F. M. Powicke (1216–1307), May McKisack (1307–1399, an excellent volume), and E. F. Jacob (1399–1485). These series should be found in all main libraries. The following bibliography is divided by chapter, though several of the works listed could have appeared under more than one heading.

CHAPTER 1   THE DEVELOPMENT OF ENGLISH SOCIETY

The student needs to develop a good visual and historical imagination. An atlas is essential; a good general atlas is H. Kinder and W. Hilgemann (eds), *Atlas of World History* (Penguin edn, 1974), 1. N. Pevsner's Buildings of England series (Penguin books) is an indispensable reference work and general guide. The Department of the Environment guides to historic monuments set a standard that is not followed by most other institutions and private owners. The books in the History of the English Landscape series (Hodder & Stoughton) are well produced and consistently interesting. To interpret documents is naturally more difficult. An idea of the structure, and something of the scale of medieval English government can be got from the questions and answers in C. Johnson (ed.), *The Dialogue of the Exchequer* (London, Nelson, 1950), and from the annual pipe rolls, published in excellent editions by the Pipe Roll Society. Biographies of the men who ran the civil service machine will be found in C. R. Cheney, *Hubert Walter* (London, Nelson, 1967), and E. F. Jacob, *Archbishop Henry Chichele* (London, Nelson, 1967). On the Angevin lands in France a useful introduction is J. Le Patourel, 'The Plantagenet dominions', *History*, 50 (1970), pp. 289–308. General reflexions on historical development are in J. R. Strayer, *On the Medieval Origins of the Modern State* (Princeton University Press, 1970). English social history is put in a European context in G. Duby, *Rural Economy and Country Life in the Medieval West*, trans. Cynthia Postan (London, Arnold; Columbia, University of South Carolina, 1968). Those not quite sure what 'social history' means could well start with M. M. Postan, 'Function and dialectic in economic history', *Economic History Review*, 2:14 (1961–2), pp. 397–407; reprinted in his *Fact and Relevance; Essays on Historical Method* (Cambridge University Press, 1971), the best introduction to the views of an influential historian.

CHAPTER 2   POPULATION AND SETTLEMENT

On the level of population the most comprehensive work is J. C. Russell, *British Medieval Population* (Albuquerque, University of New Mexico, 1948), and a valuable guide to subsequent debate is J. Hatcher, *Plague, Population and the English Economy 1348–1530* (London, Macmillan, 1977). Medieval population is set in a general perspective in J. D. Chambers, *Population, Economy, and Society in Pre-industrial England* (Oxford University Press, 1972), and T. H. Hollingsworth, *Historical Demography* (London, Hodder & Stoughton; Ithaca, Cornell University Press, 1969). On the plague P. Ziegler, *The Black Death* (London, Collins; New York, Day, 1969), and J. F. D. Shrewsbury, *A History of Bubonic Plague in the British Isles* (Cambridge University Press, 1970). For the discussion on over-population J. Z. Titow, *English Rural Society 1200–1350* (London, Allen & Unwin; New York, Barnes & Noble, 1969), and Barbara Harvey, 'The population trend in England between 1300 and 1348', *Transactions of the Royal Historical Society*, 5: 16 (1966), pp. 23–42. The history of settlement lacks either a classic or a recent general survey. The essential guide is the periodical *Medieval Archaeology*, which prints articles and a general survey of each year's excavations; through its indexes, it serves as an introduction to work published by local and national archaeological societies. For towns, there are two general histories:

C. Platt, *The English Medieval Town* (London, Secker & Warburg; New York, McKay, 1976), and Susan Reynolds, *An Introduction to the History of English Medieval Towns* (Oxford, Clarendon Press, 1977), F. Barlow et al., *Winchester in the Early Middle Ages*, Winchester Studies, Gen. Ed. Martin Biddle (Oxford, Clarendon Press, 1976) is the first in what promises to be a magnificent series. The *Victoria County History* has some valuable work on individual towns; for a city, E. Miller, 'Medieval York', *Victoria County History of Yorkshire: The City of York*, pp. 25–116, and for a town, P. D. A. Harvey, in 'Banbury', *Victoria County History of Oxfordshire*, 10 (1972), pp. 5–127. For migration to the towns E. M. Carus-Wilson, 'The first half-century of the borough of Stratford-upon-Avon', *Economic History Review*, 2:18 (1965), pp. 46–63. For villages, the essential book is M. W. Beresford and J. G. Hurst (eds), *Deserted Medieval Villages* (London, Butterworth, 1971; New York, St Martin's Press, 1972). On land reclamation, C. Platt, *The Monastic Grange in Medieval England: A Reassessment* (London, Macmillan; New York, Fordham University Press, 1969), for the forest my *Peterborough Abbey 1086–1310: A Study in the Land Market* (Cambridge University Press, 1973), chapter 4, and for the fen H. E. Hallam, *Settlement and Society: A Study of the Early Agrarian History of South Lincolnshire* (Cambridge University Press, 1965).

CHAPTER 3   LORDSHIP AND WEALTH

A translation of Domesday Book for each county will be found in the *Victoria County History*, usually in vol. 1. A new edition of individual county volumes has been started by Phillimore of Chichester. For the lords, S. Painter, *Studies in the History of the English Feudal Barony* (Baltimore, Johns Hopkins Press, 1943), and K. B. McFarlane, *The Nobility of Later Medieval England* (Oxford, Clarendon Press, 1973). McFarlane's teaching and writing has dominated recent work on later medieval English politics; on this, J. P. Cooper's introduction to *The Nobility*, pp. vii–xxxvii, should be read. For the peasants, E. A. Kosminsky, *Studies in the Agrarian History of England in the Thirteenth Century* (Oxford, Blackwell; New York, Kelley & Millman, 1956), and R. H. Hilton, *The English Peasantry in the Later Middle Ages* (Oxford, Clarendon Press, 1975). An excellent regional survey is R. H. Hilton, *A Medieval Society; the West Midlands at the end of the Thirteenth Century* (London, Weidenfeld & Nicolson; New York, Wiley, 1967). There are many valuable regional and estate studies:

e.g., F. R. H. Du Boulay, *The Lordship of Canterbury* (London, Nelson; New York, Barnes & Noble, 1966), J. Hatcher, *Rural Economy and Society in the Duchy of Cornwall 1300–1500* (Cambridge University Press, 1970), and E. Miller, *The Abbey and Bishopric of Ely* (Cambridge University Press, 1951). M. M. Postan's main articles are reprinted in his *Essays on Medieval Agriculture* (Cambridge University Press, 1973), with the important exception of 'The Famulus; the estate labourer in the twelfth and thirteenth centuries', *Economic History Review* supplement no. 2 (1954), while the most accessible synthesis of his views is *Medieval Economy and Society: Economic History of Britain, 1100–1500* (London, Weidenfeld & Nicolson, 1972; Berkeley, University of California, 1973). There are valuable articles by E. Miller, 'England in the twelfth and thirteenth centuries: an economic contrast?', *Economic History Review*, 2:24 (1971), pp. 1–14, and 'The English economy in the thirteenth century', *Past and Present*, 28 (1964), pp. 21–40, and by A. R. Bridbury, 'The Black Death', *Economic History Review*, 2:26 (1973), pp. 577–92, and 'Before the Black Death', *ibid.*, 2:30 (1977), pp. 393–410. An introduction to the work of historical geographers will be found in H. C. Darby (ed.), *A New Historical Geography of England* (Cambridge University Press, 1973).

CHAPTER 4   TRADE AND INDUSTRY

There are many good studies of English trade, most of them by scholars working at or trained at the London School of Economics. On wool, Eileen Power, *The Wool Trade in English Medieval History* (Oxford University Press, 1941), is a classic, and T. H. Lloyd, *The English Wool Trade in the Middle Ages* (Cambridge University Press, 1977), is more detailed; on wine, Margery James, *Studies in the Medieval Wine Trade* (Oxford, Clarendon Press, 1971); on tin, J. Hatcher, *English Tin Production and Trade before 1550* (Oxford, Clarendon Press, 1973); on salt, A. R. Bridbury, *England and the Salt Trade in the Later Middle Ages* (Oxford, Clarendon Press, 1955); on fur, Elspeth Veale, *The English Fur Trade in the Later Middle Ages* (Oxford, Clarendon Press, 1966). Trade statistics are in E. M. Carus-Wilson and Olive Coleman, *England's Export Trade, 1275–1547* (Oxford, Clarendon Press, 1963), an important volume. For the cloth trade, E. M. Carus-Wilson, *Medieval Merchant Venturers; Collected Studies,* 2nd edn (London, Methuen, 1967), but the best general introduction to the trade is her local study, 'The Woollen Industry before 1550', *Victoria County History of Wiltshire,* 4 (1959), pp. 115–47. For iron, lead and pottery, and for local trade in general, there are no modern surveys; see L. F. Salzman, *English Industries of the Middle Ages* (Oxford, Clarendon Press, 1923), Olive Coleman, 'Trade and prosperity in the fifteenth century; some aspects of the trade of Southampton', *Economic History Review,* 2:16 (1963–4), pp. 9–22, and for archaeological work the reports in *Medieval Archaeology.* A good study of the part played by the guilds in medieval English towns is much to be desired; G. Unwin, *The Gilds and Companies of London* (London, Methuen, 1908), is still valuable. On the merchant class, Sylvia Thrupp, *The Merchant Class of Medieval London* (University of Chicago Press, 1948). There is no general survey of the English coinage, but anyone within range of London should look at the display of coins in the British Museum. On weights and measures see P. Grierson, *English Linear Measures* (Reading, Stenton lecture, 1972), an interesting essay.

CHAPTER 5   THE COMMUNITY OF IDEAS

G. C. Homans, *English Villagers of the Thirteenth Century* (Cambridge, Mass., Harvard University Press 1941), is a marvellous book. J. M. W. Bean, *The Decline of English Feudalism, 1215–1540* (Manchester University Press; New York, Barnes & Noble, 1968) is useful. On painting, see the survey volumes by E. W. Tristram, *English Medieval Wall Painting. The Thirteenth Century,* 2 vols (London, Oxford University Press, 1950), and, more manageable in size, *English Wall Painting of the Fourteenth Century* (London, Routledge & Kegan Paul, 1955); also T. Borenius, 'The Cycle of Images in the Palaces and Castles of Henry III', *Journal of the Warburg and Courtauld Institutes,* 6 (1943), pp. 40–50. On sermons, G. R. Owst, *Literature and Pulpit in Medieval England,* 2nd edn (Oxford, Blackwell, 1961), is a work of great interest and erudition; on pilgrimage J. Sumption, *Pilgrimage: An Image of Medieval Religion* (London, Faber & Faber; Totowa, Rowman & Littlefield, 1975). On popular literature and outlaws: R. M. Wilson, *The Lost Literature of Medieval England,* 2nd edn (London, Methuen, 1970); M. H. Keen, *The Outlaws of Medieval Legend,* 2nd edn (London, Routledge & Kegan Paul, 1977); R. B. Dobson and J. Taylor, *Rymes of Robyn Hood; an Introduction to the English Outlaw* (London, Heinemann; Pittsburg University Press, 1976). On the real outlaws, J. G. Bellamy, *Crime and Public Order in England in the Later Middle Ages* (London, Routledge &

Kegan Paul, 1973). On Wyclif and Lollardy, G. Leff, 'John Wyclif: The path to dissent', *Proceedings of the British Academy*, 52 (1966), pp. 143–80, and K. B. McFarlane, *John Wycliffe and the Beginnings of English Nonconformity* (London, English Universities Press, 1952; New York, Macmillan, 1953).

CHAPTER 6   GOVERNMENT AND SOCIETY TO 1272

W. L. Warren, *Henry II* (London, Eyre & Spottiswoode; Berkeley, University of California Press, 1973), sets English history in a broad perspective. On the loss of Normandy, J. C. Holt, 'The end of the Anglo-Norman realm', *Proceedings of the British Academy*, 61 (1975), pp. 223–65, and F. M. Powicke, *The Loss of Normandy (1189–1204)* (Manchester University Press, 1913). The most important work on John's reign is J. C. Holt, *The Northerners, a Study in the Reign of King John* (Oxford, Clarendon Press, 1961); see also his *Magna Carta* (Cambridge University Press, 1965), which prints copies of the main texts, and the general survey of S. Painter, *The Reign of King John* (Baltimore, Johns Hopkins Press, 1949). The politics of Henry III's reign stands much in need of an up-to-date survey. Powicke, *King Henry the Third and the Lord Edward* (Oxford, Clarendon Press, 1947), is not a book for a beginner, who should start with one of the biographies of members of the aristocracy: S. Painter, *William Marshal, Knight-errant, Baron, and Regent of England* (Baltimore, Johns Hopkins Press, 1933); N. Denholm-Young, *Richard of Cornwall* (Oxford, Blackwell; New York, M. Salloch, 1947); C. Bemont, *Simon de Montfort* (Oxford, Clarendon Press, 1930). Denholm-Young's *Collected Papers*, new edn (Cardiff, University of Wales Press, 1969) contains much of interest. The best introduction to the history of parliament is G. O. Sayles, *The King's Parliament of England* (London, Arnold, 1975; New York, Norton, 1974), a spirited tract, and the main articles are usefully collected in E. B. Fryde and E. Miller (eds), *Historical Studies of the English Parliament*, 2 vols (Cambridge University Press, 1970). On the law, the classic survey is F. Pollock and F. W. Maitland, *The History of English Law,* new edn, introduction by S. F. C. Milsom, 2 vols (Cambridge University Press, 1968); Milsom, *The Legal Framework of English Feudalism* (Cambridge University Press, 1976), and T. F. T. Plucknett, *Early English Legal Literature* (Cambridge University Press, 1958), are of particular value.

CHAPTER 7   THE NATION UNIFIED

G. L. Harriss, *King, Parliament and Public Finance in Medieval England to 1369* (Oxford, Clarendon Press, 1975), is an important book. On Edward I: M. Prestwich, *War, Politics and Finance under Edward I* (London, Faber & Faber; Totowa, Rowman & Littlefield, 1972); D. W. Sutherland, *Quo Warranto Proceedings in the Reign of Edward I* (Oxford, Clarendon Press, 1963); T. F. T. Plucknett, *Legislation of Edward I* (Oxford, Clarendon Press, 1949). On Scotland G. W. S. Barrow, *Robert Bruce and the Community of the Realm of Scotland* (London, Eyre & Spottiswoode; Berkeley, University of California Press, 1965), and for documents E. L. G. Stones (ed.), *Anglo-Scottish Relations, 1174–1328,* new edn (Oxford, Clarendon Press, 1970). On Wales the only general survey is still J. E. Lloyd, *A History of Wales from the Earliest Times to the Edwardian Conquest,* 2 vols (London, Longman, 1911). On Edward II, T. F. Tout, *The Place of the Reign of Edward II in English History,* 2nd edn (Manchester University Press, 1936), should be read as an example of a historical tradition very influential in twentieth-century British historiography, and its approach contrasted with that of two fine studies of individual magnates, J. R. Maddicott, *Thomas of Lancaster 1307–1322* (Oxford, Clarendon Press, 1970), and J. R. S. Phillips, *Aymer de Valence Earl of Pembroke 1307–1324* (Oxford, Clarendon Press, 1972). Articles of value are Maddicott. 'The English peasantry and the demands of the crown 1294–1341', *Past and Present* Supplement no 1 (1975); I. Kershaw, 'The Great Famine and Agrarian Crisis in England 1315–22', *Past and Present,* 59 (1973), pp. 3–50; Natalie Fryde, 'Edward III's removal of his ministers and judges, 1340–1', *Bulletin of the Institute of Historical Research,* 48 (1975), pp. 149–61. On the Hundred Years' War see the essays in K. Fowler (ed.), *The Hundred Years' War* (London, Macmillan; New York, St Martin's Press, 1971). There is no general survey of the politics of Edward III's reign, but see Fowler, *The King's Lieutenant: Henry of Grosmont, First Duke of Lancaster, 1310–1361* (London, Elek; New York, Barnes & Noble, 1969); H. J. Hewitt, *The Organisation of War under Edward III, 1338–62* (Manchester University Press; New York, Barnes & Noble, 1966); G. Holmes, *The Good Parliament* (Oxford, Clarendon Press, 1975). On the *Modus Tenendi Parliamentum,* L. W. Vernon-Harcourt, *His Grace the Steward and Trial of Peers* (London, Longman, 1907), and for King Arthur, R. S. Loomis, *The Development of Arthurian Romance* (London, Hutchinson, 1963; New York, Harper & Row, 1964).

CHAPTER 8   CRISIS AND RECONSTRUCTION

On the Peasants' Revolt: for narrative, C. Oman, *The Great Revolt of 1381*, 2nd edn, introduction by E. B. Fryde (Oxford, Clarendon Press, 1969); for interpretation, R. H. Hilton, *Bond Men Made Free; Medieval Peasant Movements and the English Rising of 1381* (London, Temple Smith; New York, Viking Press, 1973); for documents, R. B. Dobson (ed.), *The Peasants' Revolt* (London, Macmillan, 1970). On Richard II, from a large literature, see first A. Tuck, *Richard II and the English Nobility* (London, Arnold, 1973; New York, St Martin's Press, 1974), and K. B. McFarlane, *Lancastrian Kings and Lollard Knights* (Oxford, Clarendon Press, 1972). On Henry IV and Henry V: McFarlane, 'England: the Lancastrian Kings, 1399–1461', *Cambridge Medieval History* (1936), 8, pp. 362–417; J. L. Kirby, *Henry IV of England* (London, Constable, 1970; Hamden, Conn., Archon, 1971); E. F. Jacob, *Henry V and the Invasion of France* (London, English Universities Press, 1947; New York, Macmillan, 1950); R. A. Newhall, *The English Conquest of Normandy 1416–1424* (New Haven, Yale University Press, 1924); S. B. Chrimes (ed.), *Fifteenth-century England 1399–1509* (Manchester University Press; New York, Barnes & Noble, 1972). On parliament: J. S. Roskell, *The Commons and their Speakers in English Parliaments, 1376–1523* (Manchester University Press; New York, Barnes & Noble, 1965), and *The Commons in the Parliament of 1422* (Manchester University Press, 1954). On historical writing in England in the middle ages: Antonia Gransden, *Historical Writing in England c. 550 to c. 1307* (London, Routledge & Kegan Paul; Ithaca, Cornell University Press, 1974), and C. L. Kingsford, *English Historical Literature in the Fifteenth Century* (Oxford, Clarendon Press, 1913).

Index